LIBRARY OF HEBREW BIBLE/ OLD TESTAMENT STUDIES

493

Formerly Journal for the Study of the Old Testament Supplement Series

LANGUAGE, POWER, AND IDENTITY
IN THE LAMENT PSALMS
OF THE INDIVIDUAL

Amy C. Cottrill

t&t clark

NEW YORK • LONDON

T & T Clark International, 80 Maiden Lane, New York, NY 10038

T & T Clark International, The Tower Building, 11 York Road, London SE1 7NX

T & T Clark International is a Continuum imprint.

Library of Congress Cataloging-in-Publication Data
Cottrill, Amy C.
  Language, power, and identity in the lament Psalms of the individual / Amy C. Cottrill.
    p. cm. -- (The library of Hebrew Bible/Old Testament studies ; #493)
  Includes bibliographical references (p.   ) and index.
  ISBN-13: 978-0-567-02728-3 (hardcover : alk. paper)
  ISBN-10: 0-567-02728-7 (hardcover : alk. paper) 1. Bible. O.T. Psalms--Criticism,
interpretation, etc. 2. Laments in the Bible. I. Title. II. Series.

  BS1445.L3C68 2008
  223'.2066--dc22

                              2007034751

06 07 08 09 10   10 9 8 7 6 5 4 3 2 1

Printed and bound in Great Britain by Biddles Ltd., King's Lynn, Norfolk

CONTENTS

Acknowledgments

One is shaped intellectually and personally by teachers and colleagues, and I have been under the care of fine thinkers and educators. First, I thank all my outstanding professors at Emory University: Carol Newsom, John Hayes, Neal Walls, Martin Buss, and Max Miller. My time at Emory was enriched by friends and colleagues, especially Katherine Turpin, Mark Roncace, Megan Moore, and Tamara Yates. Since beginning to teach at Birmingham-Southern College I have been extremely fortunate to be part of a learned and supportive community, which has been a source of intellectual stimulation and challenge.

I would like to offer special thanks to those who participated in the development of this project. Martin Buss's knowledge of the history of interpretation of the Psalms is vast, and he offered many observations that shaped the work in significant ways. I returned many times to Bill Brown's rich and thoughtful work on the Psalms throughout my research and writing, and am grateful that he was willing to lend his time to reading and commenting on this work. Finally, I thank Carol Newsom, who has the invaluable ability to see the potential of an argument and help her student articulate it to the best of her ability, which is, I believe, the hope of any student. I have benefited beyond measure from her perspicacity and exceptional generosity.

I would also like to acknowledge two important teachers from my time in seminary who are responsible for my decision to pursue further education in Hebrew Bible. I am inspired by Fred Tiffany's thoughtful connection of scholarly concerns with issues of social justice and the development of compassionate interpretive practices. I have not encountered many people with a more humane disposition, in the classroom or in life. I reserve special thanks for David Carr, whose passion for studying the Hebrew Bible was contagious. His creativity and depth as a scholar continue to be inspiring.

My family, brothers Jeremy and Joshua, sister-in-law Jennie, and especially my parents, Richard and Cheryl Cottrill, have been sources of endless encouragement. I was fortunate to be born into a home that valued learning, curiosity, humor, honesty, discussion, and compassion, all in the context of faithful commitment. I am grateful.

I dedicate this work to my spouse, Ken Wheeler, and to our daughters, Lydia and Hannah. I am thankful to be able to go through life with such a warm, generous, and humorous partner. Our two wonderfully exuberant daughters have offered much-needed perspective throughout this project. They have infused my life with laughter and tenderness. It is a great gift to live every day with these three people.

Chapter 1

LANGUAGE AND THE CREATION
OF SELFHOOD IN THE LAMENTS

1. *Introduction*

One response individuals have to situations of suffering is to create texts. Texts concerning suffering often express pain, describe the causes of the suffering, and delineate desirable means of alleviation. These texts are not simply personal stories about the experience of pain, however. The language of these texts frames the experience of suffering and provides an interpretive structure for it, all according to particular cultural values, ideological commitments, and some-times, theological assumptions.[1] Especially in self-representative language of suffering, one "tells" one's self and others who one is, one's valued structures of meaning, what one expects and desires from others, as well as one's sense of possibilities for agency. That "telling" is structured by privileged modes of speech and embedded relational narratives, a discourse that makes ideological claims about the world and the individual's place in it. These implicit and explicit stories create and sustain identity for individuals, which is particularly important when intense distress threatens previous interpretations of the self.

The lament of the individual in the book of Psalms is an example of such an identity-shaping text, created as a response to situations of acute suffering. These texts are saturated with perspective and rooted in particular cultural languages and relational narratives that organize the experience of pain. The language of the laments tells a particular story, not just of an individual's experience of pain, but about how that individual conceives of himself, his situation, others in his community, and God. The goal of this work is to describe the discursive identity created for the "I" in the laments of the individual.[2] It is

---

1. Similarly, James Boyd White argues that when individuals make texts, they organize, or reorganize, experience of the world. This happens, White maintains, "whenever a person uses language to claim a meaning for experience, to act on the world, or to establish relations with another person" (*When Words Lose Their Meaning: Constitutions and Reconstitutions of Language, Character, and Community* [Chicago: University of Chicago Press, 1984], 4).

2. Identity is created at the intersection of a variety of influences that include, among other things, economic systems, liturgy, education, and ritual. While recognizing the complex nature of the construction of the self, the present project is restricted to the ways in which language constructs the self in the laments.

my intention in the present study to describe and analyze the cultural tools the psalmist uses to represent himself and his experience of extreme suffering, position himself socially with others, and communicate his desire for and vision of social restoration. Though the psalmist's most obvious self-representation is constructed in a discourse of endangerment and powerlessness, that representation combines with a discourse of violence and aggression that affords the psalmist rhetorical and relational power. Ultimately, the psalmist's self-representative language offers the psalmist and witnesses to his prayer—including God, the enemy, and the community—different rhetorical experiences in the competing discourses of powerlessness and assertion. What emerges is not a unified, univocal self, but one that is fluid and volatile.

The question of the identity of the "I" in the laments of the individual has long been of interest in Psalms scholarship. The question has mainly been asked in the context of form criticism, with its goal of discovering the setting in life that produced these texts, or the social location of their origination. The identity of the "I," then, has largely been understood as a historical question that meant to establish the context of production of these texts in relation to the cult. While form criticism has yielded important theories about the laments' original social setting, this study is less interested in the identity of the psalmist within the original cultic setting of the Psalms, and more in identity as a discursively afforded worldview, a position from which to interpret one's self and others. This understanding of identity is also a historical endeavor, though not in the same way as traditional form criticism. The present study intersects with historical questions in the assumption that this language is historically and culturally located, not an ahistorical expression of pain. My concern is with how the psalmist articulates identity within cultural traditions of selfhood and negotiates agency through the language of the laments. That is, I view the language of the individual laments as an invitation into a perspective and am interested in how the specific language of the individual laments affords an identity for the "I."

Individuals do not create their identities *ex nihilo*. Identity-making is a culturally embedded activity, and identity-shaping languages are culturally specific. While many persons steeped in modern, Western culture assume that one's goal in life is to become "individuated," or physically and psychically independent, it is now widely recognized that cultures offer different languages of selfhood.[3] Anthropologist Clifford Geertz notes how unfamiliar most of the world is with the Western concept of the self.[4] In an oft-quoted statement, Geertz says,

3.   For further discussion of selfhood and cultural identity, see M. Carrithers, S. Collins, and S. Lukes, eds., *The Category of the Person: Anthropology, Philosophy, History* (Cambridge: Cambridge University Press, 1985); C. Davis, "Our Modern Identity: The Formation of the Self," *Modern Theology* 6 (1990): 159–71; T. C. Heller, M. Sosna, and D. E. Wellbery, eds., *Reconstructing Individualism: Autonomy, Individuality, and the Self in Western Thought* (Stanford, Calif.: Stanford University Press, 1986); C. Taylor, *Sources of the Self: The Making of Modern Identity* (Cambridge, Mass.: Harvard University Press, 1989); K. J. Weintraub, *The Value of the Individual: Self and Circumstance in Autobiography* (Chicago: University of Chicago Press, 1978).

4.   Note that some anthropologists and psychologists argue that this concept of the unitary, independent, and bounded Western self is an exaggerated and simplistic characterization. Dorothy

> The Western conception of the person as a bounded, unique, more or less integrated
> motivational and cognitive universe, a dynamic center of awareness, emotion, judg-
> ment, and action organized into a distinctive whole and set contrastively both against
> other such wholes and against its social and natural background, is, however incorrigi-
> ble it may seem to us, a rather peculiar idea within the context of the world's cultures.[5]

Ideas of selfhood in the Hebrew Bible differ greatly from Geertz's depiction of the dominant concept of the Western self. Robert Di Vito characterizes distinctions between Western conceptions of self and the ancient Israelite notions of selfhood evidenced in the Hebrew Bible and isolates four points of comparison between these constructions of personhood: (1) human dignity, in the modern sense, comes from self-sufficiency rather than social embeddedness; (2) modern constructions favor "sharply defined personal boundaries"; (3) the modern construction implies an inner life for the individual; (4) independent and autonomous action is privileged in the modern sense of personal identity. In contrast, Di Vito asserts that the identity of the Hebrew Bible subject is (1) embedded culturally; (2) has "comparatively decentered and undefined" personal boundaries; (3) lacks inner depth, but is "relatively transparent, socialized, and embodied"; (4) and has identity because of, not in spite of, obedience to relationship or dependence on other people.[6] Di Vito's comparison of selfhoods isolates important differences in biblical and Western understandings of the self and emphasizes that identity-construction is an activity rooted in specific cultures.

Because he is primarily interested in painting an overarching portrait of the self in the Hebrew Bible, Di Vito does not address the laments in particular, though he does use examples from the Psalms to illustrate his points. While discussion of selfhood on a more generalized level does have a place in explorations of the cultural uniqueness of selfhood, many cultural theorists and psychologists no longer talk about the "self" as a unified whole that is produced by a culture as a stable entity, but as a combination of loosely related subjectivities that an individual negotiates depending on the demands of the moment.[7] In fact, cultures offer many, even conflicting, languages of selfhood, and the individual's agency lies in the way he or she combines various positions of subjectivity. The present study, therefore, is not focused on generalized notions of subjectivity in the

Holland and Andrew Kipnis ("Metaphors for Embarrassment and Stories of Exposure: The Not-So-Egocentric Self in American Culture," *Ethos* 22, no. 3 [1994]: 316–42) have noted, with regard to the discourse of embarrassment, that the American self is, in practice, sociocentric rather than egocentric. They call for a more nuanced notion of Western identity that takes into consideration diverse and even competing conceptions of self that operate simultaneously. Still, for my purposes, it is helpful to characterize a dominant concept of Western personhood while also acknowledging a multiplicity of selfhoods.

5. Clifford Geertz, *Local Knowledge: Further Essays in Interpretive Anthropology* (New York: Basic, 1983), 59.

6. Robert A. Di Vito, "Old Testament Anthropology and the Construction of Personal Identity," *CBQ* 61 (1999): 221.

7. See Dorothy Holland, William Lachicotte, Jr., Debra Skinner, and Carole Cain, *Identity and Agency in Cultural Worlds* (Cambridge, Mass.: Harvard University Press, 1998), 28.

Hebrew Bible as a whole, but explores the particular shape of selfhood afforded in one discourse, that of the individual laments.

The concept of the "figured world," offered by cultural anthropologists Dorothy Holland, Debra Skinner, William Lachicotte, and Carol Cain, is a helpful tool. According to Holland and her co-authors, we create identity through participation in "figured worlds," or cultural locations of identity-making.[8] These theorists resist overarching, generalized understandings of cultural identities, but are interested in how individuals are shaped in and creatively respond to identities offered by the many different and specific cultural realms they encounter. One can recognize a figured world by its identifying symbolic practices and privileged discourses that afford modes of self and other representation.[9] A figured world may be isolated by the practices and language of that cultural world that articulate its valued assumptions, ideological perspectives, and embedded narratives. An embedded narrative is the deep structure of a cultural world, or connecting story taken for granted by participants. The story may be naïve and unacknowledged, but it is a persuasive and formative interpretation of life events, relationships, power, and personhood for individuals within that cultural realm, offering social scripts for those who participate in the figured world. The story also provides a context for assigning social worth and negotiating power among recognized characters in the figured world. Each figured world communicates its interpretation through its plot structure, characterization of participants, social scripts, and narratives, which are accessible through the artifacts of that figured world. The laments of the individual are such an artifact.

The individual laments do not articulate *the* notion of ancient Israelite selfhood; no such notion exists. Moreover, the discourse of the laments is not fully determinative of an individual's identity. Following Holland and her colleagues, the present work presumes that discourse is a highly persuasive, formative influence in identity-making, but individuals always retain improvisational ability to manipulate received discourses.[10] Just as the historical identity of the supplicant is not identifiable in any specific way, neither can we know precisely how ancient Israelites received this language and manipulated it to meet their particular needs. Nonetheless, we do have an artifact of the figured world, the language of the laments, which provides an entrance into that cultural realm, one way that individuals interpreted acute suffering and understood themselves as agents within that context. The present study approaches that language as one perspective on the world, one patterned worldview that affords an identity to anyone

8.   The concept of the "figured world" is offered by Holland and her co-authors (*Identity and Agency in Cultural Worlds*) and discussed more fully below.

9.   Language is one of the most important identity-constructing cultural tools, but Holland and her colleagues also discuss other symbolic practices: "The dialect we speak, the degree of formality we adopt in our speech, the deeds we do, the places we go, the emotions we express, and the clothes we wear are treated as indicators of claims to and identification with social categories and positions of privilege relative to those with whom we are interacting" (Holland et al., *Identity and Agency in Cultural Worlds*, 127).

10.   Holland and her colleagues (ibid., 5) are interested in how individuals are discursively formed and yet also maintain agency in figured worlds.

who assumes the position of the "I."[11] The speaker of this language, the "I," may not be historically identifiable, but the identity of the "I" is approachable as a linguistically created subject position in the discourse of the laments.[12]

The present work has two interrelated goals. First, I undertake the exegetical and descriptive task of making explicit what is implicit in the language of the laments about its construction of the individual and his situation. Second, I conduct an ideological investigation into that language, making explicit its claims about selfhood and its expectations of the relationship between that self and others. When one takes up the language of the "I," one adopts specific values, assumptions about power and relationships, and certain expectations based on a particular understanding of the world. I explore these aspects of the identity of the "I" by addressing three differing, though connected, registers of the discourse of the laments. Chapter 2 explores how the psalmist is represented in the language of the suffering body. Chapter 3 addresses the language that figures the relationship between the psalmist and the "hostile other," or the antagonists of the supplicant. Chapter 4 investigates the embedded assumptions undergirding the relationship between God and the "I." Chapter 5 integrates observations and arguments of the earlier chapters through detailed discussion of these rhetorical dynamics within one psalm, Ps 109. Finally, in Chapter 6, I offer conclusions to the study.

2. *Authorship and Social Setting of the Individual Laments*

For the purposes of this study, authorship is not of primary concern; we do not know who wrote the laments of the individual. The issue of *Sitz im Leben* is more complex and problematic. Again, we have little information upon which to base decisive arguments. The conventional nature of the language, though it

---

11.   Different figured worlds are represented in the discourses of the Hebrew Bible. One of the most obvious examples is the figured world that is cued in the discourse of Prov 1–9, which is the direct address of a father to a son. Carol Newsom notes that this is not simply a naïve family conversation, but instruction in a particular worldview. The reader of these chapters is invited to become the son being taught by the father in the ways of this cultural world, particularly with regard to gender. To enter this figured world through this discourse is to be instructed in being a certain kind of male who perceives women in specific ways. See Carol A. Newsom, "Woman and the Discourse of Patriarchal Wisdom: A Study of Proverbs 1–9," in *Gender and Difference in Ancient Israel* (ed. Peggy L. Day; Minneapolis: Fortress, 1989), 142–60.

12.   See also Judith Butler, *The Psychic Life of Power: Theories in Subjection* (Stanford, Calif.: Stanford University Press, 1997). The "subject" and the "individual" are not interchangeable concepts, though they are related. Butler defines the subject as a "linguistic category, a placeholder, a structure, or formation." Using spatial language, Butler argues that "Individuals come to occupy the site of the subject (the subject simultaneously emerges as a 'site'), and they enjoy intelligibility only to the extent that they are, as it were, first established in language. The subject is the linguistic occasion for the individual to achieve and reproduce intelligibility, the linguistic condition of its existence and agency." Two elements of Butler's definition are important to note. The first is her emphasis on the linguistic character of subjectivity. The subject is constructed in discourse. Second, Butler describes subjectivity as a site, a place, or a location, in which one is simultaneously subject to an external power and a subject having independent, though mediated, agency.

emerged from a constellation of real social systems and is embedded within a particular historical location, obscures the precise use of these texts in historical settings. The language of the texts themselves is all that we have for examination. One of the most important assumptions of this study, however, is that language is socially embedded, that discourse is both a product of and a contributor to the construction of lived social structures and personal identities. Moreover, every reader inevitably operates with assumptions about the context of language and who spoke that language. It is important to be as explicit as possible about those assumptions, as they directly shape interpretation. I offer two approaches to the question of the laments' setting in life that I think are plausible, the first relating to their origin as locally-based ritual texts and the second related to their later development as "education-enculturation" materials.[13]

Erhard Gerstenberger's construction of the *Sitz im Leben* of the individual laments is the working hypothesis that informs the present work. Gerstenberger recognizes two main groups of psalms: the personal and the public. For Gerstenberger, the laments of the individual belonged to the personal category of Psalms; he does not believe that these texts addressed the concerns of the official cult or the nation at large, but were concerned with the travails of individuals' lives. He argues that these psalms were used on a local, community level, probably originally unconnected to the official temple, and addressed the concerns of a suffering individual.[14]

Specifically, Gerstenberger imagines the use of the laments thus: in the midst of a devastating personal threat or suffering, illness, or situation of danger, an individual, probably accompanied by family or local community members, would approach a local ritual specialist. The ritual specialist would design a prayer that was intended to intercede in the situation of suffering and initiate repair. While the use of these texts was determined by immediate need, the language would have been traditional, yet flexible. The texts themselves would have differed a great deal from location to location.[15] Moreover, the psalmists themselves, Gerstenberger argues, were probably not a homogenous group, but were locally recognized specialists.[16] Gerstenberger does cite some similar examples of use of the lament form in other areas of the Hebrew Bible, but there is no exact parallel or definitive example of the ritual context.[17]

13. The term "education-enculturation" is taken from David Carr's book, *Writing on the Tablet of the Heart: Origins of Scripture and Literature* (Oxford: Oxford University Press, 2005), 12.

14. Erhard Gerstenberger, *Psalms: Part I* (Grand Rapids: Eerdmans, 1988), 33.

15. Ibid., 14: "…we may conclude that individual complaints belonged to the realm of special offices for suffering people who, probably assisted by their kinsfolk, participated in a service of supplication and curing under the guidance of a ritual expert. The liturgies of such offices very likely would vary a good deal from place to place and throughout the centuries. It is important to note that individual petition rituals were apparently independent of local shrines."

16. Ibid., 31–32.

17. Gerstenberger argues that there are several instances within the Hebrew Bible that provide some evidence of the ritualistic setting of the individual laments: Lev 13–14; Num 5:11–31; 12:9–15; Deut 17:8–13; 1 Kgs 17:17–24; 2 Kgs 4:27–37; 5:1–19; Job 5:8; 8:5–6; 11:13–14, 33; Isa 38:10–20; Jonah 2. Extra-biblically, Gerstenberger finds support in evidence of the ritual practices of the

Gerstenberger recognizes that the individual laments undoubtedly had a community function and were regulated by certain worship officials, but that they also addressed the concerns and needs of the individual in the form of ritual prayer. In other words, Gerstenberger's theory of the laments' origination is most able to account for the complexity of these texts as traditional, communal prayers that also addressed the personal and private needs of suffering individuals in a way that would powerfully shape the individual's sense of who he or she was in relation to the community and to God.

Though Gerstenberger provides what I believe to be the best model for these texts' context of origination, David Carr provides helpful insights into how the use of Psalms in general might have evolved from a worship setting to an educational setting.[18] His theory is important because he describes the Psalms as part of a corpus of education-enculturation materials that were collected with the explicit purpose of formation of individuals (probably mostly elite males). Though all language shapes individuals on some level, liturgical language may have an even more pronounced formative influence as it bears the authority of speech to God. The role of the Psalms in a more explicitly educational context in addition to a liturgical context adds another facet to their identity-shaping

---

Babylonian incantation priest as well as in the activities of shamans, medicine men, or priests and pastors in other cultures (ibid., 13–14).

18.   Others have argued that the Psalms reflect concern for education, or torah-teaching, and view education as at least one *Sitz im Leben* for the Psalms. The Jewish scholar Saadia Gaon (ca. 882–942) asserted that the Psalms were not human prayers at all, but a book of instruction, theological and moral teaching from God to David. (See Uriel Simon, *Four Approaches to the Book of Psalms: From Saadiah Gaon to Abraham Ibn Ezra* [trans. Lenn J. Schramm; Albany, N.Y.: SUNY Press, 1991], 1–57, esp. 27–31.) Recent treatments of the educational context of the Psalms include J. Clinton McCann, "The Psalms as Instruction," *Int* 46 (1992): 117–28; James L. Mays, "The Place of the Torah-Psalms in the Psalter," *JBL* 106 (1987): 3–12; idem, "The Question of Context in Psalm Interpretation," in *The Shape and Shaping of the Psalter* (ed. J. Clinton McCann; JSOTSup 159; Sheffield: Sheffield Academic Press, 1993), 14–20; Gerald T. Sheppard, "Theology and the Book of Psalms," *Int* 46 (1992): 143–55. See also William P. Brown (*Seeing the Psalms: A Theology of Metaphor* [Louisville, Ky.: Westminster John Knox, 2002], 16), who recognizes the didactic elements in the Psalms that imbue these liturgical texts with instructional purpose. In modern scholarship, the question of the didactic elements of the Psalms has often intersected with the question of the appropriateness of the category of "wisdom psalms," a designation that has recently been questioned (see especially James Crenshaw, "Wisdom Psalms?," *CurBS* 8 [2000]: 9–17). As Brown argues, however, one need not abandon the study of rhetorical connections between wisdom literature and Psalms simply because the criteria for identifying "wisdom psalms" is highly contested, even though that study may yield further recognition of their differences rather than their similarities (see William P. Brown, "'Come, O Children…I Will Teach You the Fear of the Lord' (Psalm 34:12): Comparing Psalms and Proverbs," in *Seeking Out the Wisdom of the Ancients, Essays Offered to Honor Michael V. Fox on the Occasion of His Sixty-Fifth Birthday* [ed. Ronald L. Troxel, Kelvin G. Friebel, and Dennis R. Magary; Winona Lake, Ind.: Eisenbrauns, 2005], 85–102). While the idea of the Psalms having an eventual educational context is not new, Carr's particular emphasis on how the Psalms served an identity-forming, enculturation purpose is particularly relevant to the present project. I focus on Carr's discussion of this issue because of his understanding of the Psalms as culturally valued instruction in a worldview that was part of the creation of a particular kind of subjectivity.

potential. Carr's theory that the Psalms became part of an educational curriculum, in addition to their cultic role, emphasizes the potential of the laments to form individuals in a culturally valued worldview.[19] Their identity-forming function may not have been a derived or unintentional effect of praying the laments in a liturgical context, but an intentionally desired effect of a pedagogical strategy of memorization of these texts, in which the goal was "incising key cultural-religious traditions—word for word—*on people's minds.*"[20] Internalization of language, and therefore also of ideas, values, and cultural predispositions, was the goal of this oral-written education.[21] The fact that the Psalms are so frequently cited in other texts suggests that they were internalized and became part of the way individuals viewed and responded to life situations.

Carr's theory merits some explication, though a thorough discussion of his work is not required here. Carr's basic theory is that the Hebrew Bible is a deposit of valued cultural materials collected for the explicit purpose of text-assisted memorization. Though the Psalms are not clearly marked as educational materials, Carr points to some important textual elements that indicate that they evolved into educational material at some point.[22] Though they probably retained their liturgical function, they gained another more explicitly educational function over time.[23] Carr's theory is important to the present study because it proposes another setting for the use of the laments in which they contributed explicitly to the identity-formation of ancient Israelites. The goal of this kind of education was, as Carr describes, the memorization of these texts, which is a particularly persuasive form of education because of the overt and pronounced way a student must submit her mind to that kind of study. Though my work is not dependent on the accuracy of Carr's argument, I find his work convincing, and his theory accentuates the argument I make in the present work.

Carr's theory also gives rise to an important issue regarding the gender of the "I" of the laments, which is an especially important issue because gender is a primary means of attaining and sustaining cultural identity for any individual in

---

19.   Carr does not discuss the laments in particular, but the Psalms as a whole.

20.   Carr, *Writing on the Tablet of the Heart*, 8 (emphasis original).

21.   Ibid., 160.

22.   Ibid., 152–54. Carr notes several features of the present Psalter that indicate that these texts became part of teaching materials for education in torah piety. For instance, there are several instances in the Psalter that call for recitation of Torah (see Pss 1; 78; and 119). Second, many acrostic poems (Pss 9–10; 25; 34; 119; 145) are evidence of the use of the alphabetic structure to aid in the process of memorization. Third, there is "writing on the heart" imagery, especially in Ps 40:7–9, which is an image of intentional internalization of these texts. As Carr says, "In sum, despite the cultic origins of certain psalms and genres in the book of Psalms, the Psalter as a whole is now part of a broader educational process, interlaced with scribal superscriptions of the sort we have seen so frequently elsewhere in educational long-duration literature…" (ibid., 154).

23.   It is difficult to say with precision when this might have happened with the Psalms in particular, though it was undoubtedly a gradual and complex process. Helpfully, Carr (ibid., 162, 163, 165) outlines possible stages of development of the corpus and indicates several points in time when certain groups of psalms might have made their way into a revised corpus.

any cultural setting. Carr argues that this educational curriculum was mainly reserved for elite males. As Carr says, it is possible that women would have played some role in this kind of education, but males had the most access by far to the sort of education he envisions.[24] As these educational materials gained authority as a curriculum for training and enculturating males for positions of social power, it makes sense that the ideal subjectivity embedded in the language would relate most explicitly to the formation of males. In localized, ritual use, within the kind of context Gerstenberger describes, however, it is likely that women spoke these prayers as well and addressed their suffering to God and community through that speech.[25] Gerstenberger avers that the experiences of women have undoubtedly made their way into these prayers.[26]

Here, the distinction between the historical identity and the rhetorical identity of the psalmist is vital. Though women may have adopted the language of the laments for ritual purposes, in doing so they inhabited a dominantly male subject position.[27] There may have been modification of the prayers for women's use, but the dominant rhetorical identity of the "I" is male. Throughout the present study, therefore, I refer to the psalmist as a male, though I use gender-neutral language when possible. I have not, however, attempted a thorough gender-critical analysis of these prayers. Some scholars argue that there is evidence for female composition of some of the Psalms.[28] To argue that this is a mostly male discourse is not to argue that it is uniformly so, or that there are not echoes of women's influence in this language. There is undoubtedly more work to do in this area, but that effort is beyond the present study.

---

24.   Ibid., 11–12.

25.   See, for example, the extra-psalmic examples of women's prayers: Miriam in Exod 15:20–21, Deborah in Judg 5, Hannah in 1 Sam 2:1–10, and Judith in Jdt 16:1–17.

26.   Erhard Gerstenberger, *Psalms, Part 2, and Lamentations* (FOTL 15; Grand Rapids: Eerdmans, 2001), 262.

27.   David Clines ("The Book of Psalms, Where Men are Men: On the Gender of Hebrew Piety" [paper presented at the annual meeting of the SBL, Philadelphia, November 2005]) helpfully and provocatively examines the construction of masculinity embedded in the language of the Psalms. As he says, the language of piety may at first seem gender-neutral. His analysis, however, suggests that though the "maleness" of this language may not be as overt as in other parts of the Hebrew Bible, the Psalms are "written by men for men" (p. 1). He analyzes the construction of masculinity in several categories: language of warfare, honor and shame, enemies, role of women, concept of solitariness, the metaphorical system that favors height and strength, and the presence of binary thinking. I am grateful to Professor Clines for allowing me to cite his paper.

28.   See Kathleen Farmer, "Psalms," in *Women's Bible Commentary, Expanded Edition with Apocrypha* (ed. Carol A. Newsom and Sharon H. Ringe; Louisville, Ky.: Westminster John Knox, 1998), 151; Lisa W. Davison, " 'My soul is like the weaned child that is with me': The Psalms and the Feminine Voice," *HBT* 23, no. 2 (2001): 155–67; Marc Zvi Brettler, "Women and Psalms: Toward an Understanding of the Role of Women's Prayer in the Israelite Cult," in *Gender and Law in the Hebrew Bible and the Ancient Near East* (ed. Victor H. Matthews, Bernard M. Levinson, and Tikva Simone Frymer-Kensky; JSOTSup 262; Sheffield: Sheffield Academic Press, 1998), 25–56. See also Patrick D. Miller, "Things too Wonderful: Prayers Women Prayed," in *They Cried to the Lord: The Form and Theology of Biblical Prayer* (Minneapolis: Fortress, 1994), 233–43.

3. *Selecting the Corpus*

Nearly all Psalms research is shaped to some extent by the work of form critics who have delineated categories of psalms. The very discussion of lament psalms as a category is indebted to form criticism. Few commentators agree, however, on the total number of individual laments and the specific psalms that fall into that category. As is well known, the forms of the Psalms may be manipulated in any number of ways, making it difficult at times to distinguish neat categories. This is not a form-critical study, however; thus, while I recognize that my discussion is indebted to form criticism, it is not my intention to offer a definitive list of laments of the individual.

I am interested in the psalms that deal with the individual in a situation of suffering. Therefore, I am interested in laments of the individual, the "I" of the laments, as opposed to laments of the nation or of the community, the "We" of the communal laments. Moreover, I am interested in psalms that contain elements of a plot structure that are explicitly about the individual's experience of suffering and expectation of relief. That plot structure establishes a relationship between identifiable characters—the supplicant, the hostile other, and God—and positions each character according to certain roles and characteristics. Fifty-two psalms contain an individual speaker's prayer concerning suffering and are the psalms I rely upon in this study: Pss 3; 4; 5; 6; 7; 9; 10; 11; 12; 13; 17; 22; 25; 26; 27; 28; 31; 35; 38; 39; 40; 41; 42; 43; 51; 52; 54; 55; 56; 57; 59; 61; 62; 63; 64; 69; 70; 71; 77; 86; 88; 89; 94; 102; 109; 120; 130; 139; 140; 141; 142; 143.[29] Each of these psalms contains at least some element of the plot structure of the individual laments, and I have selected illustrative examples that contribute to the overall picture of selfhood in the laments.

4. *Language and Identity: The History of the "I"*

The longstanding concern about the identity of the "I" in the laments of the individual is evident even in the superscriptions of the psalms that identify the "I" as David. These superscriptions resulted in the dominant pre-modern understanding of the laments as transparent autobiographical texts that express the sorrows and joys of one man's life.[30] The language was understood to be immediate and

29.   I compiled this list in consultation with the following treatments of the Psalms: John Day, *Psalms* (OTG; Sheffield: JSOT Press, 1993); Gerstenberger, *Psalms, Part I*; S. E. Gillingham, *The Poems and Psalms of the Hebrew Bible* (Oxford: Oxford University Press, 1994); Hermann Gunkel, *Introduction to Psalms: The Genres of the Religious Lyric of Israel* (completed by Joachim Begrich; trans. James D. Nogalski; Macon, Ga.: Mercer University Press, 1998); John Hayes, *Understanding the Psalms* (Valley Forge, Pa.: Judson, 1976); Hans-Joachim Kraus, *Psalms 1–59: A Commentary* (trans. Hilton C. Oswald; Minneapolis: Augsburg, 1988); Leopold Sabourin, *The Psalms: Their Origin and Meaning* (New York: Alba House, 1974); Klaus Seybold, *Introducing the Psalms* (trans. R. Graeme Dunphy; Edinburgh: T. & T. Clark, 1990); Artur Weiser, *The Psalms: A Commentary* (London: Westminster, 1962).

30.   James Kugel notes that the rabbis were disturbed by discrepancies in the superscriptions that seemed to indicate that someone other than David had a hand in authoring psalms. For instance,

spontaneous, the result of spiritual crisis and the consequent private communications between a man of great religious depth and his God.[31] David as the identity of the "I" has mostly been abandoned in modern scholarship, though each subsequent theory also makes specific assumptions about the relationship between identity and the language of the psalms.[32]

Other scholars have made different assumptions about identity and language, leading to diverse theories of the identity of the "I." I group these theories in three categories: the "I" as a romantic individual; the "I" as the King; and the Universal "I."[33] While these theories about the identity of the "I" differ greatly, one assumption about the language of the laments is shared. Language is understood to be a product of a particular setting as opposed to a context of perception that reflected but also contributed to the construction of the social or cultic setting of origination. Consequently, each theory has been part of a larger historical project that wanted to discover, with varying degrees of concreteness, the setting or individual responsible for the production of the laments.

Rabbi Meir gave specific instruction for reading the superscription to Ps 72:20, which most have read "The prayers of David son of Jesse are concluded." Indicating the completion of the psalms authored by David implies that other psalms were written by someone else. R. Meir said that *kalu* should be read *kol ellu*, or "All these are the prayers of David son of Jesse" (Kugel, "Topics in the History of the Spirituality of the Psalms," in *Jewish Spirituality From the Bible Through the Middle Ages* [ed. Arthur Green; New York: Crossroad, 1987], 114). See also Harry P. Nasuti (*Defining the Sacred Songs: Genre, Tradition and the Post-Critical Interpretation of the Psalms* [JSOTSup 218; Sheffield: Sheffield Academic Press, 1999], 128–62, esp. 128–41) for further discussion of Davidic authorship.

31.   Arguably, it is the assumption of Davidic authorship that has given the Psalms such authority and spiritual significance in religious tradition, especially in Judaism. See Kugel, "Topics in the History of the Spirituality of the Psalms," 113–17.

32.   Though it is not a widespread conviction, there are modern scholars who assume David is the speaker in at least some of the laments. See, for example, John Shepherd, "The Place of the Imprecatory Psalms in the Canon of Scripture," *Churchman* 111 (1997): 32. Though the assumption of Davidic authorship is not common in modern scholarly circles, Nasuti (*Defining the Sacred Songs*, 140) notes that there is renewed interest in using the figure of David as an interpretive strategy.

33.   The following review of past scholarship is not an attempt to address every answer to the question of the identity of the "I" exhaustively, but to discuss representative approaches. For instance, Rudolph Smend, in "Uber das Ich der Psalmen," *ZAW* 8 (1888): 49–147, and later Harris Birkeland, in *Die feinde des individuums in der israelitischen Psalmenliteratur* (Oslo: Grøndahl & Sons, 1933) and *The Evildoers in the Book of Psalms* (Oslo: Jacob Dybwad, 1955), argued that the "I" was not an individual speaker, but the representation of the community in the first person singular pronoun; the "I" of the laments was actually the "We" of the community. When the "I" is undoubtedly an individual speaker, Birkeland argued that it was the king praying on behalf of the nation. In effect, Birkeland denied the existence of a psalm that dealt with the private life of an individual. All of the psalms, according to Birkeland, pertained to the political situation of ancient Israel and confrontation with the enemy, also a political power. While I do not dedicate an entire section to discussion of this theory, it should be noted that Birkeland was influential in the development of Mowinckel's thought between the publishing of the latter's *Psalmenstudien* (6 vols.; Kristiania: Jacob Dybwad, 1921–24) and the original Norwegian version of *The Psalms in Israel's Worship, Offersang og Sangoffer* (Oslo: Aschehoug, 1951). Birkeland contributed to Mowinckel's designation of even more individual laments to a cultic setting.

The importance of the historical project notwithstanding, the "I" is created in the language as well. Instead of asking who the "I" was *behind* the language, I ask who the "I" *becomes* in the language. For my purposes, the "I" of these psalms is more profitably approached through the observations of linguist Emile Benveniste.[34] Benveniste argues that the pronouns "I" and "you" are linguistically unique because they do not refer to a particular external referent. Rather, these pronouns serve as placeholders for the actual participators in discourse, whoever they may be, and an identity is afforded the one who uses this language, who becomes a subject in the discourse of the laments. The "I" is the site of this construction, where the individual inhabits the psalm.[35] In this formulation of the relationship between the "I" and the language of the laments, language more than reflects identity—language affords identity. The "I" becomes a particular kind of self, a particular kind of supplicant, when he enters the discursive world of the "I" in the laments.[36] Therefore, my own assumptions about the relationship between identity and language are as follows: first, there is a difference between historical identity and rhetorical identity; second, identity is not a fixed state, but a fluctuating position relative to social context and structures of power; third, language is better conceived of as an active cultural shaping influence than as a product or a result of an individual's expression or social situation.

5. The "I" as Romantic Expressionism: Hermann Gunkel

The interest during the Romantic Movement in the expression of the individual was reflected in historical critics' search for authors and their historical setting.[37] The understanding of the "I" in the laments as an autobiographical poet in the Romantic tradition was standard in the historical-critical interpretations of the

34.   Emile Benveniste, *Problems in General Linguistics* (trans. Mary Elizabeth Meek; Miami, Fla.: University of Miami Press, 1971).

35.   See also Carol A. Newsom ("Apocalyptic Subjects: Social Construction of the Self in the Qumran Hodayot," *JSP* 12 [2001]: 9–10), who uses Benveniste as an entry into the question of the *Sitz im Leben* of the Hodayot.

36.   Throughout the present work I refer to the "I" as both the psalmist and the supplicant, and do not make distinctions between these two figures. Brown has recently pursued a more nuanced distinction between the psalmist as the architect of the language and the supplicant as the performer of the words, and he observes a dialogic tension between these figures in certain important instances (William P. Brown, "The Psalms and 'I': The Dialogical Self and the Disappearing Psalmist" [paper presented at the Baylor University Psalms Symposium, Waco, Tex., May 19, 2006]). Though the psalmist and the supplicant seem to overlap in many places, there is evidence, as Brown rightly observes, where the two may be distinguishable, especially in Pss 62 and 42/43, in which there is evident splitting of the voices of the speaking "I" and the soul or *nephesh*. Brown observes that there is a more complex relationship between the psalmist and the supplicant than is typically acknowledged, that the supplicant accepts the language of the psalmist to varying degrees, and that resistance is possible by the supplicant even within the context of the psalmist's language. Though I do not explore the distinction between the psalmist and the supplicant here, this is an important observation that contributes to an understanding of the concept of the self in the laments as a non-unified whole.

37.   See also Gillingham (*The Poems and Psalms*, 174), who notes the Romantic Movement's influence in the focus on individual authorship of Psalms.

early to middle nineteenth century, but was also quite influential in Hermann Gunkel's identification of the "I," despite his break from the historical-critical method in other ways. Historical critics' combined interest in historical reconstruction of ancient Israel and the psyche of the authors who produced these texts led scholars to focus on the "I" of the laments as an individual expressing his personal religious experience in religious lyric.[38] Commentators saw in the psalms a spiritual, aesthetic voice of an artistic poet.[39]

Though the historical-critical method could not affirm Davidic authorship of the Psalms and increasingly dated the Psalms later and later, removing any possibility of actual connection with David, the assumption of an inspired author was similar to the theory of Davidic authorship.[40] Both theories assumed an idealized individual poet who expressed the woes of his life, his inner depths, in lyric style. Both assumed a concrete historical person spontaneously uttered this language, reflected in A. F. Kirkpatrick's statement that "In the Psalms the soul turns inward on itself, and their great feature is that they are the expression of a large spiritual experience. They come straight from 'the heart to the heart,' and the several depths of the spirit."[41] According to the romantically inspired interpretation, an individual's spiritual, internal experience was the source of these texts. The language provided an immediate reflection of that religious experience.

In the late nineteenth and early twentieth centuries, Hermann Gunkel's work on the Psalms represented a shift away from historical criticism in his focus on social context and attention to form.[42] Gunkel argued for a cultic connection for psalmic language, an original *Sitz im Leben* of the cult, as opposed to the historical-critical assumption of individual authorship. Gunkel noted, however, that some psalms seemed irrelevant to the ancient Israelite cult, and were probably for private use of individuals to be prayed anywhere.[43] Gunkel imagined that the cultic poetry evolved into a private religious expression that was disconnected from the cultic tradition. Portraying the laments in a romantic light, Gunkel asserted, "out of the Cult Songs have grown Spiritual Poems. Here a kind of piety which has freed itself of all ceremonies expresses itself, a religion of the heart. Religion has cast off the shell of sacred usage, in which, until now, it has been protected and nurtured: it has come of age."[44]

38. See especially Bernard Duhm, *Die Psalmen* (Tübingen: J. C. B. Mohr [Paul Siebeck], 1922).

39. See especially W. M. L. de Wette, *Kommentar über die Psalmen* (Heidelberg: Mohr & Zimmer, 1811), who did not believe the Psalms reflected much of historical significance, but understood them to be aesthetic creations that expressed emotions of authors. The intimacy of autobiography was assumed, in which the "I" was conceived of as an individual speaking directly to the reader.

40. See also Gillingham, *The Poems and Psalms*, 175.

41. A. F. Kirkpatrick, *The Book of Psalms* (Cambridge: Cambridge University Press, 1901), v.

42. This shift reflects a broader social shift from individualism to the social. See Martin Buss, "Form Criticism," in *To Each Its Own Meaning* (ed. Steven L. McKenzie and Stephen R. Haynes; Louisville, Ky.: Westminster John Knox, 1993), 73. Moreover, it is important to note that Gunkel did not abandon aesthetic criticism in his focus on social context. His formal analysis was attentive to style and artistic features of texts.

43. Hermann Gunkel, *The Psalms: A Form-Critical Introduction* (trans. T. M. Horner; Philadelphia: Fortress, 1967), 33.

44. Ibid., 26.

For Gunkel, the laments of the individual reflected the most authentic ancient Israelite religious expression because they had been liberated from the institutional and traditional language of the cult. The identity of the "I," according to Gunkel, was an individual who adapted the language of the earlier centralized cult, personalizing it for the purposes of a mature spiritual poet. Though Gunkel sought what was patterned and typical, or determined by form, in the Psalms as a whole, he argued that the laments were not as formulaic as had been believed. He argued that the "clever images, peculiar formulations, passionate outpourings of the complaint, imploring petition, and inner personal piety" of the laments showed that they had been "freed" from the cult and had become personal literature.[45] Gunkel rightly recognized the uniqueness of some of the lament language. There are instances in which the language itself cannot be called formulaic. Psalm 38, for example, contains much rare vocabulary in its depiction of the psalmist's wounded body that is far from formulaic. The rare use of specific words, though it indicates an innovative and creative use of language, does not necessarily indicate a break from the common and embedded cultural assumptions and worldviews about selfhood in this context. That is, the particular words used in the laments may be creative, but the understanding of the self that that language articulates is part of a culturally afforded theory of the person in the context of acute suffering.

Gunkel's observation of the "inner personal piety" evident in the laments is significant. Notably, the assumption that a person is constructed of an "inner" authentic self and an "outer" existence is a primarily Western understanding of selfhood. The self in the Hebrew Bible is much more social and embodied, especially in the laments of the individual.[46] Also, Gunkel's assumption about religious lyric reflecting passionate and unique individual experience assumed that language is a tool of communication of an inner truth, which in itself has no role in the construction of those feelings. In contrast, I argue that individuals are always already formed in structures of meaning and in cultural discourses that create the possibility for certain kinds of feelings and expression. Gunkel, though he was one of the first to argue aggressively for the socially established nature of the language of the psalms, valued the laments precisely because he believed they broke free from that social location of origin, the cult. Gunkel rightly saw that human beings exhibit agency in their manipulation of cultural forms, though his analysis of the laments in particular was not balanced by the equally important recognition of the power of cultural discourses to shape individuals. The intellectual setting was not ripe for the recognition of the power of language to create selves, an understanding that would come later, most notably in the writings of Michel Foucault.[47]

---

45. Gunkel and Begrich, *Introduction to the Psalms*, 196.
46. See also Di Vito, "Old Testament Anthropology," 220.
47. See Michel Foucault, *Discipline and Punish: The Birth of the Prison* (trans. Alan Sheridan; New York: Vintage, 1979).

6. *The "I" as the King: Sigmund Mowinckel*

Gunkel's student, Sigmund Mowinckel, built on Gunkel's connection of the Psalms with the cult, but argued that even the individual laments were cultic texts.[48] Gunkel recognized royal psalms and advanced a connection between the king and the cult, but Mowinckel, influenced by Birkeland's theories of the royal nature of the Psalms, advanced the connection further by arguing for the idea of sacral kingship.[49] According to Mowinckel, in his later works, the "I" of the laments was the king speaking in the ritual context of an autumn New Year's Festival, analogous to the Babylonian New Year Festival, in which the earthly king's accession to the throne symbolically represented Yahweh's own enthronement.[50] Israel's king, like Babylon's and Egypt's, had a religious role in temple festivals. Mowinckel argued that cultic poets who worked for the king wrote psalms for use in an annual re-enthronement festival for the king. This festival, according to Mowinckel, enacted a drama between the king and enemy forces or the natural world in which the king's ability to protect and provide for the people was assured for the coming year. Mowinckel's work came to be known as "cult-functional" because he believed there was a cult function for nearly every psalm.[51]

48. In response to Mowinckel's cult-functionalism, Gunkel argued, "If all of this evidence leads to the conclusion that the genre originally belonged to the cult, this does not mean (which must be stressed again against Mowinckel) that the psalms *as we have them* which are from this genre show this connection as a whole, or even to any great degree" (Gunkel and Begrich, *Introduction to the Psalms*, 127, emphasis original).

49. Sigmund Mowinckel, *The Psalms in Israel's Worship* (trans. D. R. Ap-Thomas; 2 vols.; Grand Rapids: Eerdmans; Dearborn, Mich.: Dove, 2004).

50. Other scholars have followed Mowinckel's lead in the establishment of a cultic context for the individual laments, though there are differences in their specific conclusions. Aubrey R. Johnson argued for an annual re-enthronement festival for the king who represented Yahweh's presence on earth. Johnson's work was similar to Mowinckel's in that both argued for an annual festival in which the king was rethroned, though Johnson's approach stressed the ritual humiliation aspects of the festival and the eschatological tone of the event. See Aubrey R. Johnson, *Sacral Kingship in Ancient Israel* (Cardiff: University of Wales Press, 1967). J. H. Eaton followed Johnson's conclusions but added to the number of psalms he believed to be involved in the annual ritual. See J. H. Eaton, *Kingship and the Psalms* (London: SCM, 1976). H.-J. Kraus proposed another theory, also concerning an annual autumnal festival, in which the Yahwistic cult and the establishment of the Davidic dynasty were celebrated. The psalms used in this context, according to Kraus were mainly Zion psalms, but some royal psalms would also have been used. See Kraus, *Die Königsherrschaft Gottes im Alten Testament* (Tübingen: J. C. B. Mohr, 1951). Artur Weiser proposed the use of these "I" psalms in a covenant festival, in which the community ritualistically remembered the covenant at Sinai. See Weiser, *Psalms*. More recently, Steven J. L. Croft's work largely corroborates the identification of the "I" in the psalm as the king. Croft argues that the Psalter is a royal book that includes some psalms of the individual and some that would have been uttered by cultic officials. Croft argues that only eighteen psalms were intended for use by the common individual, as opposed to the king and cultic ministers. See Steven J. L. Croft, *The Identity of the Individual in the Psalms* (JSOTSup 44; Sheffield: JSOT Press, 1987).

51. Mowinckel (*The Psalms in Israel's Worship*, 2:1–25) did recognize the presence of some individual psalms, though he believed they were few and mainly related to the experience of illness.

Mowinckel's cult-functional approach was a direct response to Gunkel's assumption that the passionate language of the laments could only have come from an artistic individual. Mowinckel saw in Gunkel's conclusions an inaccurate understanding of traditional language as petrified and dispassionate, devoid of spiritual depth, and the product only of historical processes rather than personal experience. He believed that Gunkel failed to see certain facets of the psalmic language because of Protestant commitments to a personal religion divorced from what Gunkel perceived to be the oppressive, petrifying force of a centralized cult.[52]

Mowinckel, however, did not see the incompatibility of cultic language and personal expression. He argued that traditional language, rather, accrues the sentiments of all of its past users and becomes evocative in a different way than individual expression. He did not see passionate expression and cultic tradition as mutually exclusive, but argued that traditional language is capable of being meaningful for individuals in addition to their cultic and ritual significance.

Mowinckel's argument against Gunkel reflects a self-conscious consideration of the way ideological and theological commitments influence conclusions. Though his conclusion that the individual laments, the largest sub-category of psalms in the corpus, were mainly located in one annual ritual is extreme, his contention that even formulaic, traditional language may take on personal significance is important to the present study. Unlike Gunkel, Mowinckel sees this traditional language as vital, even if it is not the voice of one artistic individual. Though he drew different conclusions than Gunkel, Mowinckel's assumptions about the relationship between language and identity were similar to Gunkel's. Mowinckel's stated purpose at the beginning of *The Psalms in Israel's Worship* is reminiscent of Gunkel: "We wish to become acquainted with the psalms as they really were, namely, as real prayers uttered by men of flesh and blood praying in actual situations at a definite period."[53] In actuality, Mowinckel's interest is much more in the "actual situations" (setting in life) than in the "men of flesh and blood," as he understood the psalmist to be an unnamed cultic professional.[54] His interest was in the sociological circumstances that produced these texts. Like Gunkel, he was less interested in the rhetorical, shaping influence of language and how individuals in a certain cultural context conceived of themselves as sufferers and moral agents and more in language as a product of a concrete historical and social context.

These individual psalms would have been used in a cultic context for the purpose of healing. Mowinckel's primary contention about the individual laments is that they addressed issues of national concern uttered by the king on behalf of the community.

52. Ibid., 1:14–15.

53. Ibid., 1:1.

54. See also William P. Brown, Review of Sigmund Mowinckel, *The Psalms in Israel's Worship*, *RBL*, online: http://www.bookreviews.org (16 July 2005).

7. *The Universal "I": Erhard Gerstenberger*

The third approach is most readily identified in the work of Erhard Gerstenberger. I have already discussed Gerstenberger's ideas about the *Sitz im Leben* of the laments in an earlier section of this chapter, but here it is necessary to address his assumptions about language and identity in the context of the history of the understanding of the "I." Gerstenberger's work is both continuous with and different from previous understandings of the "I" in the laments. As I noted previously, Gerstenberger argues that the Psalms as a whole are divided into two categories, public and personal, which existed simultaneously. According to Gerstenberger, the public psalms would have been used in regular rituals based on the seasonal worship schedule and the personal psalms would have been used in special services that were "ad hoc" on a local basis.[55] He asserts that the personal psalms need not have evolved from the public, as Gunkel argued. Moreover, he contends that not all of the psalms originated in a public ritual, as Mowinckel maintained. Always, Gerstenberger argues, there have been individual and locally comprised forms of expression unconnected to the state or national religion.[56] Gerstenberger operates with a more broad-based understanding of cult, so that the choice is not between cultic or non-cultic psalms, but between public and private or official and local psalms.[57] He imagines a situation in which what started as a ritual of the family cult eventually became adopted by official temple religion and became part of the texts of the temple cult. This argument is important because, as Carleen Mandolfo says, Gerstenberger has "delivered us from the either/or position in which scholars have found themselves," between asserting an origin completely dependent upon or independent of the cult.[58]

Gerstenberger contributes two distinctions about the language of the laments and the identity of the "I" that are important to my project. First, Gerstenberger distinguishes between spontaneous use of the psalms and spontaneous language. He argues for the use of these texts on an ad-hoc basis, but maintains that the language itself was far from spontaneous; it was traditional and ritualized,

55. Gerstenberger, *Psalms: Part I*, 9.

56. Ibid., 7: "The evidence indicates that even the most royalist countries of the ancient Near East had religious rituals that served the daily needs of common people within their respective small social groups."

57. The development of this idea of cult as a more comprehensive cultural phenomenon than simply the institution of the temple has a history prior to Gerstenberger's development of the idea in his book on the Psalms. See especially Martin Buss's early discussion of cult, and the relationship of the laments to the cult, in which he suggests that the laments were probably not composed on the sickbed, but were used as part of a healing ritual whenever needed: "...thus they are neither tied to the great festivals nor free from the poetic process of the professional singer or composer" (Martin Buss, "The Meaning of 'Cult' and the Interpretation of the Old Testament," *JBR* 32 [1964]: 321).

58. Carleen Mandolfo, *God in the Dock: Dialogic Tension in the Psalms* (JSOTSup 357; Sheffield: Sheffield Academic Press, 2002), 155. See Mandolfo's helpful characterization of various understandings of cult and the importance of one's definition of cult to one's interpretation of, especially, the laments (pp. 150–55).

though it offered localized flexibility because it was not tied directly to the official cult.[59] The particularity of the event that required the language, then, supplied the specificity to what was otherwise rather formulaic language. Gerstenberger therefore acknowledges the social nature of even the personal use of language and understands that this language had a social function even as it addressed personal concerns. His understanding of the individual of the Psalms, therefore, differs from Gunkel's more romantic individual who created inspired religious lyric on his sick bed.[60] Gerstenberger's supplicant was embedded in a social context and used traditional language that became further endowed with significance in the specific situation dealt with by the individual and his community.[61] Most significant, Gerstenberger believes that the speaker of the language could have been anyone who suffered or had a socially perceived need for lament. In effect, the identity of the "I" was historically unlimited, a universal individual.

Gerstenberger did not, however, investigate who the "I" becomes by using this language. Gerstenberger's form-critical work is not concerned with the rhetorical formation of the identity of the "I" and the worldview implicit in that specific identity as much as he is concerned with the origin of the forms of the Psalter. Yet his work is an important segue into these questions. Anyone could have spoken these words, but the speaker becomes a particular supplicant when he takes on this language. The identity offered the speaker of this language is particular and based on certain historically embedded assumptions about self, God, and the other.

8. *The Figured World: Language and Identity-Making*

A more thorough discussion of Holland, Skinner, Lachicotte, and Cain's concept of the figured world is required at this point. Holland and her colleagues argue that identity is formed in particular locations, or figured worlds, identifiable by their languages, valued actions, and artifacts. A figured world is a venue for self-fashioning, a site of identity-making:

---

59. Gerstenberger, *Psalms: Part I*, 9.

60. Gunkel, *The Psalms*, 29.

61. Gerstenberger's depiction of the use of the laments resonates with Lila Abu-Lughod's description of the use of highly formulaic lyrics in a Bedouin community. Abu-Lughod describes poetic expression using traditional language as a means for individuals to express personal pain, negotiate complex family and community relationships, or gather community sympathy and support for action against a perceived enemy. Abu-Lughod describes spontaneous recitals of traditional poetry to express the sorrow, anger, and hurt of community members in settings where direct narrative-style description would have been condemned and would have dishonored the speaker and his or her family. Similar to Gerstenberger's theory of the use of the individual laments, Abu-Lughod observes that use of these lyrics was spontaneous, but the language was traditional and formulaic. As an observer, Abu-Lughod was often unable to gather details of the precise situation that elicited the pain of the speaker. The particularity of the situation was supplied by the hearers of the poetry who were able to understand the full contextual significance of the utterance simply because they were familiar with the life of the speaker. See Lila Abu-Lughod, *Veiled Sentiments: Honor and Poetry in a Bedouin Society* (Berkeley, Calif.: University of California Press, 1986).

> By "figured world," then, we mean a socially and culturally constructed realm of interpretation in which particular characters and actors are recognized, significance is assigned to certain acts, and particular outcomes are valued over others. Each is a simplified world populated by a set of agents...who engage in a limited range of meaningful acts or changes of state...as moved by a specific set of forces...[62]

A figured world, then, is a site in which individuals come to see themselves in a particular role, in relationship with specific other characters, and speak a certain language that identifies them with and forms them in this world. Inherent in the concept of the figured world is a different understanding of the relationship between language and identity than has typically been assumed by past scholars of the laments. The figured world emphasizes the role of language as a social tool, a cultural force of identity-construction, as opposed to the product of a previously formed individual. Every figured world has a privileged language, or a discourse, that constructs and sustains that world with its use.

Helpfully, Holland and her co-authors refer to the discourse of a cultural world as an "artifact" of that realm. They argue that individuals assume identities through use of cultural artifacts. The term "artifact" often connotes a material item, a stagnant, perhaps even abandoned, thing that was produced by a certain society. Holland et al. have a much more robust idea of the artifact in mind, however. An artifact is a public tool by which the figured world is produced and reproduced: "Artifacts 'open up' figured worlds. They are the means by which figured worlds are evoked, collectively developed, individually learned, and made socially and personally powerful."[63] An artifact may be a material production of a culture, but discourse, or the shaping language of a particular cultural realm, is equally a tool of cultural construction. Just as a material artifact, such as a hammer, enables its user to perform certain functions and do certain work, discourse as an artifact enables people to see themselves and others in particular ways as they inhabit a figured world. Inherent in the idea of language as an artifact of a figured world are important assertions about the relationship between language and identity. Discourse is not only a cultural product or a reflection of a certain social setting, it is the means by which any particular figured world reproduces itself, or recruits initiates into its developing storyline.

Though Holland and her co-authors provide several examples of figured worlds, including the cultural realms of academia, romance, and mental illness, their discussion of Alcoholics Anonymous (AA) as a figured world is the most salient heuristic illustration. In AA, individuals are afforded specific cultural artifacts and engage in an overt process of identity-formation through language. By using AA as an entry illustration into the figured world of the laments, I do not mean to suggest that they are totally analogous discursive situations. One could argue, for instance, that the identity of the participant in AA is more or less permanent, or at least a primary identity. The identity of the sufferer is, in most instances, situational and not permanent. Inhabiting these identities is surely a different experience for any participant in those respective figured

---

62. Holland et al., *Identity and Agency in Cultural Worlds*, 52.
63. Ibid., 61.

worlds. The illustration of AA is intended only to provide a means for under-
standing the identity-shaping power of language in a particular social setting.
The position of sufferer in the laments may not have been a permanent identity,
but it was a learned discursive identity afforded individuals through the use of
narrative scripts and artifacts. Learning to tell a certain kind of story about one's
self and one's experience in a language that has particular significance in that
figured world is the overlapping similarity and what makes AA a relevant entry
point into the discussion of figured worlds that are discursively signified.

Holland and her co-authors describe AA as the location in which individuals
actually *become* alcoholics, "not by drinking, but rather by learning not to
drink."[64] That is, individuals in AA become a certain kind of alcoholic, which
has less to do with the lived experience of drinking and more to do with how the
individual learns to shape that experience in language and assume the identity of
an alcoholic in AA. A critical element of the identity-making process in AA is
the personal story, which has expected plot-points, such as experiences with
extreme drinking, consequences to work and relationships, "hitting bottom," and
recovery—all of which is housed in a standardized narrative that participants in
AA learn to tell of their own lives. In that story, the participant's drinking is the
central feature of his life and defined as problematic. The narrative framework
of this figured world provides a structure for reinterpreting the past and a pattern
for life in the future. The personal story is a tool of identity transformation that
affords the participant the role of "alcoholic."

A figured world might consequently be thought of as the location in which an
individual learns to tell a specific story about her life. That identifiable narrative
is the defining feature of a figured world. Holland and her colleagues use
the term "narrativized world" as synonymous with "figured world." The term
"narrativized world" implies interconnection of elements that contribute to a
developing plot. The language, stock characters, social scripts, imagery, and
actions of participants find their meaning in the context of that culturally figured,
or narrativized world.[65] All of these elements—plot, characterization, and narra-
tive structure—are constitutive of the figured world and reveal what is desired
and rejected, expected and assumed.

The narrative provides the form that gives personal experience compre-
hensible shape in that figured world. For instance, the personal story individuals
learn to tell in AA is highly formulaic. While the personal examples may differ
greatly, the narrative structure or the plot of the story is regular and expected.[66]
The regularized plot of the stories provides cohesion to the membership; despite
individual differences, members feel that they are all alike in being alcoholics.

---

64.   Ibid., 66.
65.   Ibid., 52: "These socially generated, culturally figured worlds, many linguists believe, are
necessary for understanding the meaning of words. When talking and acting, people assume their
words and behavior will be interpreted according to a context of meaning—as indexing or pointing
to a culturally figured world."
66.   See Holland and her co-authors (ibid., 70) for more elaboration on this pattern.

Solidarity is achieved in a patterned storyline.[67] Therefore, while the stories people tell give the impression of autobiography, and they certainly are personal, they are far from spontaneous. The narrative structure is an abstraction based on the experiences of individuals, but does not reflect the experiences of one life.[68]

Though abstract, the narrativized world provides a powerful and inevitable context of meaning for individuals in that cultural realm. That "form" that individuals assume when they enter a particular figured world is their identity. Individuals who become identified with that cultural world learn to see their lives through that lens and make judgments about themselves and others according to the values and commitments of that figured world. Becoming identified with a figured world is a process that requires practice, however. Herein lies an important aspect of the figured world; identities are not natural, but learned. Holland et al. describe an acculturation process in the figured world of AA in which individuals learn to use the privileged language of that world and identify themselves with it. The degree to which one is able to fit life experiences into the figured narrative of AA is the degree to which one functions in that world successfully. For instance, resistance to calling oneself an alcoholic severely limits one's ability to participate in the figured world of AA.[69] In order to participate in this world, one must learn to accept its worldview as one's own, to allow its language to represent one's life.

The personal story of AA is a cultural artifact, a tool of identity-formation employed by that particular cultural world. Likewise, the language of the laments is an artifact of its figured world and the full significance of that discourse is understood in the context of the figured world. The laments of the individual offer an interpretation of the world that is embedded in a particular storyline. The embedded story of the laments is less overt than the personal story in AA, but the story provides the framework for interpretation of events within the figured world in like manner. Just as in AA, where the individual who drinks becomes an alcoholic, the laments of the individual provide the rhetorical location in which the individual becomes a certain kind of supplicant, a certain kind of sufferer.

The embedded storyline of the laments is the context in which to understand the actions, words, and imagery in the language of the "I." This plot structure is implicit in the language of the laments and is the context against which words and actions of the psalmist and others are understood. This narrative and its embedded theological and ideological assumptions are the background for

---

67. Ibid., 77.
68. Ibid., 53: "The production and reproduction of figured worlds involves both abstraction of significant regularities from everyday life into expectations about how particular types of events unfold and interpretation of the everyday according to distillations of past experiences. A figured world is formed and re-formed in relation to everyday activities and events that ordain happenings within it. It is certainly not divorced from these happenings, but neither is it identical to the particulars of any one event. It is an abstraction, an extraction carried out under guidance."
69. Ibid., 96–97.

understanding how particular images, words, and mini-narratives function in the laments of the individual. The following describes the plot of the laments of the individual:

> The individual is a loyal servant of God and has lived according to God's expectations.
>
> The individual is debilitated and suffering, which is often described in physical terms.
>
> The individual is socially alienated and often mocked by his community, friends, and family, resulting in intense shame.
>
> The cause of suffering is, with rare exception, oppression by an enemy and/or abandonment by God.
>
> The psalmist is utterly dependent on God for rescue.
>
> Relief is available through prayers of lament to God, who understands and attends to personal needs of individuals with whom a relationship based on loyalty has been established.
>
> God is responsible for acting on the individual's behalf. Otherwise, God shares in the shame of the individual's weakened and compromised physical and social state.
>
> The enemy who brings about the suffering of the individual should be shamed, sometimes in an extreme manner, so as to restore the individual's (and God's) honor.
>
> God receives praise and adoration from the thankful servant and God's own identity is sustained in those public praises.

This simplified narrative progresses from description of distress, to appeal to God to deliverance, or expectation of deliverance, to restoration of the speaker to health or integration into community. The distress–appeal–deliverance–restoration sequence is not realized in every lament, nor is it present in this exact sequence in every text. Some laments focus on one of the plot points primarily, such as description of distress. Also, sometimes the speaker does not achieve restoration in the psalm. Overall, however, the narrative of the laments of the individual is stable.

The most obvious aspect of the self-representation as a sufferer in this plot structure has to do with the psalmist's powerlessness, readily evident in his physical incapacitation and distress. The body in distress is a symbolic means of self-positioning that stretches far beyond a *Sitz im Leben* of disease, however. Though this language could clearly refer to physical illness as the source of the psalmist's lament, physical diminishment is also a fundamental metaphorical basis upon which selfhood is conceived in the laments.

The psalmist clearly feels his physical pain acutely and no doubt suffers, yet bodily distress as a language of powerlessness is not univocal in the laments. The subject position afforded the psalmist in the language of physical distress is one that not only affords him a culturally valued means of articulating pain, but also affords him the power to make demands and substantiate his claims to God's attention and his desires for the enemy's destruction. Bodily powerlessness also functions as a language of power and authority, an argument I develop more fully in the second chapter. For now, it is important to recognize that the role of the psalmist as a particular kind of powerless sufferer is the dominant representation of the psalmist in this language, though the representation as sufferer is multivalent and offers a particular kind of agency to the psalmist even as it expresses impaired agency.

The role of sufferer is what Holland and her colleagues would call the "figurative identity" of the psalmist, or how the psalmist is characterized in imagery and role in the narrative script. The psalmist's identity is also constructed in the language that relates him to other characters in this figured world. In the laments, the psalmist represents himself not just as physically diminished, but also as relationally powerless. He is utterly dependent upon God for deliverance and he is abandoned, pursued, and attacked by hostile foes that he cannot escape or confront on his own. As in the body-language,[70] however, these representations of relational powerlessness are simultaneously expressions of power, or part of an overall rhetorical strategy that ultimately empowers the psalmist. To be clear, the laments communicate painful experiences of community and divine abandonment, ridicule, and social abuse due to the psalmist's radical and apparently absolute loss of social worth. Those same expressions of relational powerlessness also afford the psalmist positions from which to negotiate power through specific modes of agency that relate to relational structures embedded in this discourse.

Helpfully, Holland and her colleagues discern two levels of identity-making that distinguish between the characterization of individuals in figured worlds according to their designated roles (figurative identity) and the way that social worth and relational power is negotiated among the characters in the figured world (relational identity).[71] Though these aspects of identity are intertwined, the distinction between figurative and relational identity is helpful heuristically; these categories provide a way of discussing the concept of identity as not only the position of an individual, but as part and parcel of broader social negotiations among the different characters in the figured world.

9. *Relational Identity and Negotiation of Power in Figured Worlds*

The language of the laments is infused with certain understandings of power, responsibility, and relationship. Because of the central importance of the psalmist's relationship with other characters in this figured world, the concept of relational identity is a useful means of approaching the laments. I seek to uncover the textual strategy of the laments as they construct a particular identity for the psalmist in a way that takes into consideration how identity is formed in unique cultural realms through the use of discursive social positioning.

---

70. I use "body-language" here and throughout as a less cumbersome alternative to "language of/related to the body."

71. Ibid., 125.

Two implied assumptions in the concept of relational identity merit explicit clarification. First, figured worlds offer different languages that shape relationships among recognized characters in specific cultural realms.[72] While all figured worlds have ways of negotiating social worth, not all figured worlds construct the framework for social relationships in the same way. Figured world have particular languages for social relationships, a specific way of determining relative social power, entitlement to social power, and social worth.

Consider, for example, the nomenclature designating recognized characters in the figured world of higher education as "students" and "professors."[73] Assumptions about how individuals are socially related become evident when accepted nomenclature changes. If the "student" were to be called a "customer," nomenclature borrowed from the figured world of business, the expectations of relative power in that relationship would be different. The figured world of business typically understands relationships to be based on the profitable exchange of a product. The "professor" in this new discourse might be referred to as a "customer service representative," for instance, implying concepts such as profit and customer satisfaction, a material, exchange-based representation of the "product," education, and, consequently, a radically different responsibility to the "customer." The discourse of a particular figured world frames relationships and creates the boundaries for interaction and structures of expectations for those relationships.

Second, relational identity has more to do with the stance or position one takes with regard to the other as opposed to a defining set of static attributes. Relational identity is rooted in Bakhtin's idea of the dialogic self, an understanding of selfhood that stresses the contextual and interactive nature of identity. According to Bakhtin, the self is in a constant and often unconscious process of receiving messages from its environment, discursive or physical, and responding to those messages.[74] This dialogic view of the self negates the understanding of the self as internally and autonomously generating, an already constituted and stable identity that is projected in any circumstance. Rather, Bakhtin understands

72.   Ibid., 271: "Social position has to do with entitlement to social and material resources and so to the higher deference, respect, and legitimacy accorded to those genders, races, ethnic groups, castes, and sexualities privileged by society… But the activity of positioning refers back to the cultural lay of the land, to figured world, and not only to some species-given universal frame." While it is possible for some registers of relational identity to cross figured worlds, such as identities afforded individuals according to race, gender, and class, even those seemingly enduring identities have roots in a specific cultural framework.

73.   Holland and her colleagues offer several examples of relational identity, or how individuals are placed with regard to the other in figured worlds. Among these examples are how the language of machismo adjudicates social worth in a Nicaraguan village and how modes of address index relative degrees of attractiveness in the world of romance.

74.   Gary Saul Morson and Caryl Emerson, *Mikhail Bakhtin: Creation of a Prosaics* (Stanford, Calif.: Stanford University Press, 1990), 191: "For Bakhtin, selves are creative in response to images of themselves given by others. The other bestows form, an aesthetic act, and as part of my inner life, I react to that form. I-for-myself is never identical with but always learning from the image of I-for-others, transcending that image, and so giving rise to yet other aesthetic acts that bestow on me new kinds of form."

the self always to be in conversation.[75] Relational identity is a position taken in interaction with others that indicates one's understanding of one's self and others.[76]

As Holland and her colleagues explain, "Relational identities are publicly performed through perceptible signs. People 'tell' each other who they claim to be in a society in myriad ways."[77] The story one tells about one's self in a particular social and relational context, one's perception of one's social status with regard to others, is the articulation of a relational identity. This particular self-story is contextual, a response to the stories other characters are telling about themselves and other characters in any situation. The concept of relational identity conceives of identity-making happening in the interaction between messages received about one's social position and one's acceptance or rejection of the role afforded in those received messages: "It is not only being addressed, receiving others' words, but the act of responding…that informs our world through others. Identity, as the expressible relationship to others, is dialogical at both moments of expression, listening and speaking."[78] In the reception and response to messages in the form of language, gestures, ideology, and physical stimuli, individuals communicate not only how they perceive themselves, but also how they perceive others, and their acceptance or rejection of the scripted roles that frame their relationships. The dialogical nature of relational identity, therefore, means that it is a constantly negotiated position that is contingent upon one's sense of the subject position afforded one in the figured world and one's acceptance or rejection of that subject position.

Holland and her co-writers provide an illustrative example regarding gender. They argue that gender might be more fruitfully conceived of as a verb, a process of interaction that constructs and maintains roles for the sexes in specific social settings.[79] As opposed to individuals being identified as a certain gender in essence, individuals continually "gender" themselves and others in any social interaction as one assumes or rejects the roles offered in the artifacts of any figured world. Gender identity, therefore, is not a static or essential attribute, but a dialogic, social enactment of relational positionality.

---

75.   As Bakhtin said, "The single adequate form for verbally expressing authentic human life is the open-ended dialogue. Life by its very nature is dialogic. To live means to participate in dialogue: to ask questions, to heed, to respond, to agree, and so forth. In this dialogue a person participates wholly and throughout his life: with his eyes, lips, hands, soul, spirit, with his whole body and deeds. He invests his entire self in discourse, and the discourse enters into the dialogic fabric of human life, into the world symposium" (ibid., 59–60).

76.   Holland et al., *Identity and Agency in Cultural Worlds*, 173: "In Bakhtin's system the self is somewhat analogous to 'I.' The self is a position from which meaning is made, a position that is 'addressed' by and 'answers' others and the 'world' (the physical and cultural environment). In answering (which is the stuff of existence), the self 'authors' the world—including itself and others."

77.   Ibid., 138.

78.   Ibid., 172.

79.   Ibid., 133. The authors rely on the work of sociologist R. W. Connell, *Gender and Power: Society, the Person, and Sexual Politics* (Stanford, Calif.: Stanford University Press, 1987), 140.

The dialogic character of identity-making in the concept of relational identity helps one see important elements in the laments' discourse as prayer. While Bakhtin understood the very experience of life to be dialogic, dialogue is a constitutive, generic characteristic of prayer. The laments are an intensely dialogic discourse, a form of address intended to change life events. Harold Fisch has remarked, rightly, that laments are not monologic meditations on religious topics, but prayers that desire and expect change.[80] As Carol Newsom says in her treatment of selfhood in the Qumran Hodayot, this awareness of God as one's dialogic partner inevitably influences the "verbal shape" of the utterance as one is aware of how he is and how he would like to be perceived by God.[81] The implicit understanding of dialogue is that one shapes one's speech to the specific dialogic moment. Whenever one enters into dialogue, one characterizes one's self and one's partner in dialogue in ways that reflect one's expectations of one's self and the dialogue partner within the context of a certain relational framework. It is not possible to talk with others without implying a certain characterization of one's self as well.

To say that the psalmist enacts a particular kind of dialogic identity in relation to God does not say enough about the goals of this prayer, however. The psalmist desires that something will *happen* as a result of this prayer. The laments are an individual's address to God intended to persuade, or to effect change in historical time.[82] The psalmist asks God to intervene in the situation that causes suffering and to act in a way advantageous to the psalmist. Therefore, the study of the laments' language as a rhetorical act draws on recent understandings of rhetorical criticism as the study of how worlds are created, but also on the long-standing approach to rhetorical criticism as a study in how speakers design and organize utterances in order to persuade.[83] The present study addresses the textual strategy of this dialogic address as it frames the supplicant, the situation, God, and others in order to create change. Because the

80.   Harold Fisch, "Psalms: The Limits of Subjectivity," in *Poetry With a Purpose* (Bloomington: Indiana University Press, 1988), 108–11.

81.   Newsom, "Apocalyptic Subjects," 13.

82.   Gerstenberger, *Psalms, Part I*, 5: "The purpose, then, of most ritual activity is to secure and maintain the means of survival: food, shelter, medicine, rain, etc. On the surface this definition seems to be purely materialistic. One should not forget, however, the psychological, social, and spiritual dimensions of all worship. They are intricately tied up with material concerns. In all their undertakings human beings feel the need to communicate with those beings and powers that affect daily affairs. Life, in the fullest sense of the word, is thus the goal of all religious ritual."

83.   Rhetorical criticism has traditionally been understood to be the study of language as persuasion, how a rhetor persuades an audience, or a reader, to think, believe, or act in a certain way. The study of rhetoric, however, has broadened from the study of how language persuades; it deals with rhetoric as persuasive language in the public realm, but also with rhetoric as language that constructs the very reality in which human beings act and live, publicly and privately: "The goal of studying rhetoric…[is] no longer to learn how to persuade people; rather, it is to understand how people construct the worlds in which they live and how those worlds make sense to them." (Karen A. Foss, Sonja K. Foss, and Cindy L. Griffin, *Feminist Rhetorical Theories* [London: Sage, 1999], 7.) Rhetoric, then, builds a structure of expectations, or social scripts, that are implied in that language. Yet in the laments, persuasion is also a key component to the rhetoric of these texts.

laments seek to achieve something, they are inherently about negotiating power. In order to persuade, the shape of the complaint in the psalms appeals to cultural assumptions about the nature of the relationship between God and individuals. This appeal emphasizes structures of interdependence in the relationship, defines obstacles to the relationship, as well as consequences for both God and individual in the event of failure to operate according to the responsibilities of the relationship.

The relational framework that gives shape to the God/psalmist relationship is brought into relief when read through the heuristic lens of patronage. I will explore how this personalized relational model provides the basic structure for the interaction between God and the psalmist and is the context in which the psalmist articulates his relational identity with regard to God and shapes the contours of his address to God. In describing God as a patron, the psalmist shapes his own self-representation, his desires, and negotiates power as if he were a client. The psalmist represents himself as utterly dependent upon God, relying on the relational values of loyalty and protection that characterize a patron/client relationship. That representation of dependence and powerlessness within the discourse of patronage is also tinged with ambiguity. The psalmist also represents his fate and God's fate as interconnected, a characterization of their relationship that affords the psalmist some degree of power even within this inherently vertical relationship. Because of the interconnectedness of their public fates, the extravagant claims of dependence upon God's protection is also a means of calling God to account for a failure of loyalty, failure that damages God's reputation just as it damages the psalmist's. The psalmist's extreme accounts of endangerment are not just a cry for help, but also a negotiation of relational power. The psalmist's endangerment is an implicit public accusation against a patron who shares in the shame of the psalmist unless he redeems the psalmist, and himself, from social diminishment.

Describing the laments as dialogic prayer, however, only directly identifies one of the psalmist's dialogue partners, God. As prayer, the structure of the utterance is primarily determined in relation to God. The shape of lament-selfhood is forged not only in the particular relational assumptions of the God/psalmist relationship, but also in the assumptions that frame the relationship between other characters, especially the enemy. The enemy, then, is also an addressee in this rhetorical act. Even when the psalmist does not address these characters directly, their presence is nonetheless part of the imagination of this discourse. The psalmist's negotiation of agency and relational power, therefore, occurs on several levels. On one level, power is negotiated in the attempt to motivate God to act in an advantageous way on behalf of the speaker. Further, it is a mode of address that seeks to place the supplicant with regard to the community and the enemy in specific ways that reinforce the supplicant's social value and legitimates his call for the enemy's social rejection and divine punishment. Therefore, while the dominant shape of the self is determined in relation to God, there are also other relational identities that contribute to the psalmist's discursive selfhood.

For instance, the psalmist's relationship with the hostile other is housed in the discourse of honor and shame. In the chapter dedicated to the exploration of the psalmist/enemy relationship (Chapter 3), I will explore how honor and shame as a relational discourse reflects different assumptions about social worth of individuals than does the discourse of patronage and offers a calculus of social worth that is much more rooted in agonism and achievement of social dominance. The laments reflect and construct a competitive worldview of an agonistic society. The representation of the psalmist as shamed, diminished, and powerless in relation to the hostile other is a central aspect of the laments' narrative structure, but that representation of powerlessness is part of the challenge/riposte structure of public confrontations where honor is at stake. Ultimately, honor and status can only be maintained by shaming the enemy. The psalmist represents himself as challenged by the hostile other, but that representation is connected to a more comprehensive rhetorical design of the laments in which the psalmist rejects his shamed social position and enacts a position of social worth through a language of violence, anger, and aggression. This language of dominance is a compelling language of honor that appeals to common cultural values of strength and social power. In this language, the psalmist offers himself, the community, the hostile other, and God an experience of triumphant domination that affords him a rhetorical position of respect and social value. Therefore, though the psalmist's complaint about social worthlessness and abuse by the hostile other is an authentic expression of suffering, it is only part of the psalmist's self-representation, another aspect being the rhetorically aggressive means by which he positions himself as socially worthy and powerful. The psalmist, therefore, shapes himself rhetorically in different self-representational vocabularies and relational structures that include elements of helplessness and intense vulnerability and a violent form of self-assertion and forceful claim to social and relational authority.

In saying that the psalmist enacts different relational identities and articulates identity in different relational narratives I am not arguing that one can easily parse who the psalmist addressed specifically in any given instance, or that the psalmist was conscious of all these relational dynamics. No utterance is that clearly delineated and the model of selfhood I assume is one in which identities overlap and mingle in a multifaceted intersection. One has multiple agendas in every speech act, and the same is true in the laments. In the laments, the psalmist engages in a rhetorical act in which he represents himself to himself, to God, to the enemy, and to the hearing community, using language that appeals to differing relational frameworks and self-representative strategies. Within these overlapping yet unmerged discourses, which are shaped within differing but related relational frameworks, a multifaceted subjectivity emerges in which the psalmist negotiates a rhetorical identity of powerlessness and endangerment, and one of power and potency. The identity of the psalmist exists within that complex tension.

Chapter 2

THE ARTICULATE BODY:
THE LANGUAGE OF SUFFERING IN THE LAMENTS

1. *Introduction*

A readily apparent aspect of the psalmist's self-representation as a sufferer has to do with the psalmist's powerlessness, most obvious in the many images of physical incapacitation and distress. At the heart of the laments of the individual lies a suffering body, described extensively in a language of vulnerability and pain. The psalmist suffers from wounds (Pss 38:6, 12; 39:11), is sick (41:4), and in pain (38:18; 39:3; 69:30).[1] He describes being attacked by weapons (38:3). His body loses strength, weakens, withers, and melts (6:3, 7; 22:15, 16; 31:11; 38:11). His eyes fail (6:8; 31:10; 38:11; 40:13; 69:4; 88:10) and his bones become unstable, shake, and waste away (31:10–11). He weeps (6:7, 9; 69:11; 88:9; 102:10), groans (6:7; 31:10; 38:10; 102:6, 21), and roars (22:2; 32:3–4; 38:9). The language of the suffering body is an efficient and powerful means of articulating identity. The psalmist employs a specific repertoire of imagery that characterizes the body as weakened, vulnerable, dependent, and without an effective mode of moral agency. The body rhetorically marks that site of the lamenter's public and private powerlessness, suffering, and incapacitation.

This body discourse not only expresses profound suffering, however, but also negotiates social and relational power. By adopting a discourse of suffering, the psalmist articulates his loss of power and relationship with God and community. Through this language, the psalmist organizes his suffering in a culturally acceptable idiom. The language of bodily suffering is also a cultural discourse strategy that gives the supplicant a rhetorical position from which to claim authenticity and authority. The physical circumstances of the speaker are a source of potency for the lament and become a vehicle for social positioning that demands action by the powerful on behalf of the powerless. The psalmist's physical distress is the authoritative foundation upon which he demands attention and action from God and his community.[2] Therefore, the language of physical

---

1. In addition to description of bodily conditions, the Psalter also refers to a high density of body parts. For a thorough account of the body parts used in the Psalms, as well as the frequency of their use, see Susanne Gillmayr-Bucher, "Body Images in the Psalms," *JSOT* 28 (2004): 325–26.

2. Literary scholar John Wiltshire uses Kleinman's work in his study about the body in Jane Austen's novels. There may be few areas of comparison between a lament and a Jane Austen novel,

suffering is not just a real expression of pain, but an attempt to gain social leverage to change circumstances. Indeed, the language of the suffering body confers upon the psalmist the authority to ask for God's intervention, and the destruction of the enemy. Through use of this language the psalmist attempts to gain social power and, ultimately, to dominate his foe. Finally, then, the language of the body in the laments is multivocal; it is simultaneously a language of vulnerability, powerlessness, and distress, and also a claim to authority and power.

This chapter contains three main sections. First, I provide a categorization of the body-language in these texts, a typology of imagery that groups the major elements related to the body in the laments. There are internal dynamics within each of these elements, differences in nuance and emphasis, yet they all contribute to the larger project of representing bodily powerlessness and endangerment. Second, I read this body-language as a discourse of powerlessness *and* agency. I rely on the work of medical anthropologist Arthur Kleinman, who has studied language of the body in distress as a means of not only expressing physical pain, but also as a culturally valued discourse strategy, embedded in which is a means of self and other positioning that negotiates authority in situations of disempowerment.[3] In this section I will provide examples of the way language of the body provides a mode of moral agency for the psalmist, positions the psalmist as authoritative, and substantiates his desires for the attention of God and the destruction of the hostile other. Third, I discuss the interpretive and ethical implications of reading the language of bodily powerlessness as part of a discourse strategy that simultaneously empowers the psalmist.

2. *The Language of the Suffering Body as a Discourse of Powerlessness*

The following is a categorization of the elements of the laments' somatic idiom of distress. These categories are not completely separable. For instance, language of physical diminishment is closely related to language of woundedness. The categories are arranged according to the extremity of the language, proceeding from images of diminishment and concluding with imagery that communicates the totality and absoluteness of the psalmist's suffering. These analytical categories are heuristic devices, a means of conceptualizing and analyzing the ways the body is represented in these psalms and the implications of those representations for the conception of the self.

---

yet the two works are similar in that the primary way the body is discussed is in terms of physical distress. Wiltshire employed Kleinman's work to highlight how illness simultaneously reveals and creates a language of power and negotiation of power, and how every culture uses that language differently. To speak about the cultural significance of illness is to speak about power: "Indeed such an understanding of the body cannot be disentangled from thought about power relations… Illness can be seen both as the result of lack of power, and as (sometimes compensatively) conferring power" (John Wiltshire, *Jane Austen and the Body: The Picture of Health* [Cambridge: Cambridge University Press, 1992], 19).

3.   Arthur Kleinman, *Social Origins of Distress and Disease: Depression, Neurasthenia, and Pain in Modern China* (New Haven: Yale University Press, 1986).

a. *Language of the Diminished and Overwhelmed Body*

The psalmist's most widely attested representation of his body is as diminished and overwhelmed; this portrait is prevalent and inescapable. The psalmist describes his body as weakened (עטף),[4] languishing (אמלל),[5] spent (כלה),[6] tired (יגע),[7] wasting (עשש),[8] and losing strength (עזב).[9] As opposed to the extreme images of bodily dismemberment and destruction, the language of diminishment provides the fundamental and most basic picture of the psalmist's body. The descriptions range from direct expressions of loss of power to more imagistic representations of a withering, melting, or overwhelmed body. Direct expressions of diminishment include:

> Have mercy on me, O Lord, for I languish (אמלל). (Ps 6:3)

> I am weary (יגע) with groaning. (Ps 6:7)

> My strength (כח) abandons (עזב) me. (Ps 38:11)

> From the end of the earth I call to you;
> when my heart is faint (עטף). (Ps 61:3)

> I am exhausted (יגע) from calling out. (Ps 69:4)

> When my strength fails (כלה), do not abandon me. (Ps 71:9)

In all of these instances, the psalmist is fatigued, depleted in energy. The psalmist's body is in a desperate state, at the center of his attention and urgent concern. While not as extreme as other facets of the psalmist's self-representation, this imagery effectively communicates the psalmist's feelings of debilitation, fragility, vulnerability, and powerlessness.

Psalm 31:10–11, particularly, describes the diminished body. In these verses, the psalmist uses his enfeebled and weakened body to demonstrate the distress he proclaims in v. 10a, often specifying particular body parts:

> Have mercy on me, YHWH,
> for I am in distress (צר).
> My eyes are diminished (עשש) by trouble,
> my breath and my belly as well.
> My life wastes away (כלה) in torment,
> my years in groaning.
> My strength totters (כשל) because of my iniquity,
> my bones weaken (עשש). (Ps 31:10–11)

These verses convey the diminished capacity of the total body, and repeatedly communicate the fragility, unsteadiness, and general weakness of a person

---

4. עטף is also used in Pss 61:3; 102:1 (superscription); 142:4; 143:4, as well as 77:4, which is not an individual lament.

5. אמלל is found only in Ps 6:3. In fact, the root אמל does not occur as a verb anywhere else in the Psalms.

6. כלה is found in Pss 31:11; 39:11; 69:4; 71:9; 102:4; 143:7, and also in Pss 73:26; 84:3; 119:81, 82, 123. I do not categorize Ps 119 as individual laments.

7. יגע is found only in Pss 6:7 and 69:4.

8. עשש only occurs in Pss 6:8; 31:10, 11. It is not found elsewhere in the Hebrew Bible.

9. עזב occurs, with regard to the body, in Pss 38:11 and 40:13.

who spends "years in groaning" (Ps 31:11). This physical wasting progresses
from the eyes, the external and therefore visible marker of physical vitality,
to the bones, the internal constitution of the body. The representation of the
body begins in v. 10b and ends in v. 11b with the repeated verb עשש, describing
weakened eyes, breath, belly, and culminating with weakened bones. The word
עשש occurs only three times in the Hebrew Bible, all of these occurrences in the
laments of the individual (Pss 6:8; 31:10, 11). This type of wasting away is
especially connected to the particular language of the individual lament.

The eyes typically reflect the weakening condition of the psalmist. In Pss 6:8;
31:10; 38:11; 40:13; 69:4, and 88:10, the psalmist describes eyes that become
weak (עשש),[10] fail (כלה),[11] or waste away (דאב)[12] due to affliction and suffering.
In Ps 38:11, the psalmist simply says that the light in his eyes is no longer
present; these deadened eyes have no life. In Ps 40:13, the speaker connects
suffering and failure of sight: "My misfortunes without number envelop me, my
iniquities have caught up with me, I cannot see." Trouble with sight and loss of
sight signify vexation and suffering.

The verb כלה is not only used in reference to eyes, but also depicts the entire
failing body. The eyes not only "fail" or are "consumed" (Ps 69:4), but the
psamist's body is also "consumed by the blow" (39:11), his "flesh and heart
fail" (73:26),[13] and his "strength fails" (38:11; 71:9). In Ps 31:11, the verb כלה
is combined with the verb כשל, describing the psalmist's tottering strength, and
also with the verb עשש, describing weakened bones. These examples of physical
consumption and being overwhelmed portray a body on the brink of failure.

The psalmist also represents his body more imagistically as diminishing in
power. For instance, in Ps 22, the psalmist uses images of melting (מסס)[14] to
depict his body as diminishing in power and gradually becoming overwhelmed:

> Like water I am poured out (שפך);
> All my bones separate (התפרד) from each other.
> My heart is like wax,
> melting (מסס) within my bowels. (Ps 22:15)

The potency of these images is in their representation of a body that loses boun-
daries and definition.[15] The heart's loss of form in the movement from solid to
liquid indicates the body's diminished capacity to withstand external pressures.
As strength and ability dissolve, the body also dissolves. Psalm 22:15 contains
several images of corporeal instability, especially represented by images of
formlessness. The body is not solid matter, but poured liquid without secure

10.   See Pss 6:8 and 31:10.

11.   See Ps 69:4.

12.   See Ps 88:10.

13.   Ps 73 is not considered a lament of the individual, but is here considered for its use of this
verb in a representation of the body.

14.   A different verb for "melt," מלל, occurs in Pss 37:2; 58:8, and 90:6, though these are not
individual laments. Moreover, the image of "withering" (מלל) is important to the language of Job in
14:2; 18:16, and 24:24.

15.   See also Brown, *Seeing the Psalms*, 121.

boundaries: "Like water I am poured out" (22:15). Intensifying the image of shapelessness, the psalmist's bones are disjointed, surrendering to the forces of dissolution. Finally, the psalmist's heart, the physical location of emotion, feeling, and will is like wax that melts.[16] Psalm 22:15 describes a process of dissolution, of the return of the body to unsolidified matter as opposed to a meaningful, purposeful substance.

Fluidity and permeability characterize v. 15, whereas the bodily images in v. 16 are of desiccation and aridness:[17]

> My strength dries up (יבש) like a potsherd;
> My tongue cleaves to the roof of my mouth.
> To the dust of earth you bring me down. (Ps 22:16)

In these images of desiccation, the body's strength shrivels and dries, representing physical debilitation and loss of power and vitality. The withered and parched body is also present in Ps 102, where the psalmist twice uses the verb יבש, "to dry up or wither," to describe his heart (102:5) and himself more generally as withering like grass (102:12).

The drying and dust in Ps 22:16 contrast with the images of pouring and melting in 22:15, and also with the image of the psalmist nursing at his mother's breast in 22:10. This image of quenched thirst contrasts sharply with the desiccation in 22:16, in which he is dry, thirsty, his tongue cleaving to the roof of his mouth. Thirst, in general, depicts physical vulnerability and need. In 63:2, the psalmist describes his flesh as longing for God like a "dry (ציה) and thirsty (עיף) land that has no water (בלי מים)." Again, in 143:6, the psalmist says his "throat" (נפש) is like a thirsty (עיף) land.[18] The psalmist is in many ways like the thirsty suckling of Lam 4:4 who no longer finds comfort and nourishment at the breast but languishes, unable to care for himself. The rest of the psalm, in fact, proceeds to images of desperate vulnerability as the psalmist is threatened by terrifying animals, emaciated, naked, and at the mercy of uncompassionate enemies (Ps 22:17–23). God, meanwhile, is far away, completely removed from the psalmist's bodily need and distress (v. 20). Physical desiccation, thirst, and withering, then, connote intense and terrifying social and physical vulnerability.

When water is present in the laments, there is too much; it is a symbol of threat and inundation.[19] Though water is not itself a somatic image, the threat of

---

16. See Hans Walter Wolff (*Anthropology of the Old Testament* [trans. Margaret Kohl; Philadelphia: Fortress, 1974], 40–58) for a detailed discussion of the various senses of the word "heart" in the Hebrew Bible.

17. See also John Kselman, who notes how the images progress from fluidity in Ps 22:15 to desiccation in 22:16 (John Kselman, "'Why Have You Abandoned Me?' A Rhetorical Study of Psalm 22," in *Art and Meaning: Rhetoric in Biblical Literature* [ed. David J. A. Clines, David M. Gunn, and Alan J. Hauser; JSOTSup 19; Sheffield: JSOT Press, 1982], 178). Brown also discusses the metaphorical implications of images of aridness in *Seeing the Psalms*, 121–22.

18. A contrasting image is in Isa 58:11, in which strength restored by God is like a watered garden.

19. See also Brown's thorough treatment of the complexity of water as a metaphor in the Psalms as a whole (*Seeing the Psalms*, 105–34).

drowning or being overcome and carried away by threatening waters effectively underscores the psalmist's physical distress and anxiety. Mighty, overpowering waters (מים רבים) impend disaster and loss of power and connote the panic-inducing threat of being physically overwhelmed by forces utterly out of one's control.[20] In Pss 42:8 and 88:8, the psalmist complains of God's own breakers (משבר) which threaten or sweep over the speaker. Psalm 69, however, is especially eloquent in its repeated use of threatening water to portray the psalmist's physical insecurity and anxiety:

> Deliver me, O God,
> for the waters (מים) have reached my neck.
> I am sinking into the muddy deep (יון מצולה),[21]
> and find no foothold.
> I have come into the watery depths (מעמקי מים).[22]
> The floods (שבלת)[23] sweep me away (שטף). (Ps 69:2–3)
>
> Rescue me from the mire (טיט),
> and do not let me sink (טבע)!
> Let me be rescued from my enemies,
> and from the watery depths (מעמקי מים).
> Do not let the floodwaters (שבלת מים) sweep me away (שטף);
> Do not let the deep swallow (בלע) me;
> Do not let the mouth of the pit close over me (אטר).[24] (Ps 69:15–16)

Significantly, in v. 15, deep waters and enemies are in parallel relationship, indicating the hostility and aggression with which the psalmist endows the water. Indeed, the waters in these verses terrorize the psalmist with an enemy-like focus; these verses build an elaborate and terrifying representation of physical distress and panic, as the psalmist fears suffocation and drowning (v. 2), imbalance (v. 3), being swept away (vv. 3, 16), sinking (v. 15), being swallowed (v. 16), and finally, being overwhelmed (v. 16) by floods. The psalmist has an insistent and thorough sense of physical powerlessness and lack of agency.

b. *Language of Bodily Creation and Disintegration*
The laments' distress discourse further conveys the psalmist's affliction by juxtaposing images of the making and unmaking of the psalmist's body.[25] These images escalate the intensity of the psalmist's physical vulnerability and powerlessness. The laments use a dialectic between the creation and destruction of the body that accentuates the body's material vulnerability and reinforces

---

20.   The psalmist often uses the image of overwhelming, mighty waters to characterize the past threat from which God has saved him. See Pss 18:17; 32:6; 144:7. See also Ps 124:4–5, in which the community thanks God for saving them from threatening waters.

21.   יון is a rare word, used in the Hebrew Bible only in Pss 40:3 and 69:3.

22.   מעמקים is used in Pss 69:3, 15; 130:1; Isa 51:10; Ezek 27:34.

23.   שבלת is used only in Ps 69:3, 16; and Judg 12:6 and Isa 27:12.

24.   אטר occurs only here in the Hebrew Bible.

25.   The language I use here of "making" and "unmaking" is obviously indebted to the title of Elaine Scarry's book, *The Body in Pain: The Making and Unmaking of the World* (New York: Oxford University Press, 1985).

the psalmist's self-presentation of extreme corporeal precariousness. Though instances of birth language occur only in Pss 22:10–11; 51:7; 71:5–6, and 139:13–16,[26] they are highly significant in this rhetorical context in which the body is so fundamentally important. Repeated references to the womb and birth concentrate attention on the psalmist's embodiment:

You drew me from my mother's womb (בטן). (Ps 22:10)

Upon you I was thrown from the womb (רחם).
From my mother's womb (בטן)
you have been my God. (Ps 22:11)

Indeed, I was born (חיל) in iniquity,
in guilt my mother conceived (יחם) me. (Ps 51:7)

I leaned on you from the womb (בטן). (Ps 71:6)

You constructed me in my mother's womb (בטן). (Ps 139:13)

The birth imagery in these psalms is imbued with relational assumptions, especially with regard to God and the psalmist, and I discuss the use of birth imagery as a means of relational positioning in Chapter 4.[27] This same imagery also affords the psalmist a particular kind of bodily role in the laments, as it relates the circumstances of his birth, rhetorically focusing attention on his embodiment and corporeal presence in the world. Birth imagery emphasizes the embodiment of the psalmist and his physical vulnerability. This is a body made, concrete, and vulnerable.

The "making" of the psalmist is more fully appreciated when read in the context of the more prevalent language of bodily-unmaking. The unmaking of the psalmist occurs in language of disintegration, disunity, even utter destruction, language that is far more radical than fading or becoming gradually less potent or powerful. The body here is prone to dismemberment, torn limb from limb. It is preyed upon and torn at by wild animals and devoured by enemies. Violent verbs describe the extremity of the psalmist's physical condition. For instance, in Ps 7:3, threatening lions tear (שרף)[28] and rend (פרק)[29] the body of the psalmist. Again in Ps 35:15, the psalmist's body is torn at (קרע).[30] In Ps 27:2, the body is to be utterly devoured (אכל) by the enemy. The body is the passive victim of vicious threats and extreme acts of violence and mutilation. This is a body made in birth and unmade through pain.

---

26. Ps 139 is not technically an individual lament, but has elements of those psalms and so will be considered here. It is different in tone from the laments of the individual, though it certainly asks of God vindication and action on the psalmist's behalf, shared elements of the laments of the individual.

27. Birth imagery also plays an important rhetorical role in Job, especially Job 3 and 10, which I discuss in Chapter 4, which focuses on the construction of the psalmist/God relationship.

28. For other occurrences of the verb שרף used in reference to the body of the psalmist, see Pss 17:12; 22:14; 50:22.

29. פרק is also used in Ps 136:24, though it does not refer to the individual psalmist. These are the only two instances of this root in the Psalms.

30. קרע is not used elsewhere in the Psalms.

The psalmist's description of his own heart and body are no less severe. In 38:9, the psalmist describes his body as enfeebled (פוג) and crushed (דכה). In even more violent terms, the psalmist's heart is shattered (שבר) in Pss 51:19 and 69:21, and convulsed (חיל) in Pss 55:5 and 109:22. Significantly, חיל is associated with childbirth (see Ps 51:7), so that Pss 55:5 and 109:22 overtly mingle the language of making through birth and unmaking through pain and suffering.[31] In these instances, the word חיל does not indicate writhing and convulsion that brings life, but painful shudders that signify the undoing of life.

Bones are central to the laments' language of bodily unmaking, disintegration, instability, and vulnerability.[32] Of the fifteen references to bones throughout the Psalms, twelve occur within the laments of the individual.[33] Not all references to bones represent the body of the individual directly. All references to bones in the laments, however, have to do with dramatic interiority of the individual, the basic construction of physical existence communicated by reference to the frame of the body, and contribute to the significance of the bones as representation of the suffering individual.[34]

A range of violent acts are perpetrated against the bones of the individual and the psalmist uses images of bones to articulate different aspects of physical

---

31.   See also Isa 13:8 for use of this verb in the context of birth, and Job 15:20, in which Eliphaz describes an evil man "writhing" in fear, using the Hithpolel form of this verb.

32.   Ezekiel has the highest concentration of references to bones, largely due to ch. 37, with seventeen occurrences. Significantly, Job also contains many references (thirteen) to bones in the context of personal lament and description of a suffering body, which confirms the connection between bones and lament.

33.   The references to bones in the individual laments occur in Pss 6:3; 22:15, 18; 31:11; 35:10; 38:4; 42:11; 51:10; 102:4, 6; 109:18; 141:7. The three references to bones that occur in the rest of the book of Psalms are in Pss 32:3; 34:21; 53:6. Even these occurrences have to do with physical integrity and bodily stability. In Ps 34:21, the psalmist is grateful because God will keep his bones intact, an image of rescue and safety. In Ps 32:3, the psalmist describes his bones as wasting away (בלה), an image of physical deterioration. Finally, in Ps 53:6, the psalmist rejoices because God has scattered (פזר) the bones of the enemy of the psalmist.

34.   For instance, in Ps 109:18, the psalmist prays to God that his curse against his enemy will not only be worn by the enemy like a garment, but will seep into the enemy's bones like oil. The psalmist does not want the enemy simply to be covered by the curse like he is covered by a piece of clothing, but hopes his curse will become part of the structure of the enemy's physical existence. In Ps 35:10, the psalmist prays for rescue from the enemy, promising that his bones will praise God when that happens: "All my bones will say, 'Lord, who is like you?' " Again, this example does not directly represent a disintegrating individual, but it does contribute to the significance of bones in the laments. Bones have their own voice in this verse, indeed their own words, signifying the importance of bones as a rhetorical vehicle. The psalmist's most basic material structure utters these words of praise to God, indicating the depth of praise felt by the psalmist. Finally, Ps 141:7 contains a clear reference to bones, though it is not clear whose bones are under discussion. The MT reads עצמינו, "our bones," though Bardtke, in the *BHS* apparatus, suggests עצמיהם, "their bones," according to Greek and Syriac versions. In the context of the psalm, "their bones" is more convincing, although the psalm is textually unstable at various points, especially in vv. 5–7, which directly pertain to this argument. Regardless of whose bones are discussed in the psalm, however, the bones are scattered (פזר), a clear example of bodily disintegration. This example should be noted as another instance of bones used to represent the body as disintegrating, but I have not relied heavily on this verse because of the textual uncertainty.

vulnerability. Least dramatically, the bones are described as restless or without peace (אֵין שָׁלוֹם) in Ps 38:4. Also similar is the bones consumed (עשש) in Ps 31:11, a picture of the degeneration of the body's frame. In addition, the bones are also capable of feeling terror, of quaking, in Ps 6:3 (נבהל).[35] Bones are inherently about shape and structure, and these images of threat to the psalmist's bones signify his core, skeletal instability. This is not a picture of a stable, integrated body, but one that is disintegrating, its frame at risk.

A primary aspect of bones is that they are internal, covered from sight. The psalmist, then, articulates extreme bodily vulnerability through the image of exposed bones. The bones are described as clinging (דבק) to the skin of the psalmist, indicating his wasted flesh and debilitated physical state.[36] In Ps 22:18, the psalmist describes counting his bones through his flesh. His own body is no longer a stable frame for his existence. As the body's boundaries collapse, what should be unseen is humiliatingly visible.

In other instances the bones experience extreme abuse. The psalmist describes his bones as burned (חרה) in Ps 102:4.[37] In Ps 51:10, 19, respectively, the psalmist's bones and heart are crushed (דכה). The repetition of the verb דכה in Ps 51 emphasizes the body as utterly destroyed. Also relevant is Ps 22:15, in which bones are separating from each other (התפרד), an obvious image of bodily disintegration. In Ps 42:11, the psalmist describes "murdered" (רצח) bones. The bones described here depict a body violently unmade.

The many images of the psalmist's proximity to death contrast most sharply with the images of the psalmist's birth and efficiently communicate the materiality of the psalmist's vulnerability as he is made and then unmade in suffering. In Ps 13:4, the psalmist prays that the light of his eyes be restored, before he "sleeps the sleep of death." In Ps 55:4, the psalmist says that the "terrors of death" fall upon him. Psalm 88:3, 5–7 extensively describes being at the brink of Sheol (88:3); the psalmist is cast among those in the pit, who had been slain (חלל) and now lie in a grave. Again in Ps 143:3, the psalmist describes dwelling in darkness, "like those long dead."[38] The body cast among the dead represents the body as one that only marginally exists in the living world.[39] Tellingly, William Brown refers to Sheol as the "anti-womb," aptly communicating the significance

---

35. There is a textual problem with this word in Ps 6:3. The MT has נבהלו, the root being בהל, "to terrify." The verse would have to be rendered "My bones have been frightened." Suggestions for emendation arise from the concern that bones do not feel terror. However, attributing emotion to bones is not outlandish in the context of the laments. Bones are capable of praising God and speaking their own words in Ps 35:10. There is no textual support for emendation and the repetition of the verb בהל in the next line of this psalm seems to me to be further support for its use here. Kraus argues otherwise, that the presence of בהל in the next line may have caused the copyist mistakenly to see the root בהל here, as opposed to בלה, "My bones have fallen to pieces" (Kraus, *Psalms 1–59*, 160). Bardtke, in the BHS notes, suggests בלו or נבלו.

36. See also Job 19:20. Lam 4:8 also refers to bones that are visible through the skin, though the image here is more of shriveling skin upon the bones.

37. Job refers to his bones as burned (חרה) in Job 30:30.

38. See also Pss 18:5; 22:16; 28:1; 30:10; 71:20.

39. See Kraus, *Theology of the Psalms*, 162–68, for a more thorough discussion of the significance of Sheol in the Psalms.

of this location.[40] Sheol is the location of unmaking and is everything that negates physical life or all that connotes physical integrity, strength, and security.

Significantly, the imagery of a diminishing body in Ps 31:10–11 is followed by images of the body's social isolation and proximity to death. As the culmination of a description of the social alienation that accompanies his failing physical state in Ps 31:12, the psalmist says in 31:13 that he is "put out of mind like the dead; I am like a lost object." The second line of the verse makes clear the implication of being associated with the dead. The psalmist no longer sees himself as a human being, but an object (כלי) that can be discarded and forgotten at any time. His identity as an embodied human being is lost. Proximity to death, also represented in Ps 6:6 and Ps 30:10, is the most extreme expression of bodily unmaking and powerlessness.

The imagery of the body made and unmade are not univocal expressions of powerlessness.[41] One of my central claims is that embodiment and representation of suffering, though they clearly contribute to the portrayal of the psalmist as powerless, also afford the psalmist a language of authority that enables him to seek change. The relational implications of this birth imagery are discussed in Chapter 4 about the psalmist/God relationship; birth mini-narratives underscore the psalmist's material creation and also represent the deep interdependence of God and the psalmist in responsibility for that body. That relational interdependence connects God's power and reputation to the condition of the psalmist's body and God's ability to protect that body. Nevertheless, though there are elements of empowerment in this language as well, embodiment as limitation and vulnerability is one important part of the understanding of the psalmist's rhetoric of physical suffering. The body in the laments is profoundly and unavoidably vulnerable to unmaking through pain.

c. *Language of Wounds and Weapons*
Representation of wounds and weapons intensify the psalmist's discourse of bodily endangerment and suffering. The wound is a heightened articulation of pain utilizing visually broken flesh and images of violent incursion of the skin:

My wounds (חבורה)[42] stink and fester. (Ps 38:6)

My friends and companions stand back
from my sore (נגע). (Ps 38:12)

---

40.   William P. Brown, "*Creatio Corporis* and the Rhetoric of Defense in Job 10 and Psalm 139," in *God Who Creates: Essays in Honor of W. Sibley Towner* (ed. William P. Brown and S. Dean McBride, Jr.; Grand Rapids: Eerdmans, 2000), 116.

41.   In contrast, Elaine Scarry (*The Body in Pain*, 206) argues that embodiment in the Hebrew Bible means human limitation and confinement. The Hebrew Bible, she argues, continually distinguishes and maintains the boundaries between the creator and the created by presenting a disembodied creator: "to have a body is to be describable, creatable, alterable, and woundable. To have no body, to have only a voice, is to be none of these things: it is to be the wounder but not oneself woundable, to be the creator or the one who alters but oneself neither creatable nor alterable." The issue of the Hebrew Bible's understanding of embodiment, divine and human, is far from settled; I question Scarry's broad assertion about embodiment indicating powerlessness in the Hebrew Bible.

42.   This is the only usage of this word in the Psalms.

Remove your wound (נגע) from me;
I weaken under the might of your hand. (Ps 39:11)

For they pursue him whom[43] you have wounded (נכה);[44]
they tell about the pain of those you have pierced (חלל). (Ps 69:27)

The images of the previous section about bodily creation and disintegration largely have to do with the interior of the psalmist's body, the shattered heart and crushed bones. Though exceedingly violent verbs are used, the pain endured is not overtly visible to the public. The bones imagery is somewhat more visual; part of the suffering conveyed in those images has to do with being able to see the bones through the skin, a publicly perceptible image of threatened boundaries and physical instability. Even the most extreme and violent bones imagery having to do with crushed, murdered, or burned bones, however, is more an image of profound internality than images of breached flesh in wounds language. Language of woundedness, in contrast, makes the psalmist's suffering public, visible, and uncomfortably apparent, indicated in depictions of how witnesses recoil in horror (Ps 38:12). These images, therefore, have a somatic and social significance that assists the psalmist in expressing pain while also indicating the social implications of that suffering.

Moving the representation of pain from the interior to the exterior of the psalmist's body is especially significant because part of the terror of bodily unmaking and death discussed in the previous section is the threat of social and physical nothingness and invisibility. The somatic idiom of distress in general offers a means to resist that invisibility, to make the psalmist's pain and suffering visible and evident to the sufferer as well as to witnesses, but images of wounds and weapons are especially concrete, palpable, and explicit objectifications of pain.[45] This distress discourse is about making the psalmist's pain publicly undeniable, a social and physical presence that must be addressed and engaged. The laments' language of wounds and weapons is an objectification of the psalmist's suffering, a way of taking the pain outside the internal, private body to make it publicly recognizable. Therefore, the images of wounds and weapons make an overt contribution to the psalmist's project of making his pain visible and persuasive to witnesses.

Psalm 38 serves as an important touchstone to the analysis of wounds and weapons imagery in the laments, as it uniquely concentrates these images of breached skin and woundedness in a highly articulate depiction of pain. The psalmist's pain is described with rare, stylized vocabulary that paints an exceedingly precise portrait of an injured, putrefying body. It is significant that the

---

43. MT literally reads, "For you (אתה), whom you have wounded, they pursue." More probable is that אתה should be read as את, suggested by the LXX (ὅν σὺ ἐπάταξας).

44. נכה occurs only in Ps 69:27 and in Ps 102:5 ("My heart is wounded") in reference to the individual psalmist.

45. See also David B. Morris: "our speech acts give pain a means of becoming semivisible, emerging from utter privacy into a dialogical context" (David B. Morris, "The Languages of Pain" in *Exploring the Concept of the Mind* [ed. Richard M. Caplan; Iowa City: University of Iowa Press, 1986], 90).

description of the wound occurs in such precise and rare vocabulary. In Ps 38, the psalmist's desire to "go public" with his pain in the language of wounds and weapons is aided by such elevated articulateness. Psalm 38 clearly strives to overcome the privacy of pain by making it intensely visible, not just by mention of wounds, but also by substantial, deliberate, and lengthy depiction. The precision of this language corresponds to some medical professionals' and anthropologists' observation that language often becomes the special project of those in pain, as they struggle to articulate and therefore make manifest their pain to witnesses and thereby achieve relief through verbally sharing their suffering.[46] Pain often has the effect of driving sufferers to language, as they rely on increasingly sophisticated and layered depictions of pain as a way to contain and maintain distance from the pain.[47] Far from being resistant to language, the psalmist's pain in these verses is uncomfortably apparent.

Importantly, the representation of the wounded body in Ps 38:3–12 begins with the image of an arrow piercing the psalmist's skin; weapons are inherently connected to the idea of bodily wounds and part of this language's movement toward visually accessible pain. Weapons, while not an obviously somatic image, connote injury to flesh and body. Psalm 38, dominated by descriptions of wounds and vulnerable flesh, clarifies the importance of weaponry in the articulation of the psalmist's pain:

> For your arrows (חץ) have pierced (נחת) me,
> your hand has come down (נחת) against me.
> There is no soundness in my flesh (בשר) because
> of your curse (זעם);
> There is no wholeness in my bones (עצם) because
> of my sin. (Ps 38:3–4)

The Psalms contain the most references, thirteen, to arrows (חץ) in the Hebrew Bible.[48] Six references occur in laments of the individual.[49] No other descriptions

---

46. Many who study pain's expression in language have noted the problem of articulating pain. Scarry (*The Body in Pain*, 4), most notably, argues that pain actively resists language and its fundamental unsharability is part of its essential power. For further discussion of the resistance of pain to language, see Morris, "The Languages of Pain", 89–99; Mary-Jo DelVecchio Good et al., eds., *Pain as Human Experience: An Anthropological Perspective* (Berkeley, Calif.: University of California Press, 1992). Roy Porter argues that though Scarry asserts the inexpressibility of pain, her argument is "surely contradicted by the actual accounts of pain (which, far from being 'inexpressible,' are often expressed with exactitude and eloquence) that ordinary people in the past have left us in great abundance" (Roy Porter, "History of the Body," in *New Perspectives on Historical Writing* [ed. Peter Burke; University Park, Pa.: The Pennsylvania State University Press, 1992], 209). For another thorough challenge to Scarry's argument, see also Lucy Bending, *The Representation of Bodily Pain in Late Nineteenth-Century English Culture* (Oxford: Clarendon, 2000), 82–104.
47. Of Scarry's argument that pain shatters language, Byron Good says, "For many patients, language is anything *but* shattered in this literal sense" (Byron Good, "A Body in Pain—The Making of a World of Chronic Pain," in DelVecchio Good et al., eds., *Pain as Human Experience*, 35 [emphasis original]).
48. The image of weapons used to threaten the psalmist is part of a larger military discourse that I discuss in Chapters 3 and 4. This discourse relates to the rhetorical framework of the psalmist's relationship with the enemy and with God. The prevalence of military and weaponry language

of a wound are as elaborate as in Ps 38, but the only function of an arrow is to wound or threaten to wound. When the psalmist says that his enemy's words are like arrows (Ps 64:4) or that he lies down with lions "whose teeth are spears and arrows" (Ps 57:5), the threat of wounding is implied. Weapons, then, are integral to the somatic idiom of distress, intimately tied to the expression of pain or the anticipation of pain in these texts. As Elaine Scarry observes, weaponry, and woundedness are bound together and intimately connected to the communication of pain.[50] Weapons *mean* pain: "The point here is not just that pain can be apprehended in the image of the weapon (or wound) but that it almost cannot be apprehended without it."[51]

As a place "where boundary negotiations take place," the condition of the flesh is an important indicator of bodily representation as weakened and compromised, and this is especially true of Ps 38.[52] Arrows have penetrated into (נחתו בי) and God's hand has settled upon (תנחת עלי) the psalmist. The repetition of the verb נחת emphasizes the aggressive nature of God's action against the speaker's whole body, within (בי) and upon (עלי) the speaker's flesh. Verse 4 describes the psalmist's flesh (בשר), ruptured by God's arrows, as unsound (אין מתם) and without wholeness (שלום). The condition of the flesh is so central to this psalm that the psalmist repeats in Ps 38:8 the same phrase as in v. 4: אין מתם בבשרי. The verse refers to the whole of the body, flesh and bone, indicators of boundaries and the structure of the body described as violated and unstable. God's arrows and the resulting woundedness represent the body's surface as permeable and harmable.

Following description of arrows wounding the psalmist and unsound flesh, the psalmist proceeds in vv. 6–9 with a lacerating description of an angry wound and an injured body:

> My wounds (חבורה) stink (באש) and rot (מקק)
> because of my foolishness.
> I am twisted (עוה) and bent (שחח) all the time.
> All day I walk in gloom.
> For my loins are full of burning (קלה),
> there is no soundness in my flesh.
> I am powerless (פוג) and crushed (דכה),
> I roar from the groaning of my heart. (Ps 38:6–9)

---

contributes to the general rhetorical atmosphere of threat and anxiety in the laments, some of which is somatically experienced by the psalmist, and some of which the psalmist desires to impose upon the enemy.

49. See Pss 7:14; 38:3; 57:5; 64:4, 8; 120:4.

50. Scarry, *The Body in Pain*, 16: "Both weapon (whether actual or imagined) and wound (whether actual or imagined) may be used associatively to express pain. To some extent, the inner workings of the two metaphors, as well as the perceptual complications that attend their use, overlap because the second (bodily damage) sometimes occurs as a version of the first (agency)."

51. Ibid., 16.

52. Claudia Benthien, *Skin: On the Cultural Border Between Self and the World* (trans. Thomas Dunlap; New York: Columbia University Press, 2002), ix. See also Ps 102:6, where bones show through the skin, a picture of physical deterioration, and Ps 109:24, where the flesh fails because of thinness, a sign of ill health, distress, and suffering.

This psalm's rarefied and stylized vocabulary contributes to its highly articulate representation of pain, a detailed and thorough portrait of pain that strives for visibility. The noun חבורה and three verbal roots באש, מקק, and קלה (as well as סחרחר in Ps 38:11) occur only in these verses in the Psalms, indicating the precision and meticulousness of the psalmist's language. Further, the roots עוה[53] and פוג[54] each occur in only one other instance in the Psalms. This intentional representation utilizes highly descriptive words that focus on the decay and putrefaction of the wounded body.

Moreover, these verses relentlessly build a representation of the psalmist as sick and plagued, most pronounced in Ps 38:7–9, which describe the body as burning (קלה), bent (שחח),[55] twisted (עוה), even powerless (פוג) and crushed (דכה).[56] Here, the language describing the beset body piles up so that by the end of v. 9 there is no doubt as to the state of utter suffering endured. The language is insistent and unremitting, beginning and ending in v. 7 and v. 9 with the emphatic phrase עד מאד, twice employed to emphasize extreme physical despair. The portrait presented through this language is of a body crippled by suffering, beleaguered and powerless.

In the verses following (vv. 11–12), the psalmist further articulates theological and social implications of his indisputable woundedness:

> My heart beats violently (סחרחר);[57]
> my strength abandons (עזב) me.
> The light of my eyes is also not with me (אתי);
> my loved ones and my friends
> stand back[58] from my wound (נגע).
> My kin stand far away. (Ps 38:11–12)

The psalmist's description of his woundedness begins in Ps 38:3 by naming God as the perpetrator of his injury, a clear illustration of the psalmist's sense of God's abandonment and hostility.[59] Ending the extensive representation of his woundedness and extreme physical agitation ("my heart beats violently," v. 11a),

---

53. עוה is used only in Pss 38:7 and 106:6, though the latter is not an individual lament. In Ps 106:6, the root does not refer to the body, but refers to going astray, or doing wrong.

54. פוג is used in Pss 38:9 and 77:3.

55. שחח is used in Pss 10:10; 35:14; 38:7; 42:6, 7, 12; 43:5; 107:39. (Ps 107, however, is not an individual lament.)

56. דכה is used in Pss 10:10; 38:9; 44:20; 51:10, 19.

57. סחרחר (the Pealal form of סחר) occurs only in Ps 38:11.

58. Instead of מנגד נגעי יעמדו in the MT, the LXX (ἐξ ἐναντίας μου ἤγγισαν καὶ ἔστησαν) reads, "My friends and neighbors stepped forward and took their stand." Instead of נגע, "wound," the LXX suggests נגש, "stand back," and deletes יעמדו because of the repetition in the next line. The presence of the wound in this verse, however, is wholly consistent with the progression of the previous verses; the explicit and horrifying depiction of the wounded body is the reason the community recoils. The LXX reading addresses the awkward parallelism of the verse, but misses the importance of the wound in the progression of the psalm as a whole.

59. This image of God's arrows penetrating the psalmist's skin is unique in the laments. Other texts concerned with the representation of the body in pain also refer to God's arrows, such as Job 6:4 and Lam 3:12.

the psalmist describes bodily desertion, first by strength, then by eyes that are not "with" him (v. 11). Finally, in v. 12, the psalmist represents himself as abandoned by his community, not just by strangers and enemies, but also by loved ones and others who might care for him. The somatic and social significance of the psalmist's wound come together between v. 3 and v. 12, so that by the end, the wound provides a somatic means of organizing the psalmist's sense of utter abandonment: theological, physical, and social. The wound positions the speaker physically and socially in a position of extremity, isolated and unprotected, and also in a position of powerlessness, as one who is wholly without recourse, support, or defense.

The social aspect of the somatic wound is further clarified in Ps 69, in which the psalmist describes his pursuers "telling" about his wound to others:

> For they pursue him whom you have wounded (נכה);
> they tell about (יספרו)[60] the pain
> of those you have pierced (חלל). (Ps 69:27)

In his argument for another translation of this verse, Kraus argues that "telling about" (יספרו) the pain is "senseless" in this context.[61] The psalmist's deep aversion to having others tell the story of his wounds, however, adds depth and significance to the image of the injured body in this verse, further indicating the way his physical distress is a means of social positioning.[62] The story of his bodily frailty has a social significance in the world of the psalmist, with reverberating relational implications. Though I discuss this aspect of the psalmist's sense of shame in physical and social diminishment in the context of his relationship with the hostile foe more thoroughly in the next chapter, Ps 69 effectively articulates the interconnection between the somatic and the social in the psalmist's language.

Moreover, the public report of the psalmist's injury also has relational significance in the God/psalmist relationship. God as protector is indicted by evidence of the psalmist's bodily injury, even though, and perhaps especially if, God is

---

60. The LXX (προσέθηκαν) and Syriac suggest יספיו ("they multiply the pain") instead of the MT's יספרו ("they tell about the pain"). There is no reason to emend the MT, however, as I indicate in my argument above.

61. H.-J. Kraus (*Psalms 60–150: A Commentary* [trans. Hilton C. Oswald; Minneapolis: Augsburg, 1989], 59) follows the LXX and translates Ps 69:27b, "and multiply the pain of him whom you have struck." The NRSV also follows the LXX, though the NJPS supports reading יספרו in this context, translating the line, "they talk about the pain of those You have felled." In addition, Mitchell J. Dahood (*Psalms* [3 vols.; AB 16–17A; Garden City, N.Y.: Doubleday, 1965–70], 2:155 and 163) retains the MT's יספרו in Ps 69:27: "they…told stories about the pain of him you wounded."

62. This language resonates with Job 16:8, in which Job describes his body testifying against him. As in Ps 69, the image here is of the bodily condition of the speaker resulting in public humiliation and alienation. The image in Job more directly implies corporeal alienation, since the body is the agent of the testifying; Job's own body betrays him. In Ps 69, the body itself does not do the telling, but an unsympathetic witness, though there is still a sense in which the speaker's body provides the material for the betrayal. The supplicant cannot rely on his own body for loyalty and social support. The body has its own social role, not just as the means of expressing pain, but also as a means of social positioning.

the one causing the harm, as indicated in this verse. Though this verse does represent tension between the psalmist's desire to describe his wound in specific detail, so evident in Ps 38, and the psalmist's deep chagrin that others will tell of his wound, that tension is part of the social complexity of the psalmist's rhetoric. The psalmist's pain provides authenticity and substantiates his desires for God's intervention and the hearing audience's sympathy, as well as providing the psalmist himself a means of satisfyingly expressing his experience. Simultaneously, the psalmist's public humiliation and sense of alienation involved in being both physically damaged and having stories of his physical and social diminishment publicly discussed is powerful in the world of the laments. As I will discuss in the next chapter, however, description of social diminishment by hostile foes is similar to the representation of bodily distress in that it represents disempowerment while also affording agency. The wound is a rhetorical bridge between the psalmist's somatic diminishment and his social alienation.

d. *Language of Inarticulateness*

At various points, the psalmist represents himself through audible, but non-verbal, language of agony and desperation. The psalmist renders the most extreme portrayal of physical suffering in instances in which he is reduced to inarticulateness. The portrait here is of a desperate kind of suffering that creates incapacitation.[63] He describes himself as groaning (אנחה)[64] and roaring (שאג, שאגה),[65] all descriptions of being overcome by suffering to the point of ineffable and guttural anguish:[66]

> I am exhausted with groaning (אנחה).
> Every night I flood my bed,
> I melt my couch in tears. (Ps 6:7)

> Why so far from my cry,
> the message[67] of my roaring (שאגה)?[68] (Ps 22:2)

---

63. The psalmist also describes weeping (בכה) such that his bed is drenched in Ps 6:7. See also Pss 6:9; 69:11, and 102:10 for use of the verb בכה. Weeping, however, does not connote the same kind of desperation and inarticulateness as groaning.

64. All uses of the word אנחה in the Psalms occur in the individual laments. See Pss 6:7; 31:11; 38:10; 102:6. Job, Jeremiah, and Lamentation all refer to anguished sighing (אנחה) in the context of individual lament. See Job 3:24; 23:2; Jer 45:3; Lam 1:22.

65. In the Psalms, שאג is used in 38:9; שאגה is used in Pss 22:2 and 32:3. שאג is also used in Pss 22:14; 74:4, and 104:21, though not in reference to the suffering individual.

66. In three instances, in Pss 12:6, 79:11, and 102:21, the word אנקה indicates the desperation of someone other than the psalmist; this word is not used to refer to the suffering individual.

67. Literally, דברי שאגתי is "the words (דברי) of my roaring." This example is problematic, since it contradicts my argument in this section that roaring is inarticulate, without words. I contend that roaring is an image of inarticulateness, even here, however. Relying on the flexibility of the word, I read דבר in this instance as referring to the content of the utterance, as opposed to discreet words. Roaring does contain a message, even if it is not articulated verbally. Still, the ambiguity is present.

68. The MT reads "far from my help are the words of my roaring." I have emended מישועתי ("from my help") to משועתי ("from my cry") based on the similarity of the roots ישע and שוע. This emendation also works in terms of the parallelism of the verse. Crying (שוע) is parallel to roaring

My life is spent in sorrow,
my years in groaning (אנחה). (Ps 31:11)

While I said nothing,
my bones wasted away from
my roaring (שאגה) all day long. (Ps 32:3)[69]

Because of the sound of my groaning (אנחה),
my bones cling to my flesh. (Ps 102:6)

Psalm 38, an unusually articulate example of rhetorically visible pain, is also the most poignant representation of inarticulateness. A highly specific concentration of vocabulary culminates in vv. 9–10 with the image of the most intense state of torment:

I am all benumbed and crushed;
I roar (שאג) from a raging (נהמה)[70] heart.
O Lord, my desire is before you;
my sighs (אנחה) are not hidden from you. (Ps 38:9–10)

The psalmist represents his body through nonverbal expressions of torment and pain that anyone would recognize as signs of physical suffering. The word נהמה, "raging," is quite rare, used three times in Proverbs (Prov 19:12; 20:2; 28:15) to refer to the actions of a lion and once in Isa 5:30 to refer to the sea, but only once in the Psalms. Within this one verse inarticulateness combines with high articulateness. In Ps 38 as a whole, anguished groans dramatically accentuate the psalmist's agonized and plagued body.

The significance of these images of inarticulateness as part of the psalmist's self-representation as powerless is helpfully clarified within the context of Elaine Scarry's arguments about the ability of pain to destroy language. Central to Scarry's argument is that intense pain not only defies but obliterates language: "Physical pain does not simply resist language but actively destroys it, bringing about an immediate reversion to a state anterior to language, to the sounds and cries a human being makes before language is learned."[71] Scarry addresses the agony of torture, which is not clearly the source of the psalmist's pain, yet the progression of images in Ps 38 mirrors the destruction of language through intense pain that Scarry describes. First, pain invades and monopolizes one's language, such that "complaint...becomes the exclusive mode of address."[72] The body's suffering takes up all the linguistic space available, pushing language to its limits as it struggles to capture the intensity. Finally, however, pain is too

---

(שאג) in the final line. See also Kraus, *Psalms 1–59*, 292, and Kselman, "'Why Have You Abandoned Me?,'" 175.

69. Ps 32 is not an individual lament, but in this verse the psalmist remembers his past physical suffering, the distress from which God has saved him. There are elements of the individual lament in the psalm that are relevant.

70. נהמה is another rare word found in this psalm, found only here and in Isa 5:30, where it refers to a roaring sea.

71. Scarry, *The Body in Pain*, 4.

72. Ibid., 54.

much for language: "Eventually the pain so deepens that the coherence of complaint is displaced by the sounds anterior to learned language."[73] Indeed, this is the development portrayed in this psalm. The psalmist is first highly articulate, pushing his language to capture with precision his wound, painting a highly evocative verbal portrait of breached flesh. Finally, however, the psalmist represents himself as groaning and sighing, a depiction of ultimate, absolute, and agency-robbing pain.

Some concerns must be raised about Scarry's assertion that acute pain destroys language, however. The destruction of language, for Scarry, is nothing less than the unmaking of the world, the absolute triumph of dominating power over the tortured individual's voice, creative potential, and self. For Scarry, this kind of pain does not and cannot exist in the world; she argues for the "simple and absolute incompatibility of pain and the world. The survival of each depends on its separation from the other."[74] To endure this kind of pain is to be destroyed, to have one's language, one's means of articulating selfhood, obliterated. Her argument assumes that pain is always dominant and the human body, weak and limited, always overwhelmed by pain's power; identity and selfhood cannot withstand such treatment.

What Scarry fails to observe is the way that pain can both steal and heighten human agency. Without minimizing the kind of destructive power exhibited in torture, extreme pain does not always result in the destruction of identity and worlds. In fact, in some cases intense pain may assist or generate the construction of identity. Though Scarry conceives of intense pain as always triumphant, dominating the individual and ultimately powerful, others counter with evidence that acute pain in some instances is part of the construction, not obliteration, of identity and language. Historian Janel Mueller, for instance, argues that narratives of extreme pain in torture offered a means of articulating and strengthening identity for those who resisted the demands of religious orthodoxy under Mary Tudor: "In place of unmade selves, voices, or worlds…narratives record triumphant *makings* on the part of the condemned heretics, and on the part of their prosecutors (or persecutors), correspondent unmakings that render specious any triumph that the latter may claim."[75] Likewise, in the laments, the language of pain represents unmaking even as it makes identity for those who suffer, affording a means of interpreting and acting upon situations that impose extreme physical and social suffering.

Scarry's recognition of the importance of inarticulateness in the experience and expression of pain is important, however. Though pain may not always be world-destroying in the way that Scarry describes, she recognizes the intensity

---

73. Ibid., 54.

74. Ibid., 50–51. See also Peter Singer's excellent review of this book, "Unspeakable Acts" (review of Elaine Scarry, *The Body in Pain: The Making and Unmaking of the World* and Edward Peters, *Torture*), *New York Review of Books* 33, no. 3, February 27, 1986.

75. Janel M. Mueller, "Pain, Persecution, and the Construction of Selfhood in Foxe's *Acts and Monuments*," in *Religion and Culture in Renaissance England* (ed. Claire McEachern and Debora Shuger; Cambridge: Cambridge University Press, 1997), 162 (emphasis added).

of pain that can overwhelm language, which is the means by which one interprets and creates meaning for a participant of a figured world. I distinguish, however, between overwhelming language and destroying language. Pain is always experienced within cultural artifacts, including language. That language is not static and absolute. The intense kind of pain that Scarry describes may challenge the boundaries of those artifacts, causing them to evolve and change. Pain may challenge the limitations of that language and reach the extremities of the cultural interpretations embedded therein. Yet pain is not acultural; it always exists within some framework of interpretation. Further, as Mueller suggests, interpretive frameworks are not fixed, but malleable; an interpretive framework for pain may reflect the linguistic individual's engulfment by pain, but it may also assist the individual to articulate something new.

Rhetorically, it matters that the laments represent pain that defies language in an extreme way and reduces the psalmist to groans. In fact, the experience of inarticulateness, if not an example of shattered language and worlds, is representative of encompassing pain. Inarticulateness represents the psalmist as one who is consumed by the experience of suffering in such an absolute way that he cannot see or communicate anything else. These images efficiently position the psalmist because they effectively communicate the complete absorption of the sufferer in his suffering, communicating need, desperation, and urgency. While the psalmist sometimes declares physical pain articulately, the inclusion of the psalmist's roars, sighs, and groans depicts the body in provocative and urgent pain that overwhelms vocabulary. Even though it is not the groans and sighs themselves, but the words pointing to them, the psalmist's sense of utter powerlessness is depicted in these images even as the expression of that powerlessness affords a means to organize his experience and to emerge as an agent.[76]

3. *The Language of the Suffering Body as a Discourse of Distress and Power*

Arthur Kleinman, a psychiatrist and medical anthropologist, provides the foundation for my understanding of the body-language of the laments as a cultural discourse of both distress and power, a complex of articulation of disempowerment that also functions as a mode of moral agency for the psalmist in specific ways. It is necessary to provide some background for Kleinman's conclusions. Therefore, I engage in a brief discussion of his work that concludes with discussion of three ways Kleinman understands the language of bodily suffering to empower the sufferer even as it expresses physical and social distress.

---

76. For further discussion of the way expression of pain, especially in incoherent and volatile utterances, can both witness to a sufferer's identity-robbing trauma and offer the means to remember, grieve, and testify, or begin to organize a new identity, see Serene Jones, "'Soul Anatomy': Calvin's Commentary on the Psalms," in *Psalms in Community: Jewish and Christian Textual, Liturgical, and Artistic Traditions* (ed. Harold W. Attridge and Margot E. Fassler; Atlanta: Society of Biblical Literature, 2003), 265–84, esp. 279–81. Jones's work draws on observations from trauma theory in combination with Calvin's commentary on the Psalms to discuss issues of powerlessness and development of agency in situations of intense suffering.

Kleinman's major contribution to my project is his understanding of the expression of bodily distress and illness as a discursive practice, a cultural language. Kleinman interprets the language of physical suffering as a cultural language of distress that mediates the individual's social and physical relationship to his or her cultural world. He understands physical anguish and sickness not simply as a physiological experience, but as a mode of social interaction embedded in cultural assumptions about the self, body, and larger society. Physical suffering is always deeply rooted in the culture in which it occurs, the result of an ongoing dialogue between "social world and person, cultural values and physiology."[77] No one, Kleinman argues, discovers or discusses her body "*de novo*," but always in a learned cultural language, a somatic idiom.[78] While all people share certain commonalities because of embodiment, bodies, bodily experiences, and bodily expression happen in different cultural worlds and are attributed vastly different meanings in those worlds.[79] This assumption is vital to the present project, as my intention is to understand how the language of the body functions in the particular cultural world of the laments.

Kleinman's work provides an important social and cultural lens through which to approach bodily distress and illness as not just a physical experience of one individual but also a social discourse that constructs the identity of the sufferer in a particular way. This observation enriches one of the primary ways that scholars have addressed the body-language of the laments, by locating it in a context of illness.[80] That is, the psalmist's physical suffering has often been a

---

77. Kleinman, *Social Origins of Distress and Disease*, 171. For more on pain as an acculturated, as opposed to natural, experience, see Scott E. Pincikowski, *Bodies of Pain: Suffering in the Works of Hartmann von Aue* (New York: Routledge, 2002).

78. Arthur Kleinman, *The Illness Narratives: Suffering, Healing, and the Human Condition* (New York: Basic, 1988), 13.

79. The literature about the relationship between the body, society, and discourse is extensive. The following have been most helpful:

Thomas Csordas, ed., *Embodiment and Experience: The Existential Ground of Culture and Self* (Cambridge: Cambridge University Press, 1994); Mike Featherstone, Mike Hepworth, and Bryan S. Turner, eds., *The Body: Social Process and Cultural Theory* (London: Sage, 1990); Michel Feher, Ramona Nadaff, and Nadia Tazi, eds., *Fragments for a History of the Human Body* (3 vols.; New York: Zone, 1989); Foucault, *Discipline and Punish*; Michael O'Donovan-Anderson, ed., *The Incorporated Self: Interdisciplinary Perspectives on Embodiment* (New York: Rowman & Littlefield, 1996); Porter, "History of the Body"; Chris Shilling, *The Body and Social Theory* (London: Sage, 1993); Anthony Synnott, *The Body Social: Symbolism, Self and Society* (London: Routledge, 1993); Bryan S. Turner, *The Body and Society* (New York: Blackwell, 1984); Simon J. Williams and Gillian Bendelow, eds., *The Lived Body: Sociological Themes, Embodied Issues* (London: Routledge, 1998). The increasing literature about how pain is represented and experienced differently in cultural worlds is especially relevant. See especially Bending, *The Representation of Bodily Pain*; Steven Bruhm, *Gothic Bodies: The Politics of Pain in Romantic Fiction* (Philadelphia: University of Pennsylvania Press, 1994); Florike Egmond and Robert Zwijnenberg, eds., *Bodily Extremities: Preoccupations with the Human Body in Early Modern European Culture* (Burlington, Vt.: Ashgate, 2003); Pincikowski, *Bodies of Pain*; Roselyne Rey, *The History of Pain* (Cambridge, Mass.: Harvard University Press, 1995).

80. For instance, Kraus (*Psalms 1–59*, 53) includes the following as prayer songs of a sick person, or prayers of sickness and healing: Pss 38; 41; 88 (certainly); 30; 39; 69; 102; 103 (relatively

means of categorizing particular psalms according to their historical setting in the experience of illness.[81] The discussion of illness has typically been limited to arguments for S*itz im Leben*, or to attempts to diagnose the psalmist, and not to a broader discussion of the quality of that language and how it functions rhetorically in the specific cultural context of the laments.[82] As Konrad Schaefer argues, "The poet complains of sickness and failing energies, and, given the passage of time and the foreign climate, the interpreter can do little more than list the symptoms and diagnose an underlying attitude toward illness."[83] Read from the perspective of Kleinman's understanding of illness as a cultural language, attempts to diagnose the psalmist's ailment reflect an understanding of illness as only a physical pathology. The expression of illness, according to Kleinman, is much more than a description of symptoms; it is a cultural language of embodiment that is steeped in the symbolic structure of the culture. Illness is, at once, individual and social, metaphorical and literal, physical and relational, and the way in which illness is expressed is culturally particular.

Kleinman's work is based primarily on comparative studies between the United States and China. In his research, Kleinman observed that symptoms like headache, dizziness, sleeplessness, anxiety, weakness, and fatigue are frequently diagnosed as neurasthenia in China. This diagnosis is more biological in orientation than depression, which is the diagnosis that similar symptoms frequently earn in the United States. Depression as a diagnosis orients the perception and treatment of sufferers in psychophysiological ways. Though neurasthenia as a diagnosis originated in the United States and was popular as a diagnosis between the years 1890 and 1930, it is no longer a respected or viable diagnosis

certainly); 6; 13; 31; 32; 35; 51; 71; 77; 91 (probably). Seybold (*Introducing the Psalms*, 117) does not offer a complete list, but argues that examples of "psalms of ill-health" are Pss 6; 13; 38; 39; 41; 51; 69; 102; 130.

81.   Terence Collins' work deserves special comment because it exhibits awareness of cultural differences in the psalmic and modern understanding of illness. Collins understands that modern conceptions that make clear distinction between physical and emotional distress, and associate illness with the former, do not fit the psalmist's own understanding of illness. He understands that for the psalmist, the body provides a way of talking about all kinds of distress and that the psalmist would never have made clear distinctions between physical and emotional distress. Ultimately, however, he argues that with close linguistic analysis modern interpreters could determine whether the distress was emotional or physical. He ultimately uses his in-depth discussion of the language for weeping in the Hebrew Bible as a way of deciding whether certain psalms have to do with emotional or physical distress, and so reverts to modern assumptions about illness as his basis for assigning *Sitz im Leben* (Terence Collins, "The Physiology of Tears in the Old Testament: Part I," *CBQ* 33 [1971]: 18–38; "The Physiology of Tears in the Old Testament: Part II," *CBQ* 33 [1971]: 185–97).

82.   Fredrik Lindström's work is an exception; he challenges the purely physical understanding of sickness that he feels has characterized many approaches to the psalms. His work primarily challenges the argument that illness is the result of sin and is a manifestation of God's punishing wrath (Fredrik Lindström, *Suffering and Sin: Interpretations of Illness in the Individual Complaint Psalms* [Stockholm: Almqvist & Wiksell, 1994], 19, 24–41). In addition, see Kristin M. Swenson, *Living Through Pain: Psalms and the Search for Wholeness* (Waco, Tex.: Baylor University Press, 2005), whose study of pain and the Psalms relies on an understanding that encompasses "physical, emotional, psychological, and spiritual pain" (p. 3).

83.   Konrad Schaefer, *Psalms* (Collegeville: Liturgical Press, 2001), xxxii.

and is perceived as old-fashioned and out-dated by Western medical profes-
sionals.[84] Kleinman traces a gradual series of cultural shifts that replaced the
somatic orientation of neurasthenia with an orientation that was increasingly
psychological.[85] Though the question of the exact relationship between biology,
psychology, and social factors in the experience of depression is still a topic of
research and discussion, the diagnosis of neurasthenia no longer addresses mod-
ern understandings of the self in a satisfactory fashion in the United States.[86] The
question that Kleinman addresses is why discourses of distress—physical,
social, and personal—emerge differently in diverse cultural contexts.

Kleinman's argument is that the difference in diagnostic trends has to do with
recognizing culturally privileged ways of experiencing the body and expressing
distress in order to seek assistance. In China, emotions and feelings are more
likely to be expressed through the body, which offers a more culturally salient
method of communication. This process of feeling and expressing distress
through the body is called, "somatization," in which "[l]oss, injustice, failure,
conflict—all are transformed into discourse about pain and disability that is a
metaphor for discourse and action about the self and the social world. The body
mediates the individual's perception, experience, and interpretation of problems
in social life."[87] That is, the distress caused by life situations such as loss, the
experience of injustice, stress, despair, or sadness are reflected and expressed in
physical, somatic symptoms. Significantly, Kleinman argues that the body does
not merely provide a means of representing distress. The body actually feels the
distress and interprets the social environment of the individual. According to
Kleinman, the body is a vehicle for expression of social problems as they inter-
face with the individual's interpretation: "Somatic idioms of distress…indicate
that in some nontrivial sense the body feels and expresses social problems."[88]
Kleinman observes that in socio-centric cultures such as the one found in China,
focus on the individual's internal, psychological life threatens the cultural values
of social and political harmony and is consequently not socially valued and is

84.   Kleinman (*Social Origins of Distress and Disease*, 32) notes that some Chinese medical
professionals are now uneasy with neurasthenia as a diagnosis, possibly due to Western skepticism.
    85.   Ibid., 22: "This historical transformation of neurasthenia from a somatic to a psychosomatic
to psychic state, and its ultimate dismissal as a pseudo-disease, reflects a major cultural change over
the past one hundred years. Neurasthenia's role in popular culture was superseded when psychoso-
matic and psychological constructs became acceptable means for interpreting problems in everyday
living, and euphemisms, indirection, or liminal ambiguity were no longer required." See also Klein-
man, *The Illness Narratives*, 102.
    86.   Kleinman (*Social Origins of Distress and Disease*, 39) observes that depression is only
recently viewed as psychological. The first descriptions of depression, originally called melancholia,
were somatopsychic. As he says, "Only in the West in very recent times, beginning in the Victorian
period and accelerating after Freud, have psychological and psychosomatic views of these disorders
become popular in both medical and lay circles. The recognition that biological, psychological, and
social features of depression (and neurasthenia) need to be integrated in clinical research is just
beginning to be widely shared" (ibid., 40–41).
    87.   Ibid., 51.
    88.   Ibid., 194.

even considered socially dangerous.[89] Therefore, while the Chinese individual might admit to feelings of sadness, the body provides a safe and acceptable means of experiencing and expressing distress.

The concept of somatization is relevant to reading the language of the suffering body in the laments. One cannot push comparisons between modern China and ancient Israel too far, but there are some similarities that make Kleinman's discussion of illness languages relevant and helpful. For instance, both cultures are better characterized as socio-centric than focused on the psyche of the individual. In the laments, there is no discussion of feelings or emotions, per se. Emotions, as a modern reader might think of them (and we should not assume any kind of direct correspondence between modern and ancient understandings of "feelings"), are expressed relationally and physically in a discourse of bodily suffering and alienation. Moreover, the psalmist may in fact feel physical pain and experience sickness; the psalmist's physical suffering is not "all in his head." Yet the language of bodily suffering in the laments is overdetermined, carrying multiple levels of meaning and significance for the psalmist as well as those who witness his words. The language of bodily suffering in the laments, therefore, is a way of describing physical pain, but also a means of expressing the acute anxiety, distress, loss, and anger that relate to the psalmist's sense of social alienation and experience of injustice. The psalmist's somatic idiom of distress bridges the personal and the public, the physical and the emotional.

Importantly, Kleinman observes that the rhetoric of somatization serves a significant and positive function for the sufferer. Though the somatic idiom of distress utilized in China to discuss these experiences may seem maladaptive to Western medical professionals, Kleinman argues that it is actually adaptive in Chinese cultures.[90] That is, the language of bodily suffering in China is a culturally salient means of expressing feelings and emotions that cannot safely be articulated in other ways, offering "discourse strategies to open up behavioral options."[91] The "somatic idiom"[92] of distress is not only a language of powerlessness and despair, but also a mode of social interaction that offers the individual a position of power and authority.[93] Herein lies the significance of Kleinman's work for my study. The somatic idiom of distress has a utility that is socially and personally beneficial to the psalmist. The way the psalmist expresses pain and suffering is not just a reflection of a physical state, but also a way of advantageously positioning himself in relation to others within his social world. Kleinman isolates three considerable benefits to using the culturally valued idiom of distress that are directly relevant to the psalmist's language of suffering.[94]

---

89. Kleinman, *The Illness Narratives*, 109.

90. Kleinman (*Social Origins of Distress and Disease*, 174) recognizes that somatization can be maladaptive, especially if an individual begins to construct an enduring identity upon his illness.

91. Ibid., 174.

92. Ibid., 167.

93. See also David B. Morris, *The Culture of Pain* (Berkeley, Calif.: University of California Press, 1991), 193.

94. Kleinman does not enumerate the possible benefits of articulating bodily distress in privileged idioms. I have culled these observations from his work and presented them in this fashion to

First, Kleinman observes that the body becomes a way of organizing one's feelings of despair, anxiety, hopelessness, and physical pain in a discourse that is culturally acceptable and recognized.[95] Articulation of pain in this discourse is in and of itself an act of agency that helps the individual define and characterize his suffering: "Not the least of illness's properties is the medium of communication it affords to express distress, demoralization, unhappiness, and other difficult, dangerous, and otherwise unsanctioned feelings in terms that must be heard and may lead to change."[96] The way one articulates pain and characterizes suffering is a means of containing and providing boundaries for that suffering. Likewise, in the laments, the idiom of distress affords agency and is part of the overall rhetorical intent of the prayer. In the laments, the language of pain represents unmaking even as it makes identity for those who suffer, affording a means of interpreting and acting upon situations that impose extreme physical and social suffering.

A second way Kleinman argues that the somatic idiom of distress is a means of empowerment is as a rhetorical device for persuading and exerting social authority. The use of this language sometimes empowers the sufferer by helping him control local relationships and acquire access to resources, such as medical and/or personal attention from friends, neighbors, employers, and family.[97] As Kleinman describes, being sick

> may serve to authorize and sanction failure (in work, school, marriage, sexual relations), may marshall social support otherwise unavailable (for example, love and aid from an estranged spouse), may sanction the expression of anger that is otherwise illegitimate, may provide time out and away from terribly difficult circumstances that one feels she or he can no longer tolerate.[98]

In some instances, the expression of illness opens up behavioral options that the sufferer perceives to be limited. This element of moral agency is not always a facet of using the bodily distress idiom, however. Kleinman does not argue that there is always empowerment in being ill or that sick individuals are necessarily aware of their agency when they utilize it. Being ill may, in fact, lead to increased powerlessness. Kleinman describes a situation in which the meaning of illness "oscillates between agency and structure," such that illness can convey several different meanings within the experience of one person.[99] That is, the individual's adoption of a particular idiom of distress can be, at once, a way of communicating powerlessness and despair and a mode of social interaction that affords power and authority to seek beneficial change. Neither aspect negates the other.

---

facilitate intelligibility. See also Paul E. Brodwin, "Symptoms and Social Performances: The Case of Diane Reden," in DelVecchio Good et al., eds., *Pain as Human Experience*, 78–79.

    95.   As Kleinman (*Social Origins of Distress and Disease*, 173) says, "somatization is an interpretive schema for making sense of life problems."

    96.   Ibid., 151.

    97.   Ibid., 173.

    98.   Ibid., 146.

    99.   Ibid., 146.

An example from the laments exemplifies Kleinman's argument. Above, within the analysis of the element of corporeal making and unmaking as a contribution to the discourse of bodily suffering, I described proximity to death as among the most extreme representations of bodily powerlessness. The speaker's physical relegation to the realm of the dead, however, is not without rhetorical power in the psalmist's attempts to change his situation and is, ironically, the basis upon which the psalmist makes his most blatant appeal to empower himself in his negotiation with God for physical survival. Especially in Ps 6:6, the psalmist uses his near-death location to position God socially as well, emphasizing their mutual dependence: "For there is no remembrance of you in death; in Sheol who praises you?" Similarly, in Ps 30:10, the psalmist asks, "Can dust praise you?" The psalmist reminds God that the psalmist's lack of power means diminishment for God as well. The psalmist employs the rhetoric of bodily powerlessness in a bid for some degree of relational power. In order for God to maintain God's position, praise is required from the embodied living. Physical disempowerment, then, is not unambiguously a means of expressing powerlessness. The body's suffering is also the position from which the psalmist articulates his sense of power in relation to God.[100]

Kleinman isolates a third important way the language of bodily distress often functions as a means of empowerment for disenfranchised or isolated individuals. The somatic expression of distress not only offers the suffering individual a culturally recognized discursive role, but also offers others in the social world culturally sanctioned ways of expressing support and caring for the suffering person.[101] In China, for instance, Kleinman observes that expression of distress in psychological terms often results in further alienation for the sufferer; the psychological expression of distress does not offer others a socially legitimate means of responding to the sufferer. When the sufferer adopts a somatic idiom of distress, however, relief for the individual and reintegration into the community is often achieved. The somatic idiom of distress offers others a recognizable role to play with regard to the individual's distress that is culturally respected. Expression of anxiety through the body offers the individual a position from which to communicate his or her need for social support, and also offers others a way of expressing support, of showing sympathy through concern for the individual's suffering.[102] According to Kleinman, therefore, adopting the somatic idiom of distress is a means of not only organizing one's own experience, but also of organizing others' responses, a tremendously powerful rhetorical tool. Significantly, James Boyd White describes a similar process in the interaction between a reader and an author of literature, in which the author seeks to establish a particular kind of relationship with the reader: "There is a sense in which every text may be said to define an ideal reader, which it asks its audience

---

100. I discuss the relationship between God and the psalmist implied in these verses in Chapter 4. Here, the important element to note is the way embodiment serves as a source for articulation of both powerlessness and power.

101. Kleinman, *Social Origins of Distress and Disease*, 178.

102. Ibid., 151.

to become, or to approximate, for the moment at least and perhaps forever."[103] In much the same way, the somatic language of suffering in the laments invites the hearer to become a certain kind of ideal witness, sympathetic, protective, and possibly active on behalf of the psalmist's restoration.

What Kleinman describes in the ability of the somatic idiom of distress to afford others a culturally acceptable and valued way of responding is perhaps part of simply recognizing that the laments are a persuasive discourse; a rhetorical act that seeks change in circumstances, as the laments most certainly did, often appeals to embedded values and commitments of the hearer and aligns the speaker's needs with those previous commitments. In the language of bodily suffering, the psalmist appeals to the hearer's (including God's) desire to be (or to be seen as) compassionate, protective, and kind to one who suffers. Beyond direct appeals, always to God, to act in specific ways (to save, deliver, protect, etc.) the psalmist sometimes offers rhetorical pointers to the hearing audience as to the role he would like them to assume with regard to his suffering. Descriptions of bodily distress that culminate in images of the psalmist's reintegration in the community—the psalmist offers praise to God in the "great congregation" (בקהל רב, Pss 35:18a and 22:26), and "among many people" (בעם עצום, Ps 35:18b)—are rhetorical guides to the hearing audience as well as to God.[104] The psalmist implicitly lets the audience know that his desire is reintegration and offers them the opportunity to act redemptively, to look upon him sympathetically and act in a way that would restore the psalmist to community life. The implications of this kind of role-offering persuasive rhetoric are thoroughly explored in the final chapter of the present study with regard to Ps 109, but here, it is important to recognize that the psalmist positions himself beneficially by utilizing a discourse that offers others a means of responding sympathetically that is culturally valued and recognized.

The particular ability of somatic distress to organize the responses of hearers is also evident in modern scholars' interpretations of this language. Most recently, Susanne Gillmayr-Bucher argues that the body-language of the Psalms not only adds to the passion, intensity of expression, and pathos of the psalmist, but also invites a particular response by allowing the reader to share the experience of the psalmist through body-language.[105] She repeatedly emphasizes the effect of this language on the reader and cites with approval the way body-language involves the reader in the experience of the psalmist and prohibits a voyeuristic or indifferent response to the suffering the psalmist describes. In fact, she frequently describes the intimacy the reader feels with the psalmist

---

103. White, *When Words Lose Their Meaning*, 15.

104. See also Ps 57:10, "I will thank you amidst the peoples (אודך באמים)," and Ps 109:30, "I will praise him in the midst of a throng (בתוך רבים אהללנו)."

105. Gillmayr-Bucher, "Body Images in the Psalms," 308: "Body language activates the imagination of the readers and vividly paints a communication before their eyes. They are allowed not only to hear the words spoken, but also to view the actions and reactions by means of body language. In this way the intensity of the communication described in the psalms depends in large part on the body language."

through body-language as nearly inevitable, as one is "force[d]" into engagement by the body-language.[106] According to Gillmayr-Bucher, this kind of imagery diminishes distance between the sufferer and the hearer, because humans share the experience of embodiment, so that reading the Psalms sensitizes the hearer to the psalmist's condition: "With this kind of description the readers can hardly maintain a distanced point of view; rather they are forced to add their own bodily experiences while they hear and read the text. In this way the readers are enabled to overcome the distance and to re-enact the text."[107] In Gillmayr-Bucher's view, the reader does not remain only a witness in the context of this bodily encounter with the psalmist; the reader's own physical experiences might be read into the words of the psalmist through the commonly accessible nature of the body-language.

In the context of Kleinman's discussion of the way the sufferer positions himself and others through the somatic idiom of distress, Gillmayr-Bucher's interpretation of this body-language takes on additional significance. Her analysis of the body-language of the laments strikingly demonstrates the way this discourse of powerlessness also becomes a means of empowering the psalmist by organizing the responses of others. If one is invited not only to become an engaged witness to the psalmist's suffering through this language, but also to intermingle one's own bodily experiences with the psalmist's, indeed to *re-enact* the text, one actively takes on the perspective of the psalmist. There is no more sympathetic means of responding to the suffering of the psalmist than to place one's self in his physical position, even literally, in order to take on his pain, suffering, and angst in a way that is consequential to one's own worldview. Gillmayr-Bucher values body-language precisely because it offers the reader a way into the psalmist's experience, and a way of conceiving one's own experiences through the words of the Psalms. Gillmayr-Bucher is the psalmist's ideal reader, one who envisions a merging of his suffering and her own, and advances that intimacy as a literary benefit of this language. Though Gillmayr-Bucher does not discuss the implications of this way of reading, she fully recognizes and positions herself as complicit with the power of this language of bodily distress to form sympathetic hearers and readers.

Embedded in Gillmayr-Bucher's approach is an ethical argument that to remain distant from the psalmist's physical suffering is inappropriate and undesirable.[108] Though she does not address the ethical assumptions explicitly, in her

---

106. Ibid., 310. The image of being "forced" into intense engagement with the psalmist through body-language is used four additional times in Gillmayr-Bucher's article, on pp. 311, 312, 314, and 325. In Gillmayr-Bucher's view, this language is not just highly persuasive, but constructs a compulsory experience of sympathy. Though no one can be forced to do anything in reading, I believe Gillmayr-Bucher's observation is correct that the language of bodily suffering is a particularly insistent invitation to identify with the suffering of the psalmist.

107. Ibid., 325.

108. Gillmayr-Bucher does not characterize her argument as an ethical one. Moreover, the parameters of her article do not necessarily demand that she elaborate on this idea. Yet she makes suggestive comments about the relationship between the reader and the psalmist in the context of the body-language that have important implications for my own interpretation of the laments. Therefore,

estimation body-language is a humanizing literary tool that insistently shapes readers into engaged witnesses to suffering. There is much to recommend the position Gillmayr-Bucher takes as a reader/witness to the suffering body represented in the Psalms. Her implicit commitment to reading the language of bodily suffering as an activity loaded with ethical significance is vital. Bodily distress, especially the representation of physical pain, does claim a certain natural authenticity and material authority.[109] To remain distant or unmoved in the presence of this embodied suffering and anguish seems obscene. The question that Gillmayr-Bucher does not directly address is what the psalmist would like the reader to *do* with that shared experience. If one accepts the invitation into the psalmist's world of bodily distress and even blends her own experiences with the psalmist's, what implicit worldview does one also accept?

Though there are obvious ethical implications to remaining distant in the presence of suffering, there are also ethical implications to not maintaining enough distance.[110] An example illustrates. Above, I discussed the psalmist's instances of inarticulateness as a significant aspect in the psalmist's self-representation as incapacitated and powerless. Though the psalmist may be at his most sympathetic in these descriptions of such absolute and exhausting pain, the perspective afforded in such pain is constrained and narrow; one only desires that pain cease. And the goal of alleviating pain, though of vital and irrefutable ethical and theological importance, does not necessarily give rise to ethical and theological wisdom. In the psalmist's case, alleviation of pain is defined as domination over the enemy, the one he understands to be the primary cause of his suffering. So, while identification with the psalmist's anguish may be a sympathetic position from which to engage and respond to the psalmist's suffering, that same sympathy must be balanced by recognition of the psalmist's

her work provides a ways of exploring this aspect of the empowering potential of the laments, though I recognize that I push her investigation into areas that she has not addressed directly.

109.   Lynn Meskell notes that many, especially feminist, theorists have returned to the importance of the material, biological body, which she understands as an effort to balance extreme constructionist interpretations of the body. As she says, "Bodies cannot simply be explained away" (Lynn Meskell, "The Irresistible Body and the Seduction of Archaeology," in *Changing Bodies, Changing Meanings: Studies on the Human Body in Antiquity* [ed. Dominic Montserrat; London: Routledge, 1998], 148–49). Likewise, Benthien (*Skin*, 12) argues that body-language has an authenticity that cannot be diminished by recognition of the body's construction by culture.

110.   See also Emerson and Morson's discussion of Bakhtin's insistence on the ethical significance of retaining a degree of outsidedness in the presence of another's suffering: "How shall I respond to another's suffering? What is most productive? We sometimes recommend empathy—merging as much as possible with the other's position, attempting to 'see the world from his point of view,' and renouncing one's own outsidedness and surplus of vision. But to the extent that such sympathy is possible, it is also sterile. 'What would I have to gain,' Bakhtin asks, 'if another were to fuse with me? He would see and know only what I see and know, he would only repeat to himself the inescapable closed circle of my own life; let him rather remain outside me.' Rather than empathy, we need what Bakhtin calls 'live entering' or 'living into' another. In this process one simultaneously renounces and exploits one's surplus; one brings into interaction both perspectives simultaneously and creates an 'architectonics' of vision reducible to neither" (Morson and Emerson, *Mikhail Bakhtin*, 53–54).

particular desires, expectations, and demands. When one enters into the psalmist's language of physical distress, one enters into a perspective defined by absorbing pain and the desire for its alleviation through violence against another.

4. *Conclusions*

In sum, reading the bodily suffering as a language of disempowerment and empowerment helps the reader recognize the psalmist's invitation to sympathy embedded in this self-representation while at the same time recognizing the discourse of suffering as part of a construction of identity that intends to persuade and accomplish a particular social goal. Disempowerment and empowerment function as a rhetorical complex in the laments' somatic idiom of distress, unmerged, yet not mutually exclusive aspects of the psalmist's self-representation as a sufferer. Kleinman's recognition that the expression of bodily suffering positions the speaker as powerless and also empowers the speaker is therefore crucial to understanding the kind of rhetorical identity afforded the psalmist in the language of the laments. Kleinman helps to isolate the particular way the body-language functions in the world of the laments, as part of a discourse strategy that is not only about the expression of pain, but is also, and perhaps equally, about attaining the required resources (attention from God, authority to make demands, attain the sympathetic concern of the audience) to seek the change necessary to relieve suffering. In the context of the laments, relief from suffering has a specific rhetorical form, the destruction of the hostile other, whom the psalmist holds responsible for infliction of suffering. When read as a discourse of disempowerment and empowerment, the articulate body of the laments is central to the construction of identity in this figured world. In fact, the psalmist's representation of his physical suffering not only assists him in organizing his distress, it is also the authority upon which he demands attention from God, his enemies, and his community. This socio-somatic aspect of the psalmist's rhetorical identity is only one aspect of a much more complex picture, however. In the next chapter, I explore the aspects of the psalmist's identity that are conveyed in his relationship with the enemy.

Chapter 3

RELATIONAL IDENTITY AND THE HOSTILE OTHER:
THE NEGOTIATION OF COMPETING VOICES

1. *Introduction*

The psalmist rhetorically forges his identity in a complex relational setting, including God, receptive others who will potentially support and celebrate his restoration, as well as hostile others. While the psalmist's physically vulnerable self-representation is an important factor in the psalmist's social positioning, Holland and her colleagues' concept of relational identity isolates another register of identity-making, the way individuals negotiate agency and articulate selfhood within a specific culturally afforded relational discourse. That discourse contains an implied theory of the person that recognizes and denies a certain set of possibilities for personhood and means of negotiating power in relationship with others.[1] A crucial aspect of the psalmist's relational identity is formed in the context of social conflict and personal suffering—conflict between the psalmist and the hostile others concerning the psalmist's social worth and the psalmist's suffering due to his sense of powerlessness, loss, and anger at being positioned as an object of social disdain. In that context, articulating identity becomes a way of preserving the self and combating suffering.[2] The psalmist's dominant relational narrative with regard to the foe is one of endangerment and social vulnerability, in which the psalmist is prey and utterly exposed before a pervasive and villainous enemy. Yet the laments also evidence another aspect of the relational narrative of the psalmist and the enemy, embedded in the psalmist's language of aggression and domination, which destabilizes the endangerment narrative and affords the psalmist a rhetorical position of agency and power. The present chapter includes analysis of the

---

1.   Holland et al., *Identity and Agency in Cultural Worlds*, 127.

2.   Though addressing an explicit context of warfare, historian Jill Lepore (*The Name of War, King Phillip's War and the Origins of American Identity* [New York: Knopf, 1998], ix) also argues that language of the hostile other is increasingly important in times of crisis as a way of stabilizing identity and combating pain and trauma. The language of the hostile other positions the speaker in his/her social context by creating boundaries in which the self may be understood and defended: "The words used to describe war have a great deal of work to do: they must communicate war's intensity, its traumas, fears, and glories; they must make clear who is right and who is wrong, rally support, and recruit allies; and they must document the pain of war, and in so doing, help to alleviate it."

discourse that constructs the psalmist/enemy relationship and the psalmist's use of that discourse to express social suffering and negotiate agency aimed at social restoration.

The psalmist articulates social identity in relation to the enemy in a discourse of shame and honor.[3] That is, the psalmist perceives, interprets, and responds to the hostile other from a relational and discursive worldview in which publicly recognized shame and honor offers the dominant calculus of social and personal worth. This honor/shame discourse articulates a relational worldview and offers a particular, agonistic gauge of privilege and entitlement.[4] The language of honor and shame in the laments is an artifact of a figured world in which social respect and recognition of that respect is the symbolic capital, the measure of one's social worth, the thing with regard to which one understands one's self to be entitled or not. The laments' concept of honor and shame structures social relationships as competitive and hierarchical. Because the psalmist envisions and rhetorically constructs social relationships in this way, the only possible vision of social restoration is one in which he moves from a position of social inferiority to a position of social superiority. The psalmist articulates relational identity with regard to the enemy within the context of these assumptions.

Relational identity is a helpful tool with which to read the laments' honor/shame language because it emphasizes the way that identity is an interactive process, not static, but always negotiated in one's reception of external messages about selfhood and one's response, through acceptance or rejection, of those messages. That dialogic identity-making process helpfully organizes the psalmist's construction of relationship with the enemy and is particularly relevant to the discursive features of the laments; a central feature of the laments is the psalmist's description of his treatment by the enemy, all messages of disdain, belittlement, and contempt. Mocked, hunted, abused, oppressed, and publicly humiliated, the psalmist consistently represents himself receiving painful external messages about his social worthlessness in a highly public context that results in a most intense experience of shame. The various ways he self-represents as contemptible and endangered generate a discourse of social powerlessness, a painful language of abandonment, alienation, and urgent appeal for assistance.

The discourse of social powerlessness and contempt is not the only way the psalmist positions himself in relation to the enemy, however. The psalmist

---

3. Others recognize the prevalence of shame as a major theme in the Psalms, though these works focus on the communal laments: P. J. Botha, "Shame and the Social Setting of Psalm 119," *OTE* 12 (1999): 389–400; W. Dennis Tucker, "Is Shame a Matter of Patronage in the Communal Laments?" (paper presented at the annual meeting of the SBL, Atlanta, 2003). Botha also addresses the concept of honor in the Psalms: "The 'Enthronement Psalms': A Claim to the World-Wide Honour of Yahweh," *OTE* 11 (1998): 24–39; "'The Honour of the Righteous Will Be Restored': Psalm 75 in Its Social Context," *OTE* 15 (2002): 320–34.

4. See Julian Pitt-Rivers, "Honour and Social Status," in *Honour and Shame* (ed. J. G. Peristiany; London: Weidenfeld & Nicolson, 1965), 22. Pitt-Rivers argues that honor and shame are cultural concepts used to evaluate, adjudicate, and assess one's own conduct as well as others, and are also essential to an individual's claim to privilege and entitlement.

utilizes another powerful language of personhood and relational self-identifica-
tion constituted by the many rhetorical expressions of aggression, anger, and
violence. Relational identity, as the perception of and response to messages about
position and social worth, focalizes the psalmist's discourse of dominance as a
response to his experience of shame. Much like a challenge/riposte social inter-
action that competitively determines honor, the psalmist represents the enemies'
challenge to his social worth, but also represents his aggressive response to that
challenge in a language of dominance and violence that is a rhetorical claim to
social worth and an enactment of honor. The discourse of powerlessness, though
it represents true social despair and suffering, is also part of a larger rhetorical
project rooted in the values of agonistic honor and shame in which powerless-
ness must be denied and honor asserted, often aggressively and violently.
Through images of returned shame, revenge fantasies, and imagined, aestheti-
cized violence, the psalmist constructs a "place of rage," a rhetorical position
from which to assert a counter-narrative of social triumph that undermines the
narrative of social endangerment.[5] In this rhetorical place of rage, the psalmist
rejects social contempt and enacts a position of worth and honor, all according
to the agonistic relational framework that constructs his relationship with the
hostile other.

In this chapter I explore the psalmist's negotiation of relational identity, not
as a static set of finalized identifying characteristics, but as a tensive interaction
between competing positionalities, that of shame and that of honor. In fact,
neither discourse, that of powerlessness nor that of aggression, overwhelms the
other. Both discourses are important to the psalmist's self-presentation and offer
the psalmist and the hearing audience, including God and the enemy, differing
rhetorical experiences. The major analytic sections of this chapter reflect the
dialogic identity-making process underway in the laments. After discussion of
the enemy's identity and clarification of the concepts of honor and shame, I
categorize the laments' language according to the two interrelated relational
discourses the psalmist uses to establish his position with regard to the hostile
other, the discourse of contempt and the discourse of dominance.

2. *Who* Is *the Hostile Other?*

The most obvious "hostile other" in the laments is the "enemy," designated by a
wide variety of terms.[6] The terms for "enemy," however, do not account for all

---

5. The phrase "place of rage" comes from a 1991 film about African-American women activists
entitled "A Place of Rage," directed by Pratibha Parmar. The film's name, in turn, is a quotation
from the African-American poet and Professor June Jordan. In using the phrase, I do not intend to
imply that the psalmist's social situation closely parallels that of African-American women activists
in the civil rights era up until the 1990s. I use the phrase to describe a rhetorical effect of using
language of aggression and violence as a means of asserting agency.

6. Othmar Keel lists ninety-four separate designations for "enemy" in the Psalms (*Feinde und
Gottesleugner: Studien zum Image der Widersacher in den Individualpsalmen* [Stuttgart: Katholisches
Bibelwerk, 1969], 94–98). The following is a list of the most significant terms and the number of

of the antagonistic figures in the laments. While the enemy is most prevalent, the psalmist nearly always identifies other characters as antagonistic figures who find him contemptible and socially unworthy.[7] Friends, family, and community abandon and treat the supplicant scornfully (see Pss 27:10; 31:12; 38:12; 41:10; 88:9). I employ the intentionally general term "hostile other" to encompass all of the characters the psalmist perceives to find him contemptible or who otherwise abuse, mistreat, or condemn.

The identity of the enemy, however, requires special attention. Especially in early studies, many scholars discussed the enemy's identity as part of a larger attempt to locate one psalm or the Psalms as a whole in a specific historical context. Hans Schmidt read the Psalms from a judicial perspective and argued that the laments were the words of the wrongly accused who sought redress via a verdict from God given by the priests; the enemies were those who presented false testimony against the psalmist.[8] Mowinckel asserted that the enemies were sorcerers who cursed the psalmist and caused his illness.[9] Harris Birkeland, Mowinckel's student, understood the laments to be the words of the king and argued that the enemies were national foes. He examined five psalms that use the terms גוים, עמים, and זרים and, based on his analysis, argued for an identifiable pattern of terminology that extended to all the psalms in which these terms occurred.[10] More recently, Stanley Rosenbaum adopts a similar line of argumentation, using shades of difference in different examples of enemy nomenclature to argue for an enemy-identifying schema. He argues that the two terms for the wicked (רשעים) and the enemy (איבים) are not interchangeable and consistently refer to two separate and identifiable groups; the wicked (רשעים) refer to Israelites who have gone astray, the enemies (איבים) to foreign adversaries.[11]

---

occurrences in the corpus of laments I have delineated: אויב: ×38; רשע: ×24; שנא: ×11; פועל עון: ×9; דברי כזב: ×2; רדפים: ×7; צורר: ×7; אמשי דמים: ×6; שורר: ×5; צר: ×5; איש דמים: ×3; מבקש נפשי: ×2; איש חמסים: ×2; עריץ: ×2; רע: ×2; איש לשון: ×1; צורר נפשי: ×1; צרר: ×1.

7. One exception is the character of God, who is sometimes, though not always, antagonistic to the psalmist. The relational structure between God and the psalmist is different, however, and will be discussed in Chapter 4.

8. Hans Schmidt, *Das Gebet der Angeklagten im Alten Testament* (Giessen: Töpelmann, 1928) and *Die Psalmen* (Tübingen: J. C. B. Mohr [Paul Siebeck], 1934). Schmidt did allow that some of the laments were clearly pleas in the context of sickness or despair, and not cries for divine justice. L. Delekat and Walter Beyerlin later took up this judicial line of argumentation in slightly modified ways. See L. Delekat, *Asylie und Schutzorakel am Zionheiligtum* (Leiden: Brill, 1967), and Walter Beyerlin, *Die Rettung der Bedrängten in den Feindpsalmen der Einzelnen auf institutionelle Zusammenhänge untersucht* (Göttingen: Vandenhoeck & Ruprecht, 1970).

9. Mowinckel, *The Psalms in Israel's Worship.*

10. Birkeland, *Die feinde des individuums.*

11. Stanley N. Rosenbaum, "The Concept 'Antagonist' in Hebrew Psalmography: A Semantic Field Study" (Ph.D. diss., Brandeis University, 1974). Croft (*The Identity of the Individual*, 15–48) confirms Rosenbaum's attempt to distinguish between the רשעים and the איבים, though he emends Rosenbaum's definitions of the terms. He argues that the רשעים were those who have turned away from God, as opposed to the king, and are therefore subject to God's judgment. Therefore, according to Croft, the רשעים do not represent a direct threat to the psalmist. The איבים, however, do sometimes pose direct threat to the psalmist, and are therefore not always foreign adversaries, as Rosenbaum asserts, but sometimes hostile parties within Israel. Though Croft's conclusions are

In contrast, others have rejected linguistic schemas, recognizing the enemy-terms' imprecision with regard to historical identity, and have opted for inter-pretations less historical in focus.[12] Patrick Miller argues that the stereotypical representation of the enemy in broad, negative terms provides little upon which to base a precise identification and that vagueness may have been one way the texts remained relevant over time; the language affords flexibility to the suppli-cant so that the enemy becomes whomever the suppliant perceives to be the enemy at any given time, whether national foe or personal antagonist.[13] In addi-tion, Othmar Keel argues for a psychological approach in which the hostile figure is an individual projection of antagonism as opposed to a physical, embodied enemy.[14]

My perspective is most aligned with that of Gerald Sheppard, who argues that the enemy could be a national foe, a peer of the psalmist, or a family member, and approaches the issue of identity from a socio-rhetorical perspective.[15] His interest is not in establishing historical identity, but in the socio-political context in which prayers against the enemy were spoken. Sheppard assumes a localized setting in which the psalmist spoke his complaint in the hearing of not only God and a sympathetic community, but also the enemy. In fact, Sheppard claims that one of the most understudied aspects of the Psalms is the enemies' presence at the time of the prayer, a rhetorical situation that changes one's understanding of how the prayer functioned "socially, rhetorically, religiously, and politically."[16]

---

different from both Rosenbaum and Birkeland, the methodology is similar in that he assumes that the identity of the enemy can be determined according to terminology. Moreover, like Rosenbaum and Birkeland, Croft assumes a mostly royal Psalter.

12.   In addition to those described here, see Dharmakkan Dhanaraj, *Theological Significance of the Motif of Enemies in Selected Psalms of Individual Lament* (Glückstadt: J. J. Augustin, 1992).

13.   Patrick D. Miller, "Trouble and Woe: Interpreting the Biblical Laments," *Int* 37 (1983): 34–35.

14.   Keel, *Feinde und Gottesleugner*, 1969.

15.   Gerald T. Sheppard, "'Enemies' and the Politics of Prayer in the Book of Psalms," in *The Bible and the Politics of Exegesis* (ed. David Jobling, Peggy L. Day, and Gerald T. Sheppard; Cleveland, Ohio: Pilgrim, 1991), 70: "So, if psalms often consider ruling authorities enemies…they just as often assume the enemy is a peer, a neighbor, or a member of the family." For instance, in Ps 35:13–14, the antagonist is someone with whom the psalmist had a previous relationship; the psalmist describes mourning for the antagonist when he was sick. Further, in Ps 55:14, the psalmist explicitly states that it is not an enemy or foe that hurts him, but a former friend.

16.   Sheppard, "'Enemies' and the Politics of Prayer," 72. Sheppard bases his argument on anthropological and sociological studies of enemies in preindustrial, peasant societies, especially *Peasants and Peasant Societies* (ed. T. Shanin; New York: Penguin, 1971), in which there is a "recurring pattern" of identifying "outsiders" and peers who have become antagonists as enemies. In addition, Sheppard refers to the work of anthropologists I. M. Lewis and Max Gluckman, who pursue cross-cultural studies of ritualized violence and patterned songs of hate, as foundation for his analysis of the Psalms as songs performed before an audience that included the enemy. See I. M. Lewis, *Social Anthropology in Perspective: The Relevance of Social Anthropology* (New York: Penguin, 1976), and Max Gluckman, *Order and Rebellion in Tribal Africa: Collected Essays* (London: Routledge & Kegan Paul, 1963). Sheppard's argument is supported by examples from the Psalms in which the psalmist uses second person speech and addresses the enemy directly (see, e.g., Pss 4; 52; 62).

When one understands the enemy to be part of the prayer's immediate rhetorical context, it is not just private communication between God and the psalmist, but also public discourse simultaneously addressed to the enemy and the community. Sheppard offers three functions of the indirect address to the enemy. First, the enemy is publicly exposed and the psalmist is afforded a certain degree of protection because of the public knowledge of his complaint against the enemy. Second, threats and imprecations against the enemy express the pain and suffering of the psalmist and provide some relief for that suffering. Third, the psalms often include advice to the enemy that might lead to the enemy's changed behavior.[17] In all these examples of possible implications of the enemy's presence, the prayer has theological significance as human-to-God communication, but also significance as public utterances entrenched in a socio-historical reality of dispute in which words have social, personal, and political consequences.[18] The public nature of the language as a performed discourse in the context of social conflict is essential to the psalmist's pursuit of his own social restoration.

Positing the enemy as a participant in the public utterance of the lament, however, should not cause one to expect more historical specificity about the identity of the enemy or the concrete circumstances of the conflict. The utterance, as I imagine it, is not so much designed to describe specific circumstances —this is not legal testimony—but to cast the psalmist's situation in culturally valued terms that signal the psalmist's reliance upon certain relational frameworks and lead God and the audience to sympathetic action. The psalmist's entreaty for support and sympathy appeals to embedded and emotionally potent cultural narratives about and images of an enemy who is clearly recognizable and indisputably guilty. It behooves the psalmist, then, to remain elusive about the specifics of the conflict in order to encourage the audience not to think of local individuals who are familiar to the community, and therefore inherently more particularized, but in terms of more generalized, and also perhaps more emotionally charged, conceptions of who is good and who is bad, who is right and who is to blame.

The enemy represents a "constructed counter-world," a concept Holland and her colleagues offer to describe how figured worlds define themselves for others.[19] In the emergence of a figured world, or a new identity, opposition is often figured in order to consolidate new identity. The counter-world, according to Holland and her co-authors, exists to demonstrate what the desirable figured world should *not* be. Villains, or hostile figures, oppose the desirable figured world, which is always aligned with what is good, right, and accepted in the

---

17.   Sheppard, "'Enemies' and the Politics of Prayer," 78.

18.   See ibid., 71: "Although the ritualized expressions of violence may usually dissipate and neutralize the desire actually to retaliate, to punish, or to take power from another person, the prayer does not preclude the possibility of action either on the part of the one who prays, or, as I want to call more to our attention, on the part of those who overhear... [R]itual prayers are spoken out loud or 'sung' in public; therefore, people accused in the prayers are often present, able to overhear them or at least to hear about them from others who are present."

19.   Holland et al., *Identity and Agency in Cultural Worlds*, 250.

culture.[20] Rhetorically, the speaker identifies the villain with a nightmarish opposing world that stands in threatening opposition to the values of the speaker and those sympathetic with him.[21] The primary purpose of the counter-world, in fact, is to construct identity or reinforce identity for the emerging or threatened self or community, not to establish the identity of the antagonistic forces.

Though the psalmist is not defining a new figured world, he defends a threatened identity that must be redefined and reasserted in a hostile context. Therefore, the concept of the constructed counter-world befits the function of the hostile other in the psalmist's identity-creating process. The antagonist, then, is best identified as a caricatured figure whose primary purpose is to establish the worthy social identity of the psalmist. The hostile other does not represent a figured world of his own; the laments do not offer description of the motivations or desires of the other that contextualize actions against the psalmist. The enemy exists only in threatening opposition to the psalmist's world and is "relationally inferior and perhaps beyond the pale of any imagined community we would ever want to join."[22]

3. *Honor and Shame: A Language of Relationship*

Being shamed by the hostile other and desiring to shame those antagonistic characters in return are constitutive elements of the psalmist's self and other representations.[23] The psalmist's experience of shame is acute and painful and the desire to shame the hostile other is just as palpable. Psalm 69:20, for instance, includes three shame words that communicate the suffering of the psalmist and the urgency of his plea for relief: "You know my reproach (חרפתי), my shame (בשתי), my disgrace (כלמתי). You are aware of all my foes." The call for the others' shame in Ps 70:3 is similar in word-choice, passion, and intensity: "Let those who seek my life be shamed (בשו) and disgraced (יחפרו); let those who plan to harm me fall back in reproach (יכלמו)." The dense lexical presence of shame signifies its importance in this discourse.[24] Yet various elements of the

20.　Ibid., 250.

21.　Others have described the subhuman characterization of the enemy in the Psalms and how that portrayal serves to define the character of the psalmist. Hobbs and Jackson discuss the enemy image in the laments as propaganda that seeks to strengthen the bonds of the inside group by creating a subhuman outside group (see T. R. Hobbs and P. K. Jackson, "The Enemy in the Psalms," *BTB* 21 [1991]: 26). For more conversation about the function of enemies in the creation of societies as well as individual psychologies, see the following: James A. Aho, *This Thing of Darkness: A Sociology of the Enemy* (Seattle: University of Washington Press, 1994); F. G. Bailey, *The Need for Enemies: A Bestiary of Political Forms* (Ithaca, N.Y.: Cornell University Press, 1998); Ragnhild Fiebig-von Hase and Ursula Lehmkuhl, eds., *Enemy Images in American History* (Providence, R.I.: Berghahn, 1997); Robert W. Rieber, ed., *The Psychology of War and Peace: The Image of the Enemy* (New York: Plenum, 1991).

22.　Holland et al., *Identity and Agency in Cultural Worlds*, 250.

23.　See also Lyn M. Bechtel, "Shame as Sanction of Social Control in Biblical Israel: Judicial, Political, and Social Shaming," in *Social-Scientific Old Testament Criticism* (ed. David J. Chalcraft; The Biblical Seminar 47; Sheffield; Sheffield Academic Press, 1997), 253–54.

24.　The root בוש is used in verbal form in the laments of the individual nineteen times: Pss 6:11 (×2); 22:6; 25:2, 3, 20; 31:2, 18 (×2); 35:4, 26; 40:15; 69:7; 70:3; 71:1, 13, 24; 86:17; 109:28. The discourse generate the categories of honor and shame even when specific honor and shame vocabulary is absent. For instance, I argue that honor is a powerful relational concept even though the vocabulary of honor is not nearly as frequent in the laments as is that of shame.[25] My examination of honor and shame, therefore, analyzes various discursive features that construct a relational worldview. The cultural values of honor and shame pervade the relational framework of the laments and provide a context for interpretation of the self and the hostile other.

Concepts of honor and shame are not self-contained and static, but are values that both construct and reflect assumptions of particular cultural worlds.[26] As

noun בשׁת appears five times: Pss 35:26; 40:16; 69:20; 70:4; 109:29. The root כלם appears in verbal form four times: Pss 35:4; 40:15; 69:7; 70:3. The noun כלמה is used six times: Pss 4:3; 35:26; 69:8, 20; 71:13; 109:29. The root חפר appears five times in the laments: Pss 35:4, 26; 40:15; 70:3; 71:24. The root חרף occurs seven times: Pss 42:11; 55:13; 57:4; 69:10; 89:52 (×2); 102:9. The noun חרפה occurs twelve times: Pss 22:7; 31:12; 39:9; 69:8, 10, 11, 20, 21; 71:13; 89:41, 51; 109:25. The noun קלון does not occur in the individual laments, but does occur in Ps 83.17. The verbal root קלה does not occur in the Psalms.

25. The root one might expect in a text concerned with honor is כבד, which only occurs in the individual laments in Ps 22:24, as an imperative ("All the seed of Jacob, honor him!"), in Ps 38:5, which is contextually irrelevant ("they are too heavy for me"), and in Ps 86:9, 12, which both refer to honoring the name of God. None of these references refer to the honor of the psalmist. The noun כבוד appears in the individual laments more frequently (ten times), though not nearly as frequently as shame words. See Pss 3:4; 4:3; 7:6; 26:8; 57:9, 12; 62:8; 63:3; 102:16, 17. Of these occurrences, Pss 3:4; 4:3; 7:6; 57:9; 62:8 refer to the honor of the psalmist; the other occurrences refer to God's honor. The verb הדר, another root in the same semantic field as כבד, does not occur in the individual laments; nor does הוד, the noun form.

26. The concepts of honor and shame are complex; honor and shame are discussed in the field of biblical studies with increasing sophistication. Some of the most recent and important investigations of honor and shame in biblical studies are as follows: Lyn Bechtel Huber, "The Biblical Experience of Shame/Shaming: The Social Experience of Shame/Shaming in Biblical Israel in Relation to Its Use as Religious Metaphor" (Ph.D. diss., Drew University, 1983); idem, "The Perception of Shame Within the Divine–Human Relationship in Biblical Israel," in *Uncovering Stones: Essays in Memory of H. Neil Richardson* (ed. Lewis M. Hopfe; Winona Lake, Ind.: Eisenbrauns, 1994), 79–92; idem, "Shame as Sanction"; Dianne Bergant, "The Song of Songs and Honor and Shame," *Semeia* 68 (1994): 23–40; Nancy R. Bowen, "Damage and Healing: Shame and Honor in the Old Testament," *Koinonia* 3 (1991): 29–36; John K. Chance, "The Anthropology of Honor and Shame: Culture, Values, and Practice," *Semeia* 68 (1994): 139–51; David Daube, "The Culture of Deuteronomy," *Orita* 3 (1969): 27–52; Martin A. Klopfenstein, *Scham und Schande nach dem Alten Testament* (ATNAT 62; Zurich: Theologischer Verlag, 1972); Timothy S. Laniak, *Shame and Honor in the Book of Esther* (Atlanta: Scholars Press, 1998); Jacqueline E. Lapsley, *Can These Bones Live? The Problem of the Moral Self in the Book of Ezekiel* (Berlin: W. de Gruyter, 2000); Margaret S. Odell, "The Inversion of Shame and Forgiveness in Ezekiel 16:59–63," *JSOT* 56 (1992): 101–12; Saul Olyan, "Honor, Shame, and Covenant Relations in Ancient Israel and its Environment," *JBL* 115 (1996): 201–18; Ronald A. Simkins, "'Return to Yahweh': Honor and Shame in Joel," *Semeia* 68 (1994): 41–54; Gary Stansell, "Honor and Shame in the David Narratives," *Semeia* 68 (1994): 55–79; Ken Stone, *Sex, Honor, and Power in the Deuteronomistic History* (JSOTSup 234; Sheffield: Sheffield Academic Press, 1996). Honor and shame have also received significant attention in New Testament studies. See especially Bruce J. Malina, *The New Testament World: Insights from Cultural Anthropology* (Atlanta: John Knox, 1981), and Bruce J. Malina and Jerome H. Neyrey, "Honor and Shame in Luke–Acts: Pivotal Values of the Mediterranean World," in *The Social World of Luke–Acts: Models for Interpretation* (ed. J. H. Neyrey; Peabody, Mass.: Hendrickson, 1991), 25–65.

F. Gerald Downing notes, "To assume that questions about 'honor,' 'respect,' and 'shame' are worth asking is one thing; to assume that these issues are pervasive, dominant and largely uniform, is quite another."[27] In fact, even within the laments, honor and shame are not static concepts, but differ depending upon the relational context in which one interprets the discourse. For instance, shame and honor are central to both the psalmist/hostile other relationship and the psalmist/God relationship, but are experienced and expressed differently by the psalmist. Honor and shame in the psalmist/hostile other relationship is best understood as the discourse of an intensely public and agonistic relationship. In contrast, honor and shame in the psalmist/God relationship relate to the ability and willingness of these two parties to remain in a relationship of interdependent loyalty. The concepts of honor and shame relevant to the psalmist/hostile other relationship are the primary concern of this chapter and so most of my discussion of these concepts in this section is foundation for the interpretation of that relational discourse. In order to provide as thorough an explication of the concepts of honor and shame as possible, however, it is necessary to engage in anticipatory discussion of shame resulting from failed relationship, even though that facet is most relevant to the subject of the next chapter, the psalmist/God relationship.

a. *Honor and Shame in the Agonistic Relationship*
In the agonistic relationship between the psalmist and the hostile other, public worth and the protection of reputation are centrally important. Honor is gained and protected in competitive challenge/riposte public interactions. In this social relationship, honor and shame function as oppositional categories. Saul Olyan's description of the terms is illustrative:

> In short, honor and shame communicate relative social status, which may shift over time... Honor is meant to be recognized and acknowledged; it is very much a public phenomenon. Loss of honor or diminishment results in shame; diminishment communicates a loss of social status. Like honor and its inscription, diminishment and shame also have a public dimension...[28]

Olyan draws attention to the social and public aspects of honor, in which social status is an ever-shifting struggle publicly to resist diminishment and assert social worthiness. Olyan's understanding of shame and honor is characteristic of anthropologists who have studied social negotiation of worth.[29] Shame,

---

27. F. Gerald Downing, " 'Honor' Among Exegetes," *CBQ* 61 (1999): 57.
28. Olyan, "Honor, Shame and Covenant Relations," 55.
29. For the discussion of shame and honor among anthropologists, see especially John Davis, *People of the Mediterranean* (London: Routledge & Kegan Paul, 1977); David Gilmore, "Introduction: The Shame of Dishonor," in *Honor and Shame and the Unity of the Mediterranean* (ed. D. Gilmore; A Special Publication of the American Anthropological Association 22; Washington, D.C.: American Anthropological Association, 1987); J. G. Peristiany, ed., *Honour and Shame: The Values of Mediterranean Society* (London: Weidenfeld & Nicolson, 1965); J. G. Peristiany and J. Pitt-Rivers, *Honor and Grace in Anthropology* (Cambridge: Cambridge University Press, 1992); Julian Pitt-Rivers, "The Anthropology of Honour," in *The Fate of Shechem, or The Politics of Sex:*

according to this definition, is not so much a personal feeling as a public experience in which individuals garner respect or contempt.

A central feature of the psalmist's shame experience is the other's public denial of social worth. The prayer to avoid or inflict shame is about public standing and community acknowledgment of worth. Shame in the laments nearly always involves a public recognition of unworthiness, not a personal sense of wrongdoing or inferiority. Within the psalmist/hostile other relationship, shame is best conceived of as the experience of social sanction, the public experience of rebuke or disdain, or the threat thereof, so socially significant that it is among the most horrible fates imagined by the psalmist and among the most horrible fates that he desires for his enemy.

Shame as a social sanction is also the means by which to understand the negotiation of social power operative in the psalmist/hostile other relationship. Lyn Bechtel helpfully describes shame as a social sanction as a tool for achievement of social dominance in competitive interactions.[30] The figured world implied in such language, then, is one in which imposing shame and resisting shame are indications of one's social power. Public displays of dominance or resistance to domination indicate one's social worth and establish hierarchies of power in which dominance is achieved by shaming another.

Moreover, shame as social sanction is also the lens through which to perceive the concept of honor in the laments, where honor is signified by one's ability to achieve dominance. Therefore, within the psalmist/hostile other relationship, honor and shame function as oppositional categories. Forming a binary relationship, honor is the absence of shame and the social recognition of worth, and shame is the absence of honor, and the social recognition of worthlessness.

Discussion of honor is not an obvious interpretive issue in the laments, however. Recognized honor vocabulary or descriptions of the psalmist's former social status or honorable reputation are not as fully described in the laments as shame. Unlike in Job, for instance, there are no visions of the psalmist's previous reputable social status or his future restored honor.[31] Unni Wikan argues that in some cultures in which shame is an important social category or cultural value, honor is "experience-distant," not "naturally and effortlessly" articulated

---

Essays in the Anthropology of the Mediterranean (Cambridge: Cambridge University Press, 1977). Most Hebrew Bible scholars have relied mainly upon an anthropological approach to shame. Jacqueline Lapsley's work (*Can These Bones Live?*) is one notable exception.

30. Lyn Bechtel describes three primary ways in which shame functions as a social sanction. Shame may be used "1. as a means of social control which attempts to repress aggressive or undesirable behavior; 2. as a pressure that preserves social cohesion in the community through rejection and the creation of social distance between deviant members of the group; 3. as an important means of dominating others and manipulating social status" (Bechtel, "Shame as a Sanction," 237). All three of these functions are at work in the laments' concept of shame, but the category of honor as the establishment of social worth is mostly articulated in the use of shame to dominate others.

31. For example, Job 29 entails a lengthy description of Job's previously entitled social state and provides an excellent imagistic portrait of honor in that world. See also Job 11:13–20, Zophar's description of Job's potential restoration. No such overt description occurs in the laments.

in the language or evident in the worldview.[32] Speaking of his fieldwork in Cairo and Oman, Wikan says,

> Mediterranean people do not, in their daily lives, speak of their own and each other's honour. But they do speak of shame... "Shame" accompanies negative sanctions as an exclamation and explicative, it constantly enters both into commentary and transactions. "Honour" figures mainly in "theory" discourse—it is not itself part of the give and take of interaction.[33]

He argues that scholars have become entranced by the image of masculinity in romantic notions of honor and have therefore not been attentive enough to the self-representations of people, imposing preconceived notions of honor.[34] While Wikan's methodological caution is important, I identify the category of honor as an essential part of the psalmist's relational worldview because honor in the psalmist/hostile other relationship is constructed in other ways than in vocabulary usage, just as shame is indicated in ways other than specific shame vocabulary, such as in imagistic descriptions of social diminishment and disdainful gestures. The category of honor is not marked lexically, but it is everywhere implied. Honor is brought into focus by the prevalent language of dominance, the means by which the psalmist imagines triumph and restoration. The shame and honor discourse in the laments posits human social relationships as centered around the fear of being found contemptible and the desire to attain or maintain public recognition of social worth. Inherently, in this agonistic view of social relationships dominance must be maintained by continual assertions of strength and aggression. Honor as public recognition of social worth is, therefore, exceedingly important, articulated first as a desire for reversed shame, in which the psalmist rhetorically achieves dominance through shaming the shamer, and second in a language of dominance, aggression, and violence. In both categories of honor language, the psalmist imagines social restoration as resistance to the category of contempt by dominance over the other.

The picture of honor and shame as oppositional categories that construct agonistic social relationships does not complete the picture of these categories or fully describe the psalmist's complex negotiation of differing relational selfhoods, however. Wikan urges care in assuming that honor and shame form an oppositional relationship and his caution is highly relevant to the laments.[35] Shame is not always the opposite of honor in the Hebrew Bible. Sometimes, especially where gender language and sexual imagery play a discursive role, such as in Ezek 16 and 23, honor and shame are not related oppositionally; in

32. Unni Wikan, "Shame and Honour: A Contestable Pair," *Man* 19, no. 4 (1984): 635–52. See also Johanna Stiebert, *The Construction of Shame in the Hebrew Bible: The Prophetic Contribution* (JSOTSup 346; London: Sheffield Academic Press, 2002), 34. Wikan relies on Clifford Geertz ("'From the Native's Point of View': On the Nature of Anthropological Understanding," in *Meaning in Anthropology* [ed. K. H. Basso and H. A. Selby; Albuquerque: University of New Mexico Press, 1976], 224) for the idea of "experience-distant" cultural concepts.

33. Wikan, "Shame and Honour," 638.

34. Ibid., 649.

35. Ibid., 649.

that rhetorical context, honorability is not lack of shame, but involves the ability to feel shamed.[36] Likewise, though sexual imagery is not prevalent in the laments, honor is not always articulated through a language of dominance but through the willingness to be in a diminished social position with regard to another, namely, God. That is, the language of diminishment, need, and vulnerability (e.g. "Incline your ear, Lord, and answer me. For I am poor [עָנִי] and needy [אֶבְיוֹן]. Preserve my life, for I am devoted to you. Save your servant [עֶבֶד] who trusts in you," Ps 86:1–2) is not always a mark of the psalmist's shamed relational status. In fact, the rhetorical position of diminishment that signifies the psalmist's shame in the psalmist/hostile other relationship is an articulation of relational honor and worthiness in the God/psalmist relationship, an idea I develop in the next chapter. Within the laments, the source of shame emerges from different relational frameworks; therefore, the way the psalmist negotiates relational identity through the discourse of honor and shame differs according to the specific relational framework to which the psalmist appeals. The picture of how honor and shame language reflects and creates relationships in the laments is incomplete unless one considers the shame experienced by the psalmist that results not from the hostile others' public ridicule, but from God's abandonment of the psalmist. In that relational framework, where failed relationship is the source of shame, the psalmist's response is not a language of honor as dominance, but a language of honor as continued dependence, vulnerability, and need, all rhetorical signs of the psalmist's loyalty to the particular constraints of the God/psalmist relational framework.

b. *Shame as Failed Relationship*
To this point, I have discussed honor and shame as anthropological categories, stressing the public negotiation of worth accomplished by the language and imagery of honor and shame. Shame for the psalmist does not happen entirely in the public realm, however, and its complexity is not encapsulated in an anthropological approach. Though the Hebrew language does not distinguish between public and private senses of shame, the psalmist does express a feeling of psychological shame.[37] The psalmist's experience of shame can therefore not be totally captured in the purely social model Olyan describes, though the most widespread psychological understanding of shame as related to negative evaluation of one's self and one's actions do not describe this aspect of the psalmist's shame.

Michael Lewis offers one vivid definition of the psychological experience of shame: "Shame can be defined simply as the feeling we have when we evaluate our actions, feelings, or behavior, and conclude that we have done wrong. It encompasses the whole of ourselves; it generates a wish to hide, to disappear, or

---

36. See Lapsley, *Can These Bones Live?*, 135.

37. See Michael Herzfeld's work on the complexity of the methodology needed to discuss the concept of shame in a comparative sense. Herzfeld notes that the translation of terms from culture to culture is a common theoretical problem in the analysis of shame (Michael Herzfeld, "Honour and Shame: Problems in the Contemporary Analysis of Moral Systems," *Man* 15 [1980]: 339–51).

even to die."[38] According to this understanding of shame, the criteria by which one assesses one's worth are both more internal (private) and comprehensive (involving the whole of the self) than Olyan's definition indicates. This psychological understanding focuses on shame as an individual's personal feelings of unworthiness located in one's actions, behaviors, and abilities, all of which are evaluated as painfully inadequate and leading to conclusive feelings of self-blame encompassing the global self.[39] This perception may involve a public experience of shame, but it need not.[40] In fact, even a public perception of worthiness or recognizable achievement of status would not necessarily alleviate acute feelings of shame. Regardless of public opinion, the individual comes to feel that his or her actions do not meet valued internal or external standards of worthiness.

Though the kind of psychological shame Lewis describes is found in the laments (see Ps 51 and the discussion below), shame that is grounded in the individual's profound sense of self-blame does not describe the psalmist's dominant self-representation. The psalmist, most often, does not feel ashamed for having done wrong or have a sense of painful unworthiness due to the mistakenness of his basic self and consequent erroneous behaviors. In fact, the psalmist repeatedly represents himself as innocent of wrongdoing and confidently evaluates his actions as just and righteous: "Judge me, YHWH, according to my righteousness (צדק) and the integrity (תם) that is in me" (Ps 7:9).[41] Rather, the psalmist describes the shame he feels as a result of others' acts of betrayal and abandonment, which then have definite implications for his understanding of his entire self, not the pain of feeling ashamed because of actions that miss the mark. Being shamed publicly by the failure of trusted relationships translates into feelings of internal shame. The problem is how to understand the dimension of the psalmist's personal shame that is so evidently not rooted in his sense of his personal essence and behaviors as wrong or unworthy of social respect, but that still has a profound impact on his sense of social and personal worth.

---

38. Michael Lewis, *Shame: The Exposed Self* (New York: The Free Press, 1992), 2. For more discussion of the psychological approach to shame, see W. Hobilitzelle, "Differentiating and Measuring Shame and Guilt: The Relation Between Shame and Depression," in *The Role of Shame in Emotion Formation* (ed. H. B. Lewis; Hillsdale, N.J.: Erlbaum, 1987), 207–36; A. P. Morrison, "The Eye Turned Inward: Shame and the Self," in *The Many Faces of Shame* (ed. D. L. Nathanson; New York: Guilford, 1986), 271–91; Helen Merrell Lynd, *On Shame and the Search for Identity* (New York: Harcourt Brace, 1958).

39. See June Price Tangney and Ronda L. Dearing, *Shame and Guilt* (New York: Guilford, 2002), 53.

40. Odell notes that the distinction between internal and external evaluations is misleading. The experience of shame is not dependent on a "real or imagined audience" (Odell, "Shame and Dependence in the Bible," 218). See also Tangney and Dearing, *Shame and Guilt*, 14.

41. See also Pss 17; 26; 27 and John Hayes's discussion of the "Psalms of the Accused," which exemplify this kind of confident language, in *Understanding the Psalms*, 70–74. In addition to honor and shame, guilt and innocence provide a vocabulary for self-representation as well as construction of the enemy. Guilt and innocence are categories that require more attention with regard to the laments, but are beyond the scope of this project.

Margaret Odell offers a compelling alternate psychological model well-suited to the experience of shame in the laments and also illumines the connection between the social experience of shame and the personal commitments that would make that experience of social sanction so powerful.[42] General discussion of Odell's model is a necessary precursor to understanding more fully the psalmist's sense of personal shame. In addition to shame incurred because of failed actions, Odell argues that the biblical experience evidences a kind of shame felt because of another's actions. Odell argues that in some instances shame is conceived of relationally, not as the result of one's wrong actions, but as the result of another's betrayal of trust and connection. Shame is experienced when bonds of dependence are betrayed, even if that betrayal is not of one's own doing.[43]

Odell's argument is based on a study of Japanese psychology by Takeo Doi.[44] Doi argues that Japanese culture privileges relational dependence, in contrast to modern Western notions of personhood that value individuation and independence. According to Doi's representation of the Japanese construction of shame, both personal sense of self and public recognition of social worth are derived from one's ability to maintain relations of trust and interconnection, and not from attaining autonomy from dependent relationships. Doi argues that the sense of shame in Japanese culture is not just a social concern for other's approval, "but is something extremely delicate, involving the whole inner personality."[45] Similarly, Odell writes that in some biblical instances, the power of shame is not simply in the threat of public ridicule, but also in the threat to one's sense of belonging in relationships that provide the definition for one's entire sense of self. Shame as a sanction is effective because it threatens identity-giving bonds of dependence and trust. Consequently, shame is a potent means of social control and enforcement of behavioral and moral norms because the individual *wants* to maintain those dependent relationships. In a similar manner, the power of social sanction in the laments is not only in the social realm or in the experience of being socially disdained, but also in the threat of personal shame induced by the dissolution of trusted relationships of dependency.

Most revealing about the importance of this different model of psychological shame is the individual's response to the experience of shame. Doi observes that a primary way the shamed Japanese individual attempts to reintegrate socially and restore a sense of social worth is to express continued dependence upon those relationships, despite experience of betrayal, adopting a child-like language of apology.[46] In the laments, shame as failed relationship is mostly articulated

---

42. Margaret S. Odell, "An Exploratory Study of Shame and Dependence in the Bible and Selected Near Eastern Parallels," in *The Biblical Canon in Comparative Perspective* (ed. K. L. Younger, Jr., William W. Hallo, Bernard F. Batto; ANETS 11; Lewiston: Mellen, 1991), 217–33.

43. Ibid., 220.

44. Takeo Doi, *Anatomy of Dependence* (trans. John Bester; Tokyo: Kodansha International, 1973).

45. Ibid., 55. See also Odell, "Shame and Dependence in the Bible," 220.

46. Doi, *Anatomy of Dependence*, 57–59.

in the psalmist's relationship with God; the psalmist experiences shame because of God's abandonment of relationship and betrayal of the psalmist's dependence. The psalmist's response to that experience of shame is, much like Doi observed in Japan, an elaborate discourse of dependence and need. Much of this self-presentation is explained by the discursive constraints of the patron/client relationship, the subject of the next chapter. In this chapter it is important to recognize that this rhetoric of dependency in response to the experience of shame contrasts directly with the rhetoric of aggression and dominance the psalmist adopts in response to being shamed by the hostile other, though both responses are generated by the desire for restored social and personal worth. The difference is located in the understanding of shame in varying relational frameworks. The psalmist's relationship with the hostile other is articulated primarily within the framework of an agonistic honor/shame discourse, which means the psalmist cannot demonstrate social worth by adopting a rhetoric of dependence and trust in interaction with the antagonist. However, the construction of the self in relationships of dependency *does* elucidate more clearly what is at stake in the experience of social sanction by the hostile other, though that relational framework differs substantially from that of the psalmist/God relationship. The psalmist's ultimate desire is for belongingness and reintegration into dependent relationships, not just in relationship with God, but also in relationship with his community. He must display, at least rhetorically, his strength over the enemy as a means to that end. Shame as social sanction is effective not just as a public denial of social worth, but also as a powerful psychological threat to a sense of worthiness and social belonging.

The connection between social and personal shame is evident in Ps 22:7, in which public disdain translates into a feeling of overwhelming unworthiness. The psalmist describes himself as a "worm (תּוֹלַעַת), less than human, scorned (חרף) by men, despised (בזה) by people" (Ps 22:7). Here, the psalmist represents himself as socially and personally diminished, implying an overall sense of wrongness in his existence. The feeling of internalized shame, feeling like a worm, is immediately connected to a public experience of rejection, implying both a public and private sense of shame. The psalmist is not just scorned by people in his community, but also by God, who is distant and has left him vulnerable to mockery and scornful comments (22:2, 8–9, 12, 14). The speaker accepts the public evaluation of his worth personally, even as he resists that evaluation socially by calling for deliverance and victory over the taunters (22:20–22). This example demonstrates that the complicated relationship between the public self and the private self cannot be parsed in simple categories. The threat or actual experience of social sanction and ridicule is extremely powerful in this psalm and reverberates in the psalmist's entire identity, personal and social. Yet the psalmist does not represent himself as having acted wrongly or in a way that invited this treatment by God or the taunters; he never describes his own actions that may have been perceived as deserving of sanction. The psychological aspect of his shame is due to the betrayal of trusted relationship with God that left him vulnerable to hostile attack, not due to his flawed personhood.[47]

The laments *do* include language of personal wrongdoing (see Pss 25:18–19; 38:19–20; 39:9–10; 41:5–6).[48] Importantly, however, the psalmist's acknowledgment of transgression is usually followed directly by reference to the enemy's persecution of him, as opposed to a description of an encompassing sense of unworthiness or shame that stems from that recognition of wrongdoing. For example, in Ps 25:18, the psalmist asks for forgiveness from sins (חטא), indicating acknowledgment of personal wrongdoing. The following verse refers to the vehemence of the hatred he experiences from his enemies. Again, in Ps 38:19, the psalmist acknowledges iniquity (עון) and sin (חטא) and proceeds in v. 20 to refer to his numerous enemies. The progression of thought from confession to lament about oppression at the hands of an antagonist indicates that even in the awareness of personal wrongdoing, the instigation of the psalmist's prayer is in his experience of social ridicule and antagonism, which then causes him to reflect upon and evaluate his personal actions. Moreover, the ultimate request of God is not relief from an overwhelming sense of personal unworthiness; that is not the suffering that plagues the psalmist. The supplicant's prayer is for relief from the experience of public disdain, social alienation, or persecution by enemies.

An exception is Ps 51, which does not refer to an enemy or to any public experience of disdain.[49] In fact, the psalmist states clearly that the source of the conflict is between himself and God (Ps 51:6). The language of iniquity is particularly dense in vv. 3–7, in which the vocabulary for wrongdoing (עון, פשע, חטא) repeats six times. The psalmist perceives his transgression as part of his

---

47. See also Odell's ("Shame and Dependence in the Bible," 227–28) discussion of Ps 22, in which she further explores the images of the psalmist's dependence on God.

48. The individual laments in which the psalmist consciously acknowledges transgression have often been grouped into a separate category, the seven penitential psalms (Pss 6; 32; 38; 51; 102; 130; 143), since the sixth century; see Nasuti, *Defining the Sacred Songs*, 30. Though they are traditionally understood to include confession and desires for forgiveness for personal wrongdoing, Nasuti observes that some of theses seven psalms do not actually contain an explicit acknowledgment of iniquity by the psalmist (see Ps 102) and some psalms that do (see Ps 25) are not traditionally included in this particular sub-category of laments. That fact reveals that other considerations contributed to the grouping of these psalms aside from the psalmist's acknowledgment of guilt. Nasuti rightly calls attention to the way traditions of classification emerge differently—the penitential psalms are mainly designated as such in Christian interpretive traditions—and how those designations, once established, shape the interpreter's assumptions about what a psalm does and means (ibid., 37). Here, I discuss individual laments in which the psalmist overtly acknowledges personal transgression, as opposed to declaring personal righteousness.

49. One might also consider Ps 130, in which the psalmist asks God for mercy and forgiveness: "If you keep count of sins (עונות), O Lord, Lord, who could stand?" (Ps 130:3). No mention of an enemy or public experience of shaming is evident in this psalm. The psalmist does not state as clearly as in Ps 51 that he has sinned or done wrong, though he clearly sees himself as in need of God's forgiveness, and the final verses of the psalm shift to the psalmist's admonition to Israel to look to God for redemption. Still, this psalm is similar to Ps 51 in that it does not connect sense of wrongdoing and need of redemption to public shame or mistreatment by enemies.

constitution, the wrong inherent in the circumstances of his creation (51:7). He asks God for the creation (ברא) of a new heart, an act that would transform the inner self (51:12). It is not a social experience of shame from which the psalmist seeks relief, but a personal sense of wrongdoing rooted in his being.

The distinction between anthropological and psychological shame is therefore not absolute; internal sense of worth is dependent upon or at least affected by social recognition of value. In the laments, the concepts of social and personal shame are connected. The distinction between these approaches, however, helps heuristically to isolate different registers of shame in the two primary relationships in which the psalmist represents himself, between the hostile other and God. While the dominant language of the psalmist/hostile other relationship is rooted in shame as a public sanction (both the sanction of the psalmist and the desired sanction of the antagonist), the psalmist interprets his position as sanctioned not simply in social categories, but also in terms of a broader sense of self that includes an internal, psychological sense of personal shame.

Because the shame generated by betrayed dependence is most relevant for the God/psalmist relationship and because my primary focus in this chapter is the psalmist/hostile other relationship, here I mainly focus on honor and shame as agonistic categories. Therefore, the following analysis is divided into two large sections, the elements of the laments' language that contribute to the construction of contempt and those that contribute to the construction of honor. My discussion is guided by the overall interest in how the psalmist negotiates restored social worth within the context of the honor/shame relational framework afforded by this figured world. I describe an interactive identity-making discourse discernible in the way the psalmist receives messages of contemptibility from his social environment and negotiates a rhetorical position of social worth to undermine and challenge that depiction of powerlessness.

4. *The Language of Social Diminishment: Creating the Category of Contempt*

The images of social disgrace and abandonment construct an intensely public theory of the person, in which public perception of one's social worth matters in the extreme. Much of the psalmist's description of his social situation has to do with the description of his external positioning by the hostile other as socially diminished, contemptible, and unworthy of social protection and respect. The extensive description of himself as socially diminished sends a message to God and potential sympathetic figures, engaging the interest of those who are expected to act on the psalmist's behalf. The attention and possible intervention of sympathetic or obligated others relies on this elaborate description of social diminishment. Therefore, the psalmist describes extensively the subject position afforded him by the other characters in his figured world.

The images range from expressions of the psalmist's sense of social vulnerability to images of outright social ostracism and disparagement. The discourse of social diminishment, just like the language of physical diminishment, is not univocal, however. It works on several fronts. In some of the categories described below, the language that constructs the category of shame simultaneously affords the psalmist a means of combating that social position. Therefore, even the self-representation as powerlessness is, at times, also a means of asserting rhetorical power.

a. *Language of Spatial and Relational Proxemics*
One aspect of the psalmist's discourse of powerlessness and contempt is imagery of spatial and relational remoteness and rejection.[50] He represents himself as removed from the company and protection of any supportive community through spatial distance and through gestures of disdain that physically and publicly dramatize the psalmist's social rejection. Both kinds of imagery represent the psalmist's loss of belonging in his community, though imagery of spatial distance emphasizes his abandonment and gestures of disdain emphasize, more potently, the psalmist's marginalized social position as actively scorned and condemned.

The psalmist's social identity is constructed in terms of his placement in a geographically figured relational matrix in which nearness indicates belonging and recognition of social worth and distance indicates shame and contempt. The social vulnerability involved in contemptibility is indicated in the many and repeated descriptions of the psalmist's social abandonment and community distance. In Ps 27:10 he refers to his mother and father's rejection of him and in Ps 69:9 he describes being a "stranger" to his brother and an "alien" to all of his kin. His friends stand "far off" (Ps 38:12), no one stands by his side: "Look at my right and see—I have no friend. There is no refuge for me. No one cares about me" (Ps 142:5). He is avoided on the street, an object of disgust (Ps 31:12). Again, in Ps 88:9, the psalmist describes being so despicable that even entering the public sphere is too much for him: "You remove (הרחקת) my companions from me; you make me abhorrent to them; I am shut in and do not go out." The importance of distance as a relational gauge is reasserted in Ps 88:19: "You have put friend and neighbor far (הרחקת) from me, and my companions out of my sight." In particularly bleak images of social rejection, the psalmist describes himself in Ps 102:7 as alone in the wilderness (מדבר), an owl in the wastelands (חרבות). Both of these desolate locations connote social rejection and the psalmist's residence on the margins of society. In the next verse, the psalmist describes himself as a bird alone (בודד) on a roof (Ps 102:8), an image of existence without social consolation. The devastation the psalmist describes comes from his experience of being removed from his social life, spatially isolated and separate from his community. The horror of these images of social rejection is felt only if one's conception of selfhood is largely, or at least significantly,

50. See also Barbara Korte's discussion of "proxemics," a category of nonverbal communication, as a means of literarily and rhetorically externalizing sense of social affiliation, sympathy, or condemnation. The significance of space and one's placement within it is culturally and socially embedded (Korte, *Body Language in Literature* [Toronto: University of Toronto Press, 1993], 73–77).

found in one's social identity within community. Distance is a means of figuring the psalmist's lack of social protection and inclusion, and consequent lack of social worth. Physically, the psalmist is alone, socially alienated and therefore vulnerable.

The psalmist's social powerlessness and loss of belonging is further represented in the hostile others' condemning gestures of disdain that tell a succinct and powerful story about the psalmist's social position. Gestures of disdain are among the most powerful and emotionally provocative methods of social diminishment and rejection, dramatizing and enacting a story of the others' sense of privilege and social dominance over the psalmist and the psalmist's position as socially scorned.[51] The psalmist represents himself as publicly mocked, taunted, and insulted: "I am a scornful thing (חרפה) to them. They see me and they shake (נוע) their heads" (Ps 109:25). Again, in Ps 22:8, the psalmist describes himself as an object of mockery to all he encounters: "They curl (פטר) their lips[52] and shake (נוע) their heads." Psalm 35 contains a particularly dense collection of three descriptions of hostile gestures in six verses. With vicious intent, the other gnashes his teeth (חרק עלי שנימו) at the psalmist (Ps 35:16). The psalmist describes the enemies who "wink (קרץ) their eyes" as sign of triumph and satisfaction in the psalmist's diminished state (35:19). Finally, in 35:21, the psalmist describes the wide mouths of those who mock and speak condemning words: "They open their mouths wide against me (ירחיבו עלי פיהם). They say 'Aha! Aha! Our eyes have seen.'" The hostile community and identified enemy symbolically mark distance through repeated withering actions and gestures that condemn and isolate the psalmist. Disdain for the psalmist is publicly performed in embodied gestures of disgust and acts of scorn.

51.   To my knowledge, the significance of these gestures has not been studied explicitly, though other types of gestures in the Hebrew Bible and other ancient Near Eastern literature have received attention. For instance, see Nili S. Fox, "Clapping Hands as a Gesture of Anguish and Anger in Mesopotamia and in Israel," *JANES* 23 (1996): 49–60; Scott C. Layton, "'Head on Lap' in Sumero-Akkadian Literature," *JANES* 15 (1983): 59–62; David P. Wright, "The Gesture of Hand Placement in the Hebrew Bible and in Hittite Literature," *JAOS* 106 (1986): 433–46. M. I. Gruber's work is the most extensive treatment of nonverbal communication in the Hebrew Bible, though he does not analyze the gestures of contempt in the Psalms (Mayer I. Gruber, *Aspects of Nonverbal Communication in the Ancient Near East* [Rome: Biblical Institute, 1980]). P. A. Kruger offers the most focused treatment of gesture in the Psalms, encouraging caution in translation and attention to the context in which gestures occur (P. A. Kruger, "Nonverbal Communication and Symbolic Gestures in the Psalms," *BT* 45 [1994]: 213–22). As he notes, a gesture used in one culture might have a very different, even opposite, social meaning in another culture (p. 214). Kruger does not offer alternative readings of the gestures described above as indications of something other than contempt, however; their context is clearly one of demonstrating disdain. These gestures are not nearly as ambiguous in their meaning as, for instance, the "hand on the mouth" gesture in Job 40:4, which could indicate "astonishment, reverence, respect, repentance, humiliation, and obeisance" (see Gregory Yuri Glazov, "The Significance of the 'Hand on the Mouth' Gesture in Job XL 4," *VT* 52 [2002]: 31).

52.   This is the only instance of פטר in the Hiphil in the Hebrew Bible. In the Qal, פטר has to do with separation, departing, or removing. In the context of the next phrase, "they shake their heads," it seems clear that the action of the lips is a gesture of contempt as well. Hilton Oswald translates Kraus's original German translation of יפטירו בשפה as "screw up their mouth" (Kraus, *Psalms 1–59*, 291).

The hostile others' gestures of disdain are so rhetorically powerful for two reasons. First, they communicate on a more immediate level than verbal condemnation, though words are obviously extremely important to the psalmist's sense of social rejection. Barbara Korte, a literary theorist of nonverbal communication, suggests that textual representation of bodily gesture affords emotional authenticity to communicative acts. In fact, Korte argues that nonverbal gestures are more effective than verbal communications for the expression of states of mind or emotional responses because individuals are typically less in control of their bodily responses than their verbal ones.[53] Therefore, there is a stronger connection between feeling and non-verbal expression, making gesture more effective at conveying the "unspeakable," nonverbal aspects of emotional responses.[54] In the laments, the nonverbal gestures of the hostile others authenticate both the other's disdain and disassociation and the intensity with which the psalmist feels that disavowal.

Second, gestures are especially powerful indicators of social alienation because they are a recognizable social performance of contempt that makes use of conventional community understandings of these actions. These gestures are part of a social and cultural choreography of establishing interpersonal affiliation, and group membership or rejection. Their use in the laments emphasizes the hostile others' sense of social security, safety, and confidence, thereby reinforcing the psalmist's social alienation, vulnerability, and unprotected position in the community.[55] Gestures of contempt are therefore a means of establishing and reinforcing social dominance over the psalmist.[56] The psalmist's representation of himself as the object of such humiliating gestures of contempt emphasizes the community's heightened emotional and visceral rejection of the psalmist and their intention to relegate him to absolute social isolation through public displays of his unworthiness and repugnance. Concrete, physical enactments of distance and social rejection rhetorically concretize the psalmist's sense of social powerlessness.

53.   See also Michael Argyle (*Bodily Communication* [2d ed.; London: Methuen, 1988], 305–6). Argyle is a theorist of nonverbal communication who argues that nonverbal signs are far more effective in communication of interpersonal attitudes and are often perceived to be more genuine because they are a more immediate and less controlled response to a social encounter.

54.   Korte, *Body Language in Literature*, 40–41.

55.   See ibid., 50.

56.   Gilles Kirouac and Ursula Hess ("Group Membership and Decoding Nonverbal Behavior," in *The Social Context of Nonverbal Behavior* [ed. Pierre Philippot, Robert S. Feldman, and Erik J. Coats; Cambridge: Cambridge University Press, 1999], 193) discuss bodily communication as a means of establishing social dominance. See also Steve L. Ellyson and John F. Dovidio, eds., *Power, Dominance, and Nonverbal Communication* (New York: Springer, 1985), especially the article by Nancy M. Henley and Sean Harmon included in this volume: "The Nonverbal Semantics of Power and Gender: A Perceptual Study," 151–64. Though Henley and Harmon do not analyze gestures of disdain specifically, their work provides helpful analysis of dominance gestures more generally, and I assume gestures of disdain fall into the category of a dominance gesture since the intention is to ostracize and reject. These authors argue that dominance gestures have a strong effect in the appearance of dominance and power and that being the target of such a gesture creates the appearance of submission (pp. 153, 161).

b. *Images of Undesirable Social Affiliation*

While social and relational isolation is a constitutive part of this discourse, the psalmist also makes reference to other characters in this figured world who serve as a gauge of his own social position and assist the psalmist as he establishes a relational identity. Social affiliation is as important as social distance in this rhetorical world as a way of identifying social placement as well as articulating claims to social worth.

References to social affiliations serve three different purposes. First, the psalmist refers to his social position relative to groups of people he considers socially beneath him as a means of describing his own diminished social position and extent of his social contemptibility. For instance, in Ps 39:9 the psalmist prays not to be made the "reproach of the foolish (נבל)." In Ps 35:15, the psalmist refers to the "beaten down" (נכים)[57] who tear (קרע) at him endlessly. Here the psalmist communicates the extent of his diminished social status by referring to his position relative to other recognized outsiders in this society. The extent of his social diminishment is expressed in being found contemptible even by those who have no respectable social status. Reference to others who are marginalized vividly communicates the extent of the psalmist's fall from social worth—the psalmist is rejected even by the rejected.[58]

Another illustrative example is Ps 69:13, in which the psalmist refers to two different groups of people who find him contemptible, thereby establishing the social parameters of his rejection: "Those who sit at the gate complain (שיח) about me; the drunkards (שותי שכר) sing mocking songs (נגינות)[59] about me." The gate is the seat of patriarchal social power and an image of honor and social respectability.[60] Those who sit at the gate are the adjudicators of justice, the decision makers and bearers of wisdom for the community, while the drunkard signifies the disdained members of this society (see, e.g., Prov 20:1; 23:29–33). The psalmist's loss of social status could not be depicted more thoroughly. He is not only shunned by the honorable of his community, but is scorned by the scorned, the outcast of this society.

57. I read נכים as a Hophal adjective from נכה (so BDB), though this is the only occurrence of this word in the Hebrew Bible and translation is problematic. Similar translations to mine occur in the RSV, which reads "cripples," and the NJPS, which reads "wretches." Some emend this word to an active participle, מכים, "the smiters" (see Dahood, *Psalms*, 1:213; D. Winton Thomas, "Psalm XXXV. 15f," *JTS* 12 [1961]: 50–51). Bardtke, in the *BHS* apparatus, suggests נכרים, "strangers." See also Kraus, *Psalms 1–59*, 391; Brown, *Seeing the Psalms*, 250. I translate the word, "the beaten down," though the psalmist's sense of indignation and rejection at being "gathered against" (נאספו עלי) by this group is the same independent of one's translation of נכים. In any of the proposed translations, נכים refers to a group of social outsiders; the psalmist uses this group's actions against him to demonstrate the extent of his social diminishment.

58. A similar technique for describing social diminishment in Job 30. See Carol A. Newsom, "The Moral Sense of Nature: Ethics in the Light of God's Speech to Job," *PSB* 15 (1994): 13.

59. The reference to נגינות indicates drunken songs. See also Job 30:9 and Lam 3:14 for instances in which this word is used in a mocking context. Job describes being mocked by those over whom he once was socially superior. Lamentations does not specify to whom the speaker has become an object of mockery, but simply says the speaker is the taunt of "all people."

60. For images of the gate as the location and symbol of authority and power, see Deut 21:19; 22:15; 25:7; Ruth 4:1; 2 Sam 18:4; Amos 5:10, 12, 15.

A second way that references to social affiliations contribute to the psalmist's representation as contemptible is in protestations of innocence. In Ps 26:4–5, the force of the psalmist's plea of innocence is based on his claim of right social affiliations: "I do not sit with frauds (מְתֵי שָׁוְא), or mix with the treacherous (נַעֲלָמִים).[61] I hate the company of evil men (מְרֵעִים), and do not consort with the wicked (רְשָׁעִים)." The protest the psalmist believes will motivate God to act on his behalf is that he did not consort with the socially unfavorable. One way that the psalmist knew his own social worth was in his rejection of those who were not considered socially valuable. Social worth is indicated, in part, by the merit of one's social affiliations. In his supplication, the psalmist surely means simply to represent himself as unjustly accused and as entitled to social justice and restoration of his place in the community. In so doing, he reflects his assumptions about his social world, that social worth is established in one's affiliation with the honorable and rejection of the contemptible.

A third example of the discursive use of references to social affiliation is in the psalmist's pleas not to be associated with certain people in his society. In Ps 26:9 he pleads: "Do not gather me with sinners (חַטָּאִים), my life with men of blood (אַנְשֵׁי דָמִים)." Again, in Ps 28:3, the psalmist prays, "Do not count me with the wicked (רְשָׁעִים) and evildoers (פֹּעֲלֵי אָוֶן) who speak goodwill toward their neighbors while evil is in their heart." The psalmist's central plea is not to be unjustly accused. But, significantly, he places his plea for fair treatment in terms of the threat of undesirable social affiliations; he wants to be judged fairly, and he also wants to avoid association with those who are socially condemned. His reference to other disdained groups is of import here as an articulation of his vision of society and his rightful place in that society. The psalmist perceives people in terms of those who are contemptible or honorable, and his association with those in either category as an indication of his own social worth.

Importantly, the psalmist does not challenge the relational system in which one's own social worth is measured relative to others. That is, the psalmist does not make a plea about the plight of the socially contemptible; the psalmist's suffering lies merely in his inclusion among them. In fact, he depends on the category of contempt to understand and identify himself socially. The psalmist affirms and reinforces the hierarchical social structure in his claim to social worth based on his rejection of some and right affiliation with others. Threat of association with the disenfranchised of his society is a rhetorical method of representing his social diminishment, one that reflects and creates the agonistic social and relational structures in which he crafts his supplication.

c. *Images of Verbal Threat and Malicious Speech*
The kind of language an individual uses with others indicates a sense of relative social position and articulates relational identity.[62] One constructs relational

---

61. נַעֲלָמִים is literally "the hidden ones."
62. Holland et al., *Identity and Agency in Cultural Worlds*, 127: "Relational identities have to do with behavior as indexical claims to social relationships with others. They have to do with how one identifies one's position relative to others, mediated through the way one feels comfortable or

identity in the language one adopts and, when being addressed, in one's perception of the language others employ. In the socially competitive world of the laments, words and speech matter in the extreme. The many images of words and speech as threatening and dangerous are another way the psalmist articulates the fragility of his social world and his unstable position in it. Words and quality of speech are central to the discourse of the laments and a fundamental way the psalmist represents himself as socially diminished and vulnerable to hostile, malicious, and deceitful forces.

The psalmist frequently characterizes the others' speech as untrustworthy, deceptive, and deceitful: "With their mouths they bless, but inwardly, they curse" (Ps 62:5; see also Pss 38:13; 64:6; 109:2–3; 120:2–3). Mouths speak arrogance, contempt, and deceit (Pss 10:7; 17:10; 31:19; 62:5). The tongue is an instrument of evil and treachery (Ps 10:7). The psalmist describes insincere lips, throats like an open grave, slippery, deceitful tongues (Pss 3:10; 12:3–4; 120:2–3).

The hostile other, however, is not just deceitful and untrustworthy; his speech is actually a tool of violence, a weapon of attack. Speech is a means of violently wounding. In Ps 59:8 the psalmist describes swords (חרב) on the lips of his attackers. The psalmist in Ps 55:22 equates words with weapons of attack: "His talk was smoother than butter, but his mind was on war (קרב), his words were more soothing than oil, but they were drawn swords (פתחות)." The relationship construed in this example is one of embattled warriors, fighting verbally for social dominance. The war concerns public reputation and perception of social worth, wherein publicly uttered words have the power to wound.

Further intensifying the image of words as violent tools of diminishment, the psalmist in Ps 57:5 conflates imagery of speech, predatory animals, and military weaponry: "In the midst of man-eating lions I lie down; their teeth are spears and arrows, their tongue a sharp sword." The foe created in this imagery is a word-wielding predator, pursuing and attacking the psalmist with cutting speech. As I will describe below in the section on predatory language, the lion was an especially recognizable and powerful cultural symbol of strength and skill in hunting and attack in the ancient Near East.[63] To describe social threat as a lion with weapon-like methods of speaking is to grant words a tremendous amount of wounding, predatory power. Threat and social powerlessness, represented as an attack by a super-powerful, mythically strong beast with the easy ability to damage, maim, and even kill, is heightened to extreme levels of intensity.

The psalmist does not only heavily characterize his own social vulnerability through characterization of the hostile other's words, but also through direct

---

constrained, for example, to speak to another, to command another, to enter into the space of another, to touch the possessions of another, to dress for another...."

63. See Brent A. Strawn, *What is Stronger than a Lion? Leonine Image and Metaphor in the Hebrew Bible and the Ancient Near East* (Fribourg: Academic Press; Göttingen: Vandenhoeck & Ruprecht, 2005), 35–36.

quotation.[64] The psalmist's quotation of other characters in this figured world is prominent. While Bakhtin understood the self to be always receiving and responding to messages, even unconsciously, the psalmist's reception of external messages about his social position and response to those messages is writ large.[65] In fact, the psalmist reports speech from every character in the figured world, including himself, God, the hostile other, and the sympathetic community. The hostile other is, by far, the most quoted figure; the psalmist uses quotation dramatically and directly to represent the other as arrogant and himself as viciously and unjustly designated as socially contemptible.[66] The psalmist represented in the hostile others' words is an object of disdain and mockery, often because the hostile other perceives the psalmist as abandoned by God and without hope of God's assistance. Twice in Ps 42 the psalmist refers to the taunts of foes who say, "Where is your God?" (Ps 42:4, 11). The psalmist reports, "Many say to me, 'There is no deliverance of him by God'" (Ps 3:3). Again, in Ps 10:4, the wicked (רשע) says, "He (God) does not care (דרש). There is no God." Psalm 22:9 is one of the most potent examples of the other's derision of the psalmist, as he taunts the psalmist with God's clear absence in spite of the psalmist's claim to special relationship with God: "Roll onto[67] God! Let him rescue him. Let him save him. For he is pleased with him." In these words, the psalmist represents himself as an object of disdain and rebuke, someone whom others feel they can abuse. The hostile other in these examples, moreover, is construed as merciless and arrogant in his assurance of God's abandonment of the psalmist and the psalmist's clear and humiliating overestimation of God's commitment.

The psalmist asserts the strongest control as orchestrator of voices in his characterization of the other's internal thoughts, which typically depict the foe's extreme arrogance. According to the psalmist, the wicked is brashly sure of his

64. See also Rolf A. Jacobson, *"Many are Saying": The Function of Direct Discourse in the Hebrew Psalter* (JSOTSup 397; London: T&T Clark International, 2004), for further discussion of the use of direct quotations in the Psalter.

65. Others have studied the multi-voiced, dialogic elements of the Psalms. See especially Herbert Levine, "The Dialogic Discourse of Psalms," in *Hermeneutics, the Bible and Literary Criticism* (ed. Ann Loades and Michael McLain; New York: St. Martin's, 1992), 145–61; idem, "An Audience with the King: The Perspective of Dialogue," in *Sing Unto God a New Song: A Contemporary Reading of the Psalms* (Bloomington: Indiana University Press, 1995), 79–129; Mandolfo, *God in the Dock*.

66. See Pss 3:2; 10:4, 6, 11; 12:5; 13:5; 22:9; 35:21, 25; 41:6, 8–9; 42:4, 11; 59:8–9; 64:4–6; 70:4; 71:11; 94:7.

67. Numerous textual fixes have been offered to account for the abrupt transition in the MT from the second person imperative form of the root גלל ("Roll onto God!") to the third person verbal forms in the rest of the verse. Dahood (*Psalms 1–50*, 139) proposes that the root is not גלל but גיל and offers a slightly obscure sense of this root, "He lived for Yahweh." Kselman ("'Why Have You Abandoned Me?,'" 176) follows Dahood in this reading. My translation is influenced by Gesenius's observation that this abrupt change in person in poetic texts is well-attested and not always due to a textual problem. As evidence, he cites Isa 22:16; 47:8; 48:1; 54:1, 11; Jer 22:16; Amos 5:6; Mal 3:9, among other examples (W. Gesenius and E. Kautzch, *Genesius' Hebrew Grammar* [trans. A. E. Cowley; 2d. English ed.; Oxford: Clarendon, 1910], 462).

triumph over the psalmist when he "says in his heart" that they will not stagger or experience trouble "from generation to generation" (Ps 10:6). In Ps 12:5 the psalmist characterizes the hostile other as, again, overly confident of his triumph: "They say, 'By our tongues we will be strong; with our lips, who can be our master?' "[68]

Through use of quotations, the psalmist effectively communicates his social humiliation as well as his foe's arrogance and injustice. While the instances of reported speech depict the words and intentions of the hostile other, the psalmist utilizes those words in his own rhetorical project of defining the identity of the hostile other, and thereby also defining himself in relation to the hostile other. Quotations always "serve a second master," and therefore serve the rhetorical purposes of the psalmist, offering an efficient means of self-authoring through other-authoring.[69] This repeated rhetorical element allows him to put words in another's mouth and, by extension, author his thoughts, motives, and utterances. By orchestrating the direct speech of the hostile other, the psalmist simultaneously constructs himself as contemptible and rejects that external positioning by claiming a position of rhetorical authority.

It is significant, however, that the psalmist goes so far as to include the hostile other's words, a rhetorical act that implicitly attributes importance to his thoughts and utterances. Would not the other's silence within the context of the prayer be a better means of usurping his social and personal power? The inclusion of these quotations does evidence the importance of external evaluation in the psalmist's dialogic selfhood. The other's negative evaluation clearly does matter to the psalmist greatly, as it challenges his sense of social worth, belonging, and entitlement. Yet, the other's words do not enjoy equal discursive authority. Rather, the psalmist employs quotation to establish control over the other, an anti-dialogic rhetorical practice.[70] The psalmist uses the other's speech to regain rhetorical control and construct identity in opposition to and juxtaposition with the representation of the self in the other's speech. Therefore, though the psalmist includes the other's words, there is no true contest of voices.[71] The

---

68. At other times, the reported speech of the other indicates what the psalmist would like to prohibit the other from being able to say: "Let not my enemy say, 'I have overcome him.' My foes exult when I totter" (Ps 13:5).

69. See Bakhtin's description of the prose writer's use of voices in novels: "The prose writer makes use of words that are already populated with the social intentions of others and compels them to serve his own intentions, to serve a second master" (Mikhail Bakhtin, *The Dialogic Imagination: Four Essays by M. M. Bakhtin* [ed. M. E. Holquist; trans. Caryl Emerson and Michael Holquist; Austin: University of Texas Press, 1981], 299–300).

70. Bakhtin imagined certain rare cases, mainly in the novels of Dostoevsky, in which the presence of another's discourse through quotation might be allowed to challenge the narrator's words and produce opportunity for true dialogue between equally valued worldviews. In this scenario, the narrator must cede monologic control and allow the other's discourse to enjoy that same authority as the narrator's. See Mikhail Bakhtin, *Problems of Dostoevsky's Poetics* (ed. and trans. Caryl Emerson; Minneapolis: University of Minnesota Press, 1984), 5.

71. Levine (*Sing Unto God a New Song*, 110) accords more authority to the other voices in the Psalms and argues that the presence of quotations is evidence of an internal struggle within the

hostile other's words do not enjoy the same authority as the psalmist's and do not invite the audience to consider the worthiness of the foe's opinion. The psalmist's many descriptions of the enemy's tongue, mouth, and throat as deceitful and lying and the enemy's speech as duplicitous and arrogant instruct God and the hearing audience to greet the enemy's words with suspicion and distrust.[72] The psalmist orchestrates the interaction between himself and the hostile other in order to illustrate the enemy's depravity and allow the psalmist to self-author in a way that engages the sympathy of God and the potentially sympathetic audience who might act to the psalmist's benefit.

The extent of the psalmist's claim to rhetorical power through use of quotations is evident in his use of God's and the community's words further to condemn the hostile other. That is, the psalmist uses the voices of others in the community to enact the foe's fall from honor and his own social ascendance. The psalmist's orchestration of his own social restoration through juxtaposition of the authority of contrasting voices is clear in Ps 12, in which the psalmist directly places in competition the hostile other's words and God's words. The foes say, "By our tongues we will be strong; with our lips, who can be our master?" (Ps 12:5). Following this, God's words are reported, establishing a direct contrast with the words of the wicked: "'Because of the violence endured by the poor and the groans of the needy, now I will rise up,' says YHWH. 'I will provide as salvation a witness for him'" (Ps 12:6).[73] Then, in Ps 12:7, the psalmist describes God's words, emphasizing and clarifying the significance of the juxtaposition: "The words of YHWH are pure words, silver refined in an earthen crucible, purified seven times." The psalmist exhibits clear rhetorical control in these verses. There is no contest between the authority of God's pure words and the hostile other's arrogant ones. The psalmist's social dominance is

psalmist. According to Levine, the psalmist does not control the voices of others, but allows quarrel, which provides an "ideological fulcrum," in the Psalms. In his example (Ps 12), however, he argues that it is really only God's voice that enjoys equal authority as the psalmist's voice. The words of the wicked are presented through the "prejudicial view of the psalmist" (p. 112). That God's voice prevails in the argument in Ps 12 is only further evidence of the psalmist's rhetorical control of these voices. The psalmist may depict a verbal competition, but he is fully in control and the hostile others' viewpoint is never present in any other way than to prove his wickedness and the necessity of his destruction.

72. See Pss 3:10; 10:7; 12:3–4; 17:10; 31:19; 38:13; 62:5; 64:6; 109:2–3; 120:2–3.

73. The phrase in Ps 12:6, אָשִׁית בְּיֵשַׁע יָפִיחַ לוֹ, is a textual puzzle. Patrick D. Miller ("*Yāpiaḥ* in Psalm XII 6," *VT* 29 [1979]: 495–501) offers a thorough analysis that results in the following translation: "I will place in safety the witness in his behalf." J. Gerald Janzen ("Another Look at Psalm XII 6," *VT* 54 [2004]: 157–64) builds on Miller's work. He accepts Miller's construal of יָפִיחַ as "witness," but offers a slightly different interpretation of אָשִׁית בְּיֵשַׁע: "I will provide as salvation a witness for him." Full discussions of the arguments of each scholar are beyond the scope of this work; both translations are plausible, though I follow Janzen's interpretation in the present chapter. Though each scholar discusses the significant implications of his translation, for my purposes it is simply important to recognize that this line is the psalmist's quotation of God's speech in which God promises either to provide or protect a witness who will act beneficially for the psalmist. The psalmist identifies himself with the poor and needy whom God will defend. In response, God promises salvific assistance.

enacted in his God's verbal proclamations of affiliation with the poor and needy, designations the psalmist applies to himself.

In like manner, the psalmist also includes the speech of the larger community who will condemn the hostile other, returning his taunts and making the other the object of disdain: "The righteous, seeing it (God's obliteration of the other), will be awestruck; they will laugh (שׂחק) at him, saying, 'Here is a man who did not make God his refuge, but trusted in his great wealth, was strong in his wickedness'" (Ps 52:7–8). The psalmist's use of the community's words for his own purposes of achieving social restoration is clear. Here, the psalmist orchestrates the words of the sympathetic community to imagine and enact the social diminishment of the hostile other and his own consequent social restoration.

The psalmist stages another similar interaction, though on a more gruesome scale, in Ps 58.[74] After describing in gory detail the enemy's slaughter, the psalmist quotes the community's response as final compensation for the other's downfall. The psalmist enthusiastically imagines public recognition of God's justice and recognition of the righteous person's (i.e. the psalmist's) worth: "Men will say, 'Indeed, there is a reward for the righteous. Indeed, the justice of God exists on earth'" (Ps 58:12). Through use of reported speech, the psalmist not only instructs the audience to perceive the other as diminished, but also to perceive the psalmist as dominating and triumphant through his association with God. The words of sympathetic onlookers play a crucial role in the psalmist's fantasies of restored social worth and public recognition of strength.

In these instances, God and the community serve as the psalmist's super-addressee, a concept Bakhtin used to describe the imagined sympathetic audience that uncritically and unreservedly sees, or will see, the validity of the speaker's viewpoint.[75] The superaddressee embodies the "principle of hope" in an utterance, the hope of just understanding and supportive response.[76] In these fantasies of future social restoration, the presence of sympathetic onlookers who re-evaluate their understanding of the psalmist is crucial to the psalmist's rhetorical goals. The psalmist's quotation of the onlookers' affirming words functions on several levels. First, these words speak to the foe, articulating a threat and a promise of what is in store for him socially if he does not change his ways. Second, they speak to the community and to God. They educate the listening audience as to the desired and correct response to the psalmist and his social antagonist, modeling sympathy for the psalmist and disdain for the hostile other. Third, they are a means of self-speaking. They afford the psalmist a position of restored socio-rhetorical power in visions of the hostile other's diminishment and his own publicly recognized restored worth.

The degree of importance attributed to speech and the significance of the mechanism of speech is an important way the psalmist generates a category of contempt. These words not only characterize the maliciousness of the enemy,

---

74. Ps 58 is not an individual lament, but I include it as an example because it further illustrates a psalmic pattern in which the psalmist uses the other's speech to support his rhetorical goals.

75. Morson and Emerson, *Mikhail Bakhtin*, 135–36.

76. Ibid., 135.

but also reflect the psalmist's position as socially powerless and shamed. The psalmist, however, in the characterization and quotation of the other's speech, as well as God's and the community's speech, both constructs and refuses the category of contempt. If the social power lies with the other in this discourse, rhetorical power lies with the psalmist. The psalmist, in other words, fashions his own identity of social worth, even as he narrates words that portray him as disgraceful. Orchestration of voices that define the self in particular ways is part of a process of self-formation in the laments.

d. *Images of Predation and Attack*

Two dominant metaphors construct the relationship between the hostile other and the psalmist, one construing the relationship as a hunt and one as a battle.[77] The implications of these metaphors as part of a relational framework are best understood when interpreted as part of the honor and shame discourse in the laments. Both sets of imagery represent the psalmist in a socially diminished and unprotected role, vulnerable and exposed. The psalmist's status as socially unprotected indicates his loss of honor and respect in this cultural world. Honor and respect afford an individual social protection and the privilege of social safety, though this safety must always be guarded against diminishing attacks. In the relational framework offered by the images of pursuit and attack, the psalmist represents himself as outside the protections of social honor. While the images of the hunt and battle both position the psalmist as endangered and socially vulnerable, the two sets of images offer the psalmist different modes of response to that social positioning. The image of the hunt implies a passive position for the psalmist, who is simply prey to the hunter. Battle imagery, however, implies warfare that offers the psalmist, through God, an aggressive mode of response to attack.

The relational metaphor of the hunt offers two simple roles to the principal characters; the hostile other is the hunter and the psalmist is the prey. The sense of threat is heightened by metaphorically likening the hostile other to various menacing and carnivorous animals; he is a lion (אריה: Pss 7:3; 10:9; 17:12; 22:14, 22; ארי: Ps 22:17;[78] כפירים: Ps 35:17;[79] לבאם: Ps 57:5[80]), dog (כלב: Pss

---

77. See also Peter Riede (*Im Netz des Jägers: Studien zur Feindmetaphorik der Individual-psalmen* [WMANT 85; Neukirchen–Vluyn: Neukirchener, 2000], 20–149, 339–76), who discusses the enemy metaphors, and associated God metaphors, related to warfare and to the hunt.

78. The word כארי in the MT has provoked a great deal of discussion. My argument does not depend on this word meaning "like a lion" and so I do not fully engage the increasingly sophisticated arguments about this textual issue here. My assumption is that the MT's phrase, literally "like a lion my hands and feet," is the most likely reading and that a verb probably dropped out of this phrase at some point. The references to other lions and leonine behavior in the psalm seem to support this argument, but this assertion is by no means unchallenged. For a more complete discussion of this issue, see J. J. M. Roberts, "A New Root for an Old Crux, Ps XXII 17c," *VT* 23 (1973): 246–52; R. Tournay, "Note sur le Psaume 22:17," *VT* 23 (1973): 111–12; Gregory Vall, "Psalm 22:17b: 'The Old Guess,'" *JBL* 116 (1997): 45–56; John Kaltner, "Psalm 22:17b: Second Guessing 'the Old Guess,'" *JBL* 117 (1998): 503–6; Brent A. Strawn, "Psalm 22:17b: More Guessing," *JBL* 119 (2000): 439–451; Kristin Swenson, "Psalm 22:17: Circling around the Problem Again," *JBL* 123 (2004): 637–48; James R. Linville, "Psalm 22:17B: A New Guess," *JBL* 124 (2005): 733–44.

22:17, 21; 59:7, 15), wild oxen (רמים: Ps 22:22), and bull (פרים: Ps 22:13).[81] In this imagery, the hostile other's motivations and goals are simple and finite; the ferocious animal desires to hunt and kill.[82] An enemy that is a menacing animal is one with a predisposed aggressive nature.[83] The image of the foe as a threatening beast implies a level of inevitability in the interaction of these characters, in which the enemy acts as the aggressor and the psalmist is a powerless victim.[84]

The lion is the most frequently invoked animal in the laments, significant because of the lion's status in the ancient Near East as a predator par excellence.[85] The psalmist is most often hunted by *the* symbol of animalistic potency and power. In fact, because the lion was used so often in the ancient Near East to describe royalty and symbolize deities, the lion as a metaphor for the psalmist's personal antagonist accrues that heightened power as well. Brent Strawn argues as much in his work on the lion as metaphor: "When the psalmists describe their personal enemies as lions…they are employing a metaphor of power and dominance reserved for gods and kings."[86] In this metaphor, the enemy is granted extraordinary, god-like powers. The ultimate strength of the lion effectively and necessarily implies the ultimate powerlessness of the psalmist.[87] Before this animal, above all animals, the psalmist is terrifyingly helpless. To imagine any individual having recourse against this rapacious, god-like animal, endowed with mythic levels of strength and potency, borders on the ridiculous, in fact. The psalmist's agency is therefore severely impaired by this construction of the psalmist/hostile other relationship.

The terror of the hunt is illustrated clearly in the dramatic images of the psalmist being ripped apart (טרף) by a lion (Ps 7:3). A less dramatic yet equally significant part of the predation imagery is the hostile others' relentless observance and strategic planning for the downfall of the psalmist.[88] The psalmist's social diminishment is articulated in his vulnerability to external hostile pursuit and lack of strength with which to combat affront. The enemy sets traps (פח: Pss 69:23; 140:6; 141:9; 142:4), nets (רשת: Pss 9:16; 10:9; 25:15; 31:5; 35:7, 8; 57:7; 140:6), snares (מוקש: Pss 69:23; 140:6; 141:9; נקש: Ps 38:13), and uses ditches (שחת: Pss 7:16; 9:16; 35:7; 55:24), pits (שיחה: Ps 57:7), and rope

---

79. See also Ps 58:7.

80. This form of לביא is a defective masculine plural.

81. See also Brown, *Seeing the Psalms*, 136–44; Katharine J. Dell, "The Use of Animal Imagery in the Psalms and Wisdom Literature of Ancient Israel," *Scottish Journal of Theology* 53 (2000): 275–91; Brian Doyle, "Howling Like Dogs: Metaphorical Language in Psalm LIX," *VT* 54 (2004): 61–82; Riede, *Im Netz des Jägers*, 150–230.

82. See also Keel, *The Symbolism of the Biblical World*, 88.

83. The enemy is also referred to as a snake (נחש: Ps 140:4) and a horned viper (עכשוב: Ps 140:4), decidedly not carnivorous images, but still potentially deadly and definitely threatening.

84. See also Hobbs and Jackson, "The Enemy in the Psalms," 24.

85. See also Brown, *Seeing the Psalms*, 136.

86. Strawn, *What is Stronger than a Lion?*, 274.

87. See also ibid., 275, and Brown, *Seeing the Psalms*, 139.

88. Hobbs and Jackson also note that conspiracy is part of the enemy image in the Psalms. See Hobbs and Jackson, "The Enemy in the Psalms," 24.

(חבלים: Ps 140:6) to capture the psalmist. He lies in wait (ארב: Pss 10:9; 59:4) and insistently pursues (רדף: Pss 69:27; 143:3). The psalmist represents himself as the object of plots and schemes (Pss 31:14; 56:6–7; 59:4–5; 62:5; 140:3, 5). He perceives himself as evaluated for weakness and possible attack throughout the laments: "I hear the words of many, horror on every side, as they conspire (יסד) together against me, plotting (זמם) to take my life" (Ps 31:14).

Even when the psalmist is not describing the threat of physical attack, anxiety associated with being the object of constant scrutiny, observation, and evaluation for weakness heightens the portrayal of the psalmist as socially unprotected, marginalized, and contemptible. Referring to the hostile other as a "watcher (שורר),"[89] the psalmist establishes the power of the other versus his own sense of relative powerlessness when he characterizes the enemy as an aggressive and strategic observer who evaluates the psalmist for vulnerability. The psalmist's description of the hostile other's merciless behavior in Ps 10:8–9 is illustrative:

> He sits in the ambush (in) enclosed places;
> from hiding places he slays the innocent;
> his eyes furtively look for the unfortunate.
> He waits in hiding like a lion in its thicket,
> he waits to seize the poor;
> he drags the poor into his net.

Attributing to the other the immense power in looking and secret observance, especially implied in the voracious powers of the lion, the psalmist represents himself as the object of the unsympathetic gaze. Looking, as is already firmly established in feminist biblical criticism, connotes power, control, and dominance.[90] In the laments, being observed is an indication of social vulnerability, a public act of contempt that reflects the other's perception of the psalmist as lacking the protections of social honor and reputation.[91] To be the object of such evaluation and assessment indicates one's inferior status with regard to the observer. Moreover, Michael Lewis argues that the sometimes painful awareness of the other's gaze is a powerful initiator of personal shame for some.[92] Therefore, the gaze is significant not just for the psalmist's sense of vulnerable social status but also in terms of his more comprehensive self-awareness and

---

89.   See Pss 5:9; 27:11; 54:7; 56:3; 59:11. The word שורר only occurs in the psalms, and only in one psalm that is not a lament of the individual, Ps 92:12.

90.   Feminist biblical scholars, especially J. Cheryl Exum (*Fragmented Women: Feminist [Sub]Versions of Biblical Narratives* [Valley Forge, Pa.: Trinity Press, 1993], 172–76, 194–98), have discussed the connection between the gaze and the negotiation and assertion of power in narrative contexts, especially with regard to the Bathsheba story. Exum's major contribution to this discussion is her recognition that actively looking or being looked upon are indications of a character's power and are integral to the construction of subjectivity. Korte (*Body Language in Literature*, 60) also connects the gaze to expression of power.

91.   In Ps 35:21, the psalmist connects being watched with an opportunity for public ridicule and taunting: "They open their mouths wide against me. They say 'Aha! Aha! Our eyes have seen.'"

92.   Lewis, *Shame*, 30: "It was the social significance of the act, the eye of the other, that produced shame."

consequent feeling of shame. Being observed unsympathetically represents threat on numerous levels. The psalmist symbolizes his intense social and personal vulnerability, shame, and loss of position through the hostile other's strategic observation, which is the enemy;s assertion of social dominance.

The imagery related to battle posits the enemy as a predatory warrior, affording the enemy much the same powerful position as the hunting imagery. Military imagery and weaponry characterize the hostile other's speech and body parts that produce speech, as described above (פְּתחוֹת: Ps 55:22; חָנִית, חרב, חֵץ: Ps 57:5; חרב: Ps 59:8; 64:4). The other's words are weapons of attack, yet the enemy does not just wage a verbal war. The enemy readies weaponry (קֶשֶׁת: Ps 7:13; חֵץ: Ps 7:14; קֶשׁת, חֵץ: Ps 11:2; קֶשׁת, חרב: Ps 37:14–15), whets his sword (חרב: Ps 7:13), and plans battle (מלחמה: Pss 120:7; 140:3; קרב: Ps 55:22).[93]

While the enemy is an aggressor in the imagery of battle and weaponry in much the same way as in the hunting imagery, the role afforded the psalmist is not as clearly the role of the powerless victim. Though the hunter does not expect to be hunted in return by his prey, a context of warfare implies a competitive battle. The language of warfare affords the psalmist an imagistic foundation upon which to confront the hostile other on at least a rhetorical battlefield. The psalmist does not describe himself as a warrior, however, but does encourage God to be a military force to combat the other.[94] He refers to the God of armies (צבא: Pss 59:6; 69:7; 89:90), to God as a shield (מָגֵן: Pss 3:4; 7:11; 28:7; 35:2; 59:12; 89:19), to God's sword (חרב: Pss 7:13; 17:13), spear (חָנִית: Ps 35:3), javelin (סגר: Ps 35:3), and arrows (חֵץ: Pss 38:3; 64:8).[95] The psalmist adopts military language, albeit assuming God as the aggressor, as a response to the socially diminishing affronts of the other.

The relational metaphors of the hunt and battle posit a one-dimensional hostile other, ruthless and volatile, with no motive other than to harm the supplicant. Both sets of images construct a perilous, violent social world in which the psalmist is endangered. Both groups of images contribute to the emotional framework of the laments, depicting the psalmist as endangered, pursued, on the verge of death, and in need of sympathetic assistance. The immediacy of the psalmist's suffering and need is evident in the emotional and physical terror of being hunted or attacked in battle. Most importantly, both sets of imagery afford the psalmist a position as socially unprotected by the privilege of social respect and vulnerable to shaming acts of social diminishment.

---

93.   For further discussion of the imagery of weaponry, see Riede, *Im Netz des Jägers*, 123–49.

94.   Again, the significance of the psalmist's consistent denial of instrumental agency in the language of violence is a facet of the discourse that is fully developed in the next chapter. Here, however, it is important to recognize the cultivated neediness and lack of agency in the psalmist's self-description, even as the rhetoric itself affords him a position of socio-rhetorical power.

95.   For further discussion of God as a warrior, see also Marc Brettler, "Images of YHWH the Warrior in Psalms," *Semeia* 61 (1993): 135–65; Brown, *Seeing the Psalms*, 189–91; Martin Klingbeil, *Yahweh Fighting from Heaven: God as Warrior and as God of Heaven in the Hebrew Psalter and Ancient Near Eastern Iconography* (Fribourg, Switzerland: University Press; Göttingen: Vandenhoeck & Ruprecht, 1999); Riede, *Im Netz des Jägers*, 83–93, 117–22, 140–49.

The opportunities for the psalmist's agency and empowerment are vastly different in each of these relational metaphors, however. Succinctly, the psalmist's agency is impaired in one relational metaphor and supplied in the other. The metaphor of the hunt depicts a vulnerable, weakened, and ineffective supplicant, in addition to being socially alienated and unprotected by the social securities of honorability. Warfare as a relational metaphor, however, affords the psalmist a different role, as one capable of aggressive response in returning (socio-rhetorical) violence in a competitive battle for dominance. Even if the psalmist's power lies in God as the military champion, the relational metaphor of battle moves the psalmist away from a self-representation of powerlessness.

I have argued that the psalmist's ultimate goal is to restore social honor through dominance over the hostile other. The logical question arises, then: Why would the psalmist so willingly play the role of the utterly powerless prey, incapable of response to the other's predatory aggression, if his social restoration lies in asserting his claim to self- and social-worth in a discourse of strength and triumph? In a culture that supposedly values those social characteristics, why does the psalmist cultivate an image of himself as needy and vulnerable?

The answer to this question lies in the psalmist's need rhetorically to balance the justice and necessity of his appeal for God's (and the community's) help with a picture of himself as worthy of that help. That is, the language of predation and powerlessness intends to stir sympathy and support on the part of sympathetic witnesses and God, and affirms the justice of the psalmist's request for God's assistance in the obliteration of a foe. The rhetorical strategy involves making that plea in such a way that also appeals to the cultural values of dominance in an agonistic social world. The psalmist has to be needy enough to deserve sympathy and active support, but not so needy as to provoke further derision and disdain. The psalmist as a rhetorical agent has to walk a fine line between the neediness that establishes the hostile other's wickedness and the justice of his claim of suffering at the other's hands and a rhetoric of strength that establishes his worthiness according to privileged relational values of honor.

At least two relational agendas are served in this language, therefore. One emotional structure of the story is served by the depiction of the psalmist as powerless before fierce predators. (Who would not cower before a carnivorous lion or not sympathize with one who does?) The cultural values that privilege strength, triumph, and military prowess are served by the agonistic battle imagery. To be successful in his ultimate goal of social restoration, the psalmist must achieve a position of ascendancy; the military relational metaphor is a step toward that desirable self-representation, the topic of the next section. Even though the psalmist does not depict himself as a warrior, but casts God in that role, his language is often verbally aggressive, a rhetorical position of empowerment. The relational metaphor of battle that frames the psalmist/other relationship is therefore critical for this analysis of honor/shame discourse because it exemplifies the way the psalmist negotiates self-representation as socially diminished and socially dominant. The following discussion provides further analysis of the overtly aggressive language through which the psalmist claims another relational position, that of honor and respect.

5. *The Language of Dominance and Aggression:*
Creating the Category of Honor

The laments construct the category of shame in a rich variety of vocabulary, images, and metaphors. While the vocabulary of honor is not substantial in the laments, the importance of honor is implied in the psalmist's extensive descriptions of suffering he endures due to his lack of social respect. The discursive negotiation for social worth is brought into relief when read through the lens of the competitive relational structure created in the language of honor and shame. The psalmist describes his social diminishment, yet also tells a destabilizing, competing story that asserts his social worth. In this alternate story, the psalmist employs language of aggression and dominance to reject shame and enact a position of honor and respect. The language of anger and aggression is a language of agency and empowerment, a means of self-bolstering and refusal of a disdained social position.[96]

The following is an analysis of two elements of the psalmist's language of dominance that afford the psalmist a position of agency and honor, the language of returned shame and the language of violence and aggression. In the language of returned shame, the psalmist represents himself as triumphant over the hostile other in the ability to turn the tables on the shaming other, a position of dominance entailed in the rhetorical reversal of shame. The language of violence and aggression escalates the psalmist's response to the hostile other. While the degrees of violence range in intensity, all aspects of the language posit a social relationship in which the psalmist's restoration can only be achieved in the subordination of the other. Whether in images of returned shame or more explicitly violent images of revenge or destruction, the language of anger is the psalmist's means of establishing himself, socially and psychologically, as powerful and potent, necessary components of restored honor.

a. *Images of Returned Shame and Reversed Position*
One obvious way the psalmist refuses his placement in the category of contempt is to impose it rhetorically on the hostile other. Repeatedly, the psalmist expresses his desire for the others' mortification, that he be shamed in his attempts to destroy the psalmist, fall back in humiliation, and experience disgrace:

> All my enemies will be shamed (בוש)
> and terrified (בהל);
> they will turn back suddenly, shamed (בוש). (Ps 6:11)

> Let those who seek my life be shamed (בוש)
> and humiliated (כלם),
> let those who plan to harm me shrink back (סוג)
> and be mortified (חפר). (Ps 35:4)

---

96. Tangney and Dearing (*Shame and Guilt*, 93) convincingly argue that shame, as one of the most painful and intense feelings of globalized self-blame, often leads to blaming others in an angry and aggressive fashion: "Anger is an emotion of potency and authority. In contrast, shame is an emotion of the worthless, the paralyzed, the ineffective."

Let those who seek my life be shamed (בוש)
and disgraced (חפר);
let those who wish me harm shrink back (סוג)
in shame (כלם). (Ps 40:15)

Let those who seek my life be shamed (בוש)
and disgraced (חפר);
let those who wish me harm shrink back (סוג)
and be ashamed (כלם). (Ps 70:3)

The degree of similarity between these verses indicates the importance of this mode of response for the psalmist. He escapes shame by imposing shame.

Images of the others' shame, therefore, indicate the psalmist's understanding of his own social restoration. This vision of restoration is articulated clearly in Ps 31:18–19:

O Lord, let me not be shamed (בוש) when I call you.
Let the wicked be shamed (בוש).
Let them be silenced (דמם) in Sheol.
Let lying lips be stilled (אלם)
that speak insolently against the righteous
with arrogance and contempt.

The repetition of the verb בוש in v. 18 illustrates the reversal of position the psalmist envisions; as a response to his own shame (בוש) he prays for the shame (בוש) of the other.[97] The psalmist further describes the shame he desires for the other in the next lines. The psalmist responds to the others' haughty speech with a prayer that their speech, or their lying lips, be stilled (אלם, v. 19) and that they themselves be silenced (דמם) in Sheol (v. 18). Restoration for the shamed psalmist is envisioned in terms of the shame of the enemy, which is achieved through God's aggressive action. In response to the malicious speech of the hostile other, the psalmist adopts a language of elevated hostility that affords him a position of dominance.

In another image of reversed social fortune, the psalmist wishes upon the hostile other the same kind of intensely public and inescapable humiliation that he himself experienced. The psalmist represents himself experiencing disgrace (כלם) that covers (כסה) his face in Ps 69:8 and as being covered (כסה) in shame (בוש) in Ps 44:16.[98] In like manner, the psalmist in Ps 35:26 desires that the hostile other experience the same kind of publicly recognizable disgrace: "May those who rejoice at my misfortune be shamed (בוש) and utterly disgraced (חפר); may those who vaunt themselves over me be clothed (לבש) in shame

---

97. A similar desire for a simple reversal of position is found in Ps 71, where the psalmist prays that he not be shamed (בוש: Ps 71:1), but that the hostile other be shamed (בוש) and consumed (כלה: Ps 71:13). The rhetorical effect of the repetition of the verb בוש constructs a situation in which the psalmist's social restoration is envisioned as a reversal of position accomplished with God's assistance.

98. Ps 44:16 is not a lament of the individual. This psalm, however, contains a first-person singular representation of the shamed self and so is applicable here.

(בשת) and ignominy (כלמה)."[99] The psalmist desires that the others' shame and humiliation be as publicly evident as clothing, as obvious and indisputable as one's public appearance so that the enemy will be easily identified as socially unworthy by any who encounter him.

The psalmist also enacts a position of dominance through reversed shame in the explicit images of his triumph over the hostile other. Part of his self-representation as contemptible is in the depiction of the enemy looking over him, implying a spatial position of control and superiority. In Ps 25:2 the psalmist asks that the enemy be prohibited from celebration of superiority: "May my enemy not rejoice (עלץ) over me." Similarly, in Ps 35:19, the psalmist prays, "Let not my treacherous enemies rejoice (שמח) over me." In Ps 59:11, however, he imagines a position reversal, saying that God will let him "gloat over (ראה) [his] watchful foes."[100] Again, in Ps 54:9, the psalmist imagines being saved from his foes and being allowed to "gaze triumphantly (ראה) upon [his] enemies." Being in the position to look upon and evaluate the enemy is part of the psalmist's vision of triumph, a vision that implies the psalmist's ascendance to superiority over the subordinated enemy. Triumph is portrayed as the ability to, finally, be the agent in looking as opposed to the object of the unsympathetic gaze.

The rhetorical move involved in reversed shame is rather simple, but important in the psalmist's articulation of a relational worldview. The psalmist does not object to the social world implied in the need to shame as a means of achieving social rehabilitation. The psalmist imagines a role-reversal, but not a change in structures of relationship in which someone must be shamed in order for another to be respected or honored. The social vision here is one in which the domination of someone through social shaming is inevitable and expected. The psalmist is not dissatisfied with the structure of his social relationships, but with his placement in those relationships. Thoroughly embedded in this agonistic figured world, rhetorically envisioning the shame of the other is how the psalmist rejects his own position of social inferiority and claims an identity of strength and honorability. Shame itself, sometimes violently imposed, is not negative. When under the rhetorical control of the psalmist, in fact, the shame that wielded such threatening power to belittle and dehumanize is re-envisioned as restoration and deliverance.

b. *Images of Violent and Aggressive Subordination of the Hostile Other*
The psalmist articulates his claim to social respect and honor in an angry discourse of violence and aggression. The laments contain some of the most violent and notorious speech desiring the destruction of the hostile other in the Hebrew

99. See also Pss 71:13; 109:29. In addition, see Ps 132:18 for another example of the psalmist's desires to clothe his enemies in shame, though this is not a lament of the individual.

100. J. A. Emerton ("Looking on One's Enemies," *VT* 51 [2001]: 195) urges caution in using the translation "to gloat" for ראה. He argues that while the translation may be fitting in some instances, it is not an acceptable translation in all cases and should be used carefully because of the forcefulness of the English verb. The sense of gloating comes from context, however, and is an appropriate translation in this case.

Bible. Violence perpetrated by God against the oppressive other is a central focus of desire in the psalmist's prayer and is therefore one of the most important elements indicating concepts of self and other.[101] Importantly, the violent actions the psalmist envisions are not perpetrated, even rhetorically, by his own hand, but are the desired actions of God. That fact, however, should not lead one to conclude that the psalmist is not personally an agent of violence, though his prayer that God be the agent does obscure his own actions. As John Collins notes, "the line between actual killing and verbal, symbolic, or imaginary violence is thin and permeable."[102] Violent utterances and imagistic representations, whether or not they lead to "real," material harm of another, have real social and personal ramifications, creating structures of desire that empower and embolden individuals through shaping emotional experiences. Though the connection is not always direct, discourses of violence, including and perhaps especially violence that is God's prerogative, creates a world of possibilities for violence. This language is not merely a tool of cathartic expression, though it may function as such, but is also the psalmist's means of rhetorically creating a counter-reality in which his experience of himself and others' experience of him might be altered in language of domination. Even though the psalmist posits God as the instrument of violence and aggression, the elaborate and highly articulated hopes for violence against the hostile other is a means of self-construction for the psalmist as potent and powerful. The only critical question, therefore, is not whether the prayer resulted in real, as opposed to linguistic, imagined, or rhetorical, violence; though there are obviously differences between material and representational violence, the later is quite real.[103] I ask to what effect,

101. The following are among the most significant interpretations of violence in the Psalms: D. G. Firth, "Responses to Violence in Some Lament Psalms of the Individual," *SK* 17, no. 2 (1996): 317–28; idem, "Context and Violence in Individual Prayers for Protection," *SK* 18, no. 1 (1997): 86–96; Erich Zenger, *A God of Vengeance? Understanding the Psalms of Divine Wrath* (trans. Linda M. Maloney; Louisville, Ky.: Westminster John Knox, 1996). See also Ingvar Fløysvik, "When God Behaves Strangely: A Study in the Complaint Psalms," *Concordia Journal* 21 (1995): 298–304; Patrick D. Miller, "The Hermeneutics of Imprecation," in *Theology in the Service of the Church* (ed. Wallace M. Alston, Jr.; Grand Rapids: Eerdmans, 2000), 153–63.

102. John J. Collins, "The Zeal of Phinehas: The Bible and the Legitimation of Violence," *JBL* 122 (2003): 4. In his article, Collins treats the "most obvious, even crude, forms of violence," killing, specifically (p. 4). He recognizes as accurate, however, the broader definition of violence Craig Nessan offers; violence is "the attempt of an individual or group to impose its will on others through any nonverbal, verbal, or physical means that inflict psychological or physical injury" (Craig Nessan, "Sex, Aggression, and Pain: Sociobiological Implications for Theological Anthropology," *Zygon* 33 [1998]: 451).

103. The relationship between material and representational violence and the particular interpretive issues posed to and negotiated by readers of violence is an issue of increasing importance in literary criticism and one that I address in greater detail in relation to the laments in the final chapter. The following have been the most important to this project: Nancy Armstrong and Leonard Tennenhouse, eds., *The Violence of Representation: Literature and the History of Violence* (New York: Routledge, 1989); Laura E. Tanner, *Intimate Violence: Reading Rape and Torture in Twentieth-Century Fiction* (Bloomington: Indiana University Press, 1994); Jana Howlett and Rod Mengham, eds., *The Violent Muse: Violence and the Artistic Imagination in Europe, 1910–1939* (Manchester: Manchester University Press, 1994).

rhetorically, socially, and personally, the psalmist employs rhetorical violence.
Who is the self that prays thus and why?

Violence is evident in the psalmist's discourse in several ways. The most
obvious examples are in the psalmist's direct requests to God for the hostile
other's destruction. The vocabulary of eradication and destruction in the laments
is extensive and varied. Repeatedly, the palmist asks that God kill (קטל: Ps
139:19), destroy (אבד: Pss 9:4, 6; 143:12), annihilate (צמת: Pss 54:7; 94:23
[×2]; 143:12), demolish (הרס: Pss 28:5; 58:7), obliterate (נתץ: Ps 52:7), or end
(כלה: Ps 71:13) the hostile other, the cause of his suffering:

> Rise, YHWH! Deliver me, O my God!
> For you strike (נכה) all my enemies in the face;
> you break (שבר) the teeth of the wicked. (Ps 3:8)

> He will rain down on the wicked fiery coals[104]
> and sulfur; a raging (זלעפות)[105] wind
> will be the portion of their cup. (Ps 11:6)

> He will demolish (הרס) them,
> and he will not rebuild them. (Ps 28:5)

> So God will obliterate (נתץ) you for good.
> He will take you out and tear you from your tent,
> and root you out of the land of the living. (Ps 52:7)

At times, the other's destruction is imagined less decisively, yet still violently,
as in Ps 64:8 when the psalmist imagines God shooting the enemy with arrows,
or in Ps 63:10–11 when the psalmist prays that those who have pursued him will
enter the depths of the earth, fall to the sword, and be prey to jackals. In some
instances the level of violence escalates from destruction of the person of the
other to destruction of his family and entire community.[106] Psalm 69:25–26 imag-
ines desolate encampments, emptied through God's anger and wrathful action.
Repeatedly, the psalmist fantasizes God acting violently, even murderously, on
his behalf.[107]

---

104.   I read פהם ("charcoal" or "coals") for פהים. See Kraus, *Psalms 1–59*, 201. Dahood
(*Psalms 1–50*, 68–70) reads the MTs פהים as a form of פוח, "to blow," and so translates the phrase
"bellows, fire, and sulphur." This translation also seems possible, considering the reference to a
raging wind in the next line.

105.   See also Ps 119:53 for use of this word in the context of rage, though the rage in this psalm
is the psalmist's and not God's.

106.   Images of mass destruction are typical of communal laments as well, especially Pss 58 and
137. The psalmist's desire in Ps 137:9, the final verse of the psalm, to smash (נפץ) the children of
the Edomites against a rock is infamous, a ruthless and unapologetic desire that indicates complete
dehumanization of the other. Ps 58:7–12 is an extended description of violent acts the psalmist
desires that God perpetrate against the irredeemable other, culminating in the enthusiastic image of
righteous man who "bathes (רחץ) his feet in the blood of the wicked" (Ps 58:11). Here is a picture of
abundant violence that mixes images of profuse blood, pleasure, and annihilation, all orchestrated by
God on behalf of the psalmist and his community.

107.   The instances of this kind of language are too many to discuss. See also Pss 7:7; 9:6–7;
10:12; 11:6; 17:13; 28:5; 31:18; 35:1–3; 52:7; 55:16, 24; 56:8; 140:10–13.

The priority of dominance as a social and relational display of power and self-assertion is embedded in other images and concepts. For instance, the concept of revenge is intrinsically connected to acts of violence.[108] In Ps 94:1, נקם is used twice to address and name God: "Yahweh, God of revenge (נקם), God of revenge (נקם), appear!"[109] The next verse promises the arrogant their reward (גמול). Finally, the last verse of the psalm promises that God will annihilate (צמת) the other. In fact, the verb צמת is used twice in this verse, just as נקם is used twice in the first verse, creating a rhetorical connection between the repeated address to a vengeful God and the repeated promise of God's violent eradication of the other. Here, the language of revenge, while also a language of justice and righteousness (v. 15), is part of a discourse that affords the psalmist a position of violently achieved dominance over the enemy.[110] Ability to inflict revenge portends restored honor and an identity of social worth.

Further, the language of violence and aggression in the laments provides concrete content for the concept of deliverance in this world. The psalmist's goal is deliverance from suffering; his requests for deliverance (נצל),[111] salvation (ישע),[112] or rescue (פלט)[113] are many and a central element of the rhetorical

---

108. Several scholars have interpreted the picture of revenge as something other than violent and vindictive. H. G. L. Peels, in an extensive study on the root נקם, argues that modern associations of vindictiveness and lustful blood-thirstiness do not apply to the biblical concept of revenge. Rather, he contends that revenge in the Bible is a sign of God's justice and covenantal loyalty to God's people. According to Peels, the joy described in the particularly bloody vision of נקם in Ps 58:11 is a celebration of God's justice, not the violent downfall of the enemy (H. G. L. Peels, *The Vengeance of God: The Meaning of the Root NQM and the Function of NQM-Texts in the Context of Divine Revelation in the Old Testament* [Leiden: Brill, 1995], 218). Sakenfeld and Brueggemann do not interpret the desire for revenge as a positive expression of God's justice, but both argue that the desire for vengeance or destruction of the enemy in the laments is a real expression of how people feel about their enemies, and those feelings find their proper articulation in the context of prayer that can lead to redemptive construction of righteous individuals and communities. Both Sakenfeld and Brueggemann stress that the psalmist always puts revenge in God's hands; the psalmist's prayer is not for his own empowerment to seek revenge upon the other. See Katherine D. Sakenfeld, *Faithfulness in Action: Loyalty in Biblical Perspective* (Philadelphia: Fortress, 1985), 88, and Walter Brueggemann, "Psalm 109: Three Times 'Steadfast Love,'" *Word and World* 5, no. 2 (1985): 152. For similar views, see also Firth, "Responses to Violence," and "Context and Violence"; Zenger, *A God of Vengeance?*

109. The Hebrew root most often discussed in the context of revenge is נקם, though this root is only found in one of the designated laments, Ps 94. Other usages of the root נקם occur in Pss 8:3; 18:48; 44:17; 49:7; 58:11; 79:10; 94:1; 99:8.

110. Ps 54:7 makes a similar connection between revenge and annihilation of the enemy, as the psalmist prays that God will repay (literally "return the evil") his foes and destroy them (הצמיתם). See also Ps 28:4–5, where the psalmist asks that God repay the hostile others and "tear them down, never to rebuild them." Ps 41:11–12 is a possible exception to the connection between violence and revenge. While clearly a fantasy of revenge, there is no explicitly violent language. Aggression is implied in the description of the psalmist's repayment to the roaring enemy, but it is not explicit.

111. נצל occurs in verbal form in Pss 7:2, 3; 22:9, 21; 25:20; 31:3, 16; 35:10; 39:9; 40:14; 51:16; 54:9; 56:14; 59:2, 3, 15 (×2); 70:2; 71:2, 11; 86:13; 109:21; 120:2; 142:7; 143:9.

112. ישע occurs in verbal form in Pss 3:8; 6:5; 7:2, 11; 12:2; 17:7; 22:2; 28:9; 31:3, 17; 54:3; 55:17; 57:4; 59:3; 69:2, 36; 71:2, 3; 86:2, 16; 109:26, 31.

113. פלט occurs in verbal form in Pss 17:3; 22:5, 9; 31:2; 43:1; 71:2, 4.

design. In the laments, deliverance is not an abstract concept, but concrete, almost always envisioned as the domination of the hostile other through aggressive and sometimes violent acts.[114] As an aspect of dominance, deliverance is part of the relational framework afforded by the language of honor and shame, a rhetorical enactment of the shaming and subordination of the other that socially elevates the psalmist.

The association between deliverance and the other's subordination is most readily evident in military imagery frequently accompanying this language. Military terms associated with requests for deliverance create a direct connection between the other's domination and the psalmist's salvation and contribute to the construction of the psalmist/enemy relationship in terms of the agonistic assumptions of the world of warfare. Psalm 35:1–3 is a prime example of the connection between deliverance and domination in the laments:

> Lord, contend with my adversaries,
> battle my foes.
> Seize the shield and buckler,
> and rise up to my defense.
> Draw the spear and javelin
> against my pursuers.
> Tell me, "I am your deliverance!"

Military images, including weaponry and tools of defense, construct a situation of warfare in which the adversaries are aggressors and must be defeated and/or eradicated in order to save the psalmist. Verse 3 is especially telling. The psalmist, after urging God to take up warfare accoutrements, pleas to God, "Tell me, 'I am your deliverance'" (אמר לנפשי ישעתך אני)! Similarly, Ps 59:3 includes a repeated appeal for deliverance (נצל, ישע) from "doers of evil" (פעלי און) and "men of blood" (אנשי דמים) that is followed by address to the God of armies (צבאות: Ps 59:6).

In other places, the imagery accompanying the terms for deliverance is not explicitly military but is nonetheless violent and aggressive, connecting the psalmist's rescue and the other's subjection. In Ps 12:2, for instance, the psalmist asks for deliverance and then asks that God cut off the lips of the one who spoke malicious words against him (vv. 3–4). In Ps 71:2, the psalmist repeatedly asks for deliverance. Then, in Ps 71:13, he asks God to let his accusers "perish in shame" (יבשו יכלו). In Ps 143:9, the psalmist asks to be saved from his foes,

---

114. There are exceptions, which I note below. Deliverance is a flexible term, used in military, juridical contexts, as well as in a more general sense of salvation in the Hebrew Bible. For instance, Ps 43:1 contains juridical language in the context of deliverance: "Vindicate (שפט) me, O God, champion (ריב) my cause against faithless people; rescue (פלט) me from the treacherous, dishonest man." While the psalmist does refer to God as a stronghold (מעוז) in Ps 43:2, which has military connotations, this is not an overtly violent or aggressive vision of deliverance. See Sawyer for a detailed semantic discussion of the terms for deliverance: John F. A. Sawyer, *Semantics in Biblical Research: New Methods of Defining Hebrew Words for Salvation* (London: SCM, 1972). See also Brettler, "Images of YHWH the Warrior in Psalms," 135–65, for a discussion of deliverance in a military context.

which is followed in v. 12, the last verse of the psalm, with requests for the destruction (צמת) and eradication (אבד) of those enemies.

Moreover, the psalmist directly connects deliverance as dominance with the other's shame. The psalmist in Ps 6:5 repeatedly asks for deliverance: "O Lord, turn, rescue (נצל) me. Deliver me (ישע) as befits your faithfulness." Then, in Ps 6:11, the psalmist concretely envisions that deliverance: "All my enemies will be shamed (בוש) and stricken with terror; they will turn back in an instant, shamed (בוש)." Similarly, in Ps 70:2, the psalmist says, "Hasten O God to save (נצל) me; O lord to aid (עזר) me." In the next verses (vv. 3–4), he overtly describes deliverance as a means of imposing shame: "Let those who seek my life be frustrated (בוש) and disgraced (חפר); let those who wish me harm fall back in shame (כלם). Let those who say 'Aha, Aha' turn back because of their frustration (בוש)." Deliverance is the psalmist's rescue and return to social respect, but also results in the hostile other's shame.

In a few psalms, requests for deliverance are not accompanied by discussion of an enemy (see Ps 51) or by language that imposes subordination upon the hostile other through aggressive or violent language (see Pss 22:20–22; 38:22; 43:1; 57:4; 62:2; 71:2). The few instances in which this is the case, however, only further illustrate the degree to which deliverance in the laments is either explicitly military or subordinates the other to the psalmist. Deliverance in the laments, therefore, is not a generic image of rescue but is more concretely imagined as rescue through the aggressive subordination of the other, a display of dominating strength and violent potential that restores the psalmist's social worth. Psalm 62:8 directly relates God's deliverance to the psalmist's honor: "I rely on God, my deliverance (ישע) and my honor (כבוד), my rock of strength (צור עזי), in God is my refuge (מחס)." In the request for deliverance, the psalmist imagines an agonistic encounter in which the psalmist's honor is restored through the domination of the other.

Not every lament contains violent imagery (see Pss 13; 26; 51; 61; 77; 102; 130), but in the laments that do not contain explicitly violent language there is also no mention of an enemy or hostile other, which confirms the connection between the foe and violence.[115] In the laments that feature enemies, social restoration happens at the expense of the other and is central to the recuperation of the psalmist's honor and social worth in his figured world. Fantasies of violence and threats of aggression are key elements in the construction of the agonistic social world posited in the laments and the psalmist's negotiation of social worth in that context.[116] It is part of the worldview embedded in this

---

115. Ps 102 does mention an enemy, though most of the lament is concerned with the psalmist's physical debilitation and does not express a desire for violence against an enemy. Further, Ps 77 does not mention an enemy, but the psalmist does recall past instances in which he was mocked and received the jibes of others; the lament is conceived within a context of public scorn.

116. Two laments, Pss 62 and 120, problematize the use of violence and evidence caution and restraint, however subtle, on the psalmist's part. The psalmist advises in Ps 62:11, "Do not trust in violence (עשק)," and says that force and retribution are the attributes of a faithful God (אדני חסד) in Ps 62:12–13. The language still creates a world in which subordination of the other through force

language and therefore part of the moral imagination of the speaker, an acceptable means by which social restoration and social worth are enacted. The language of violence affords the psalmist a mode of agency and potency, yet also perpetuates the structures of an agonistic social world to which the psalmist also represents himself as victim.

6. *Conclusions*

Self-fashioning occurs in the laments in the psalmist's self-representation through the eyes of others and in the articulation of a response to that positioning. The concept of relational identity is a particularly helpful reading tool because it emphasizes the dialogic quality of relational identity-making; the concept brings together the psalmist's representation of himself as socially powerless with his self-representation as aggressive, assertive, and strong, often indicated in decidedly violent language. Representing himself as contemptible and shamed, the psalmist describes the messages given him in the words, actions, and gestures of others that assign him to a position of social powerlessness. To focus on the psalmist's self-representation as socially powerless, however, is to miss another highly articulated aspect of the psalmist's identity with regard to the hostile other embedded in the many expressions of rhetorical anger, aggression, and violence directed at the enemy. In the world of the laments, verbal ferocity is a vocabulary of agency, a way of enacting a position of social respect and dominance, as opposed to accepting a subject position of contempt and condemnation. The language reflects and creates a world in which contempt, as a necessary companion to respect and social honor, must not only be resisted, but also imposed on others in order to achieve social restoration.

The psalmist's sense of self in relation to the enemy should not be characterized purely as one of triumphant rejection of shame, however. Though the psalmist articulates social identity in the way he refuses external messages about his selfhood and social worth, that articulation does not always occur as an absolute denial of the hostile others' messages. In fact, in rare instances, the psalmist seems to accept the hostile others' imposition of shame. Psalm 22, in which the psalmist refers to himself as a worm who is hated and despised by all,

---

and violence is the means of restoration, and creates structures of violence that are the framework for negotiating antagonistic relationships. In Ps 120, the psalmist compares his peaceful ways, describing himself simply as "peace" in v. 7 (אני שלום), in contrast to the warring and violence of those who "hate peace" in v. 6. In Ps 120:3–4, the psalmist asks rhetorical questions of those who speak treachery and deceit, and then answers that they will reap violent rewards for their lies and malicious words: "What can he give to you, what can he add to you, deceitful tongue? A warrior's sharpened arrows, hot coals of broom-wood." Violent action, signaled in the warrior's arrows, is here seen as an inevitable result of malicious speech. In v. 6 the psalmist represents himself as exhausted by violence ("A long time I lived with those who hate peace"), but also presents violence as the inevitable result of publicly spoken lies or treachery (vv. 2–4). This is a different, less enthusiastic position with regard to violence against the enemy, but the threat of violence is present nonetheless.

evidences the psalmist's apparent internalization of the hostile others' judgments. Though this is not a frequently repeated theme, this example is important because it complicates the psalmist's concept of self in relation to the enemy. Even when publicly refuted, the hostile others' judgments are still critical to the psalmist's self-understanding and self-representation. Though the language of dominance as honor, in my estimation, is a clear response to the experience of social powerlessness and a means of exerting rhetorical agency and power, that language of dominance does not decisively and finally override the narrative of endangerment and powerlessness.

I imagine the psalmist's sense of self in relation to the hostile other as constantly and indecisively negotiated between two rhetorical poles, self-representation as socially powerlessness and self-representation as socially dominant. As he moves between these two poles, the psalmist establishes a dialogic tension that is necessary and effective on different levels. In the narrative of social powerlessness, the psalmist engages the interest of God and possibly the community, real or imagined, casting himself as a sympathetic victim whose circumstances of painful and unjust social diminishment require intervention. His situation requires and demands that action be taken on his behalf and that the hostile other be subjugated. He involves others as potential protectors and affords himself a position as innocent, appealing to cultural values of justice and a common understanding of the humiliation of unjustly inflicted social condemnation. The language of dominance also appeals to different common cultural values. In this language, the psalmist offers himself, the community, the enemy, and God an experience of triumphant domination. Through this self-presentation he does not appeal to sympathy, but to another emotional structure having to do with respect for strength and culturally embedded desires for recognized social dominance. The psalmist appeals to a common respect for acts of assertion that consolidate one's honor and perhaps to a sense of the rightfulness of justice in which the powerless overcome their oppressing enemy even if only through acts of rhetorical violence in which that enemy is socially and physically shamed and destroyed. This is, in fact, the psalmist's vision of social restoration. In the laments, therefore, there is sustained and unresolved tension between a self that must be represented and perceived as an object of sympathy and protection and also a subject of strength and aggression.

This picture of the psalmist's relational identity is only one aspect of the psalmist's representation of social and personal identity. The psalmist/God relationship is equally important, especially as the psalmist posits God as the underwriter of his social restoration through dominance. The following chapter investigates the relational assumptions embedded in the framework of the psalmist/God affiliation.

Chapter 4

ANXIOUS SELFHOOD: IDENTITY AND AGENCY IN THE PSALMIST/GOD RELATIONSHIP

1. *Introduction*

At a basic level, the laments are prayers to God that intend to solicit God's assistance in alleviating the psalmist's suffering. Therefore, the psalmist/God relationship provides the most immediate framework in which the psalmist constructs his address. The psalmist addresses, expects, anticipates, and demands, all according to a specific framework that organizes the psalmist/God relationship. These relational assumptions and expectations are not universal, but are rooted in a particular and culturally embedded discourse that affords certain roles to God and the supplicant. This chapter investigates how the psalmist discursively establishes his relationship with God and analyzes that relational framework for the theological and ideological assumptions within which the psalmist articulates selfhood and negotiates agency. One way to approach this relational framework is to use the patron/client model of relationship as a heuristic device that brings into relief important aspects of the psalmist/God relationship in the laments.[1] The psalmist's subject position, when viewed through the lens of patronage, is one in which he is empowered and disempowered in particular ways. The patronage model of relationship brings into relief vital aspects of the psalmist's selfhood, illuminating a relational context that affords the psalmist an alternately assertive and deferential subject position that is based in both relational interdependence and pronounced power imbalance. The psalmist articulates selfhood and negotiates agency within his God-relationship in a context of continually shifting alliance and ambivalence.

Through encounter with the psalmist/God relationship, one enters a figured world in which God and the individual are represented within a certain cultural "frame of meaning." That the psalmist/God relationship is not a universally transferable construction, but culturally particular, is not a new observation. Thorkild Jacobsen, for instance, in his investigation of the development of religious ideas in ancient Mesopotamia, discusses the psalmist/God relationship in the context of the rise of personal religion. Jacobsen defines personal religion as follows:

---

1. Dennis Tucker of Baylor University has also addressed the dynamics of patronage in the Psalms and I am indebted to him for sharing his work with me. See Tucker, "Is Shame a Matter of Patronage?"

> We use it [the term "personal religion"] to designate a particular, easily recognized, religious attitude in which the religious individual sees himself as standing in close relationship to the divine, expecting help and guidance in his personal life and personal affairs, expecting divine anger and punishment if he sins, but also profoundly trusting to divine compassion, forgiveness, and love for him if he sincerely repents. In sum: the individual matters to God, God cares about him personally and deeply.[2]

Jacobsen observes that individuals have not always addressed God with an assumption of God's care and involvement in their individual lives. The laments, a product of personal religion, offer a specific mode of address and set of operative assumptions about the place of the individual in relation to God, according to Jacobsen.[3]

Jacobsen notes that within the Hebrew Bible, and within the Psalms themselves, there are texts that posit a different psalmist/God relationship than that characteristic of personal religion. Jacobsen prefers the language of Ps 8:3–9, which he feels exemplifies "more real humility"[4] in the question "What is man, that thou art mindful of him?"[5] He further cites Job as Israel's attempt to redress the focus on the individual through God's speech, in which "The personal, egocentric view of the sufferer—however righteous—is rejected."[6] In both examples, Jacobsen sees a response to the presumptions of the individual's importance that illustrates the different assumptions of the individual's place in the laments.[7] According to Jacobsen, Ps 8 and the book of Job, among other examples, preserve the majesty and power of God, as opposed to the individual laments' "almost limitless presumption of self-importance" and their "approach to the highest, the most awesome, and the terrifying in such an easy and familiar manner."[8] The relationship between the individual and God is not uniform and static; the laments represent a particular line of thought.

Jacobsen contributes important observations about the individual's self-representation in the laments. He acknowledges a cultural world cued in the language of the laments that authorizes the relational framework for this discourse, locating the laments' assumptions in the development of personal religion. What his treatment lacks is recognition of the specific socio-rhetorical

---

2. Thorkild Jacobsen, *The Treasures of Darkness: A History of Mesopotamian Religion* (New Haven: Yale University Press, 1976), 147.

3. Ibid., 20–21. The assumptions of Roman religion bring into relief the particular assumptions of personal religion. As Helmut Koester describes, ancient Roman religion did not posit personal gods, but conceived of divinities as abstract powers. Though the Roman conception of the gods became more anthropomorphic under the early Etruscan and the later Greek influences, Roman religion remained more concerned with "exact observation of established rites on behalf of the political community" than with the religious experience of the individual (Helmut Koester, *Introduction to the New Testament: History, Culture, and Religion of the Hellenistic* Age [2d ed.; 2 vols.; New York: de Gruyter, 1995], 1:347–48).

4. Jacobsen, *The Treasures of Darkness*, 151.

5. Ibid., 150 (Jacobsen's translation).

6. Ibid., 163.

7. Within the Hebrew Bible, Jacobsen (ibid., 151) also cites Exod 20:18–19 and Isa 6:5 as examples of the preservation of God's majesty over the individual's concern.

8. Jacobsen, *The Treasures of Darkness*, 161.

world in which the psalmist/God relationship was conceived. The patronage model reconfigures the relational framework in which this language is shaped and attributes a different significance to the psalmist's self-representation and address to God than Jacobsen recognizes. His understanding of personal religion as the context in which to read the laments is compatible with the ideology of patronage, especially in the heightened focus on the individual's personal needs and assumption of God's concern for the individual. When read through the lens of the patron/client relational model, however, the features of the laments Jacobsen notes surface as something different than presumptuous self-importance, though this relational model is, as Jacobsen observes, highly personal. Patronage enables one to see a relational structure in which the psalmist balances asserting claims on God's attention and articulating pronounced subservience and submission, all in an attempt not only to achieve his own personal restoration but also to maintain the interdependence with God that is a cornerstone to his identity. What emerges is not an assured or presuming selfhood, but one that is anxious and ambivalent, simultaneously assertive and deferential, coercive and dependent, empowered and defenseless.

2. *Language and Power in the Psalmist/God Relationship*

The patron/client model of affiliation is a helpful means to clarify the relational worldview of the laments and identify structures of power, entitlement, and expectation that are part of the discourse of the psalmist/God relationship. Embedded in this model of interpersonal interaction are specific relational assumptions about each party's obligation to the other, reflected in the language that shapes their interaction. Because the patron/client relational model is an organizing heuristic device, it is necessary to describe that model at the outset. The following discussion of the core characteristics of patron/client relationships provides orientation to the dynamics of the relationship described in the subsequent rhetorical analysis.[9]

a. *Describing the Model: Core Characteristics of Patronage*
J. M. Bourne succinctly describes patronage's essence as "inequality, reciprocity and intimacy."[10] A patron/client relationship is a personal relationship between social unequals that involves the exchange of resources within a context of loyalty and ongoing commitment.[11] The patron/client relationship is particular,

---

9. S. N. Eisenstadt and L. Roniger's (*Patrons, Clients, and Friends: Interpersonal Relations and the Structure of Trust in Society* [Cambridge: Cambridge University Press, 1985], 48–49) description of patronage's core characteristics is the most comprehensive and is the foundation for my description.

10. J. M. Bourne, *Patronage and Society in Nineteenth-Century England* (London: Edward Arnold, 1986), 5. See also Richard P. Saller, *Personal Patronage Under the Early Empire* (Cambridge: Cambridge University Press, 1982), 1.

11. Wallace-Hadrill (*Patronage in Ancient Society*, 1989, 3) offers the following definition of patronage: "patronage is a social relationship which is essentially (i) reciprocal, involving exchanges

not general or bureaucratic, and is characterized by intimacy that is often figured in terms of fictive kinships or familial language.[12] The language of such a personal relationship constructs a "realm of trust" that creates a meaningful context in which to negotiate power and distribute resources. The construction of such intimacy fosters a perception of "unconditionality and of long-range credit and obligations."[13]

Though this relationship is personal, it is also inherently vertical, between parties of different social standing. This type of relationship is distinguishable from a friendship, which may also involve reciprocal exchange of emotional and instrumental resources, because a friendship occurs between social equals. Further, the patron/client relationship is distinguishable from a master/servant relationship because it is reciprocal. Patrons are those who have access to goods and services, or more generalized social power; clients are those who are in need of social or material resources controlled by the patron and commit themselves to the service and support, often political or social, of the patron.

In spite of the social inequality of the committed parties, the relationship is based on mutual benefit and reciprocity. The identities of the patron and the client are formed in relationship to each other in a web of mutual exchange and hierarchical social positioning that often affords each of the parties a long-term relational identification. A defining element of this relationship is that it is based on the reciprocal exchange of goods and services, both parties promising services and expecting services in return.[14] The resources exchanged may be tangible, the patron offering protection in exchange for votes or political support. The resources are also intangible, the patron offering security, status, loyalty, and respectability to the client in exchange for honor, public praise, and loyalty.[15] Moreover, the exchange of resources is not a simple or wooden one. There is an emotional structure to this relationship that meets needs for security and protection not simply on a physical or material level, but also on a meta-level, for both the patron and the client. The bonds created in the patron/client relationship provide "personal-emotional security."[16] The emotional needs of the client for

---

of services over time between two parties, (ii) personal as opposed to e.g. commercial, and (iii) asymmetrical, i.e. between parties of different status. Most would accept a fourth element...namely that it is voluntary, not legally enforceable."

12.　See S. N. Eisenstadt's description of a "particularist" relationship: "By particularist I mean that the incumbents of the relationship act towards one another in terms of their respective personal properties and not in terms of general universal categories" (S. N. Eisenstadt, "Ritualized Personal Relations, Blood Brotherhood, Best Friends, Compadres, Etc.: Some Comparative Hypotheses and Suggestions," *Man* 56 [1956]: 90).

13.　S. N. Eisenstadt and L. Roniger, "Patron–Client Relations as Model of Structuring Social Exchange," *Comparative Studies in Society and History* 22 (1980): 50.

14.　This exchange is not necessarily simultaneous, but is based on the expectation of an enduring relationship. This is a relationship of enduring memory and ongoing exchange, not a one-time offering of mutual assistance.

15.　See also Ronald A. Simkins, "Patronage and the Political Economy of Monarchic Israel," *Semeia* 87 (1999): 134.

16.　Eisenstadt, "Ritualized Personal Relations," 93.

security may be more readily recognizable, because of his inferior social position, but the emotional structure of the relationship is significant for the patron as well.

The logic of exchange is central to the personal identity-formation that is afforded both parties in this relationship.[17] What often originates as an instrumental relationship, in which needed resources are exchanged, evolves into a relationship with personal, identity-shaping significance. As J. K. Campbell explains, what may begin as a "utilitarian" exchange takes on a "strong moral quality" over time.[18] The "moral quality" of the relationship, as Campbell puts it, has to do with the strong sense of personal honor and social identity that is afforded both the patron and the client in this relationship.[19] Both parties derive personal honor from being loyal to the relationship, which means maintaining the terms of the exchange.[20] Importantly, the committed parties do not derive honor merely from their own loyalty to the relationship, but also from "reflected" honor, the willingness and ability of the other party to be loyal to the roles assigned to them in the relationship.[21] This sense of derived honor creates mutual interdependence that has to do with personal identity established not only in one's own actions, but also in the actions of the other committed party. Campbell describes the interconnectedness particularly well:

> The patron in accepting the dependence of his client, who thus admits, implicitly, the inferiority of his status, himself recognizes moral obligations toward the client. The dependence of the client draws attention to the power of his patron, while the protection of the patron suggests that the client is a man of some standing and respectability in his own community. The social reputations of the two men are now linked. If a patron cannot effectively protect his clients his prestige is diminished; and in his own community the client, too, suffers for the incapacity of his patron, since the potential of his strength from this source is seen to be less than was supposed. But when the protection is effective, both patron and client gain prestige from the relationship.[22]

The exchange-based ideal links the personal and social identities of the connected parties. The client gains social respect though his social connection with a reputable patron and through the patron's willingness to be his patron as well as his faithfulness in playing the role of the client. The patron gains social respect from adhering to his commitments and from the client's willingness to

---

17.   L. Roniger, *Hierarchy and Trust in Mexico and Brazil* (New York: Praeger, 1990), 31.

18.   J. K. Campbell, *Honour, Family and Patronage: A Study of Institutions and Moral Values in a Greek Mountain Community* (Oxford: Clarendon, 1970), 259.

19.   Eisenstadt and Roniger, "Patron–Client Relations," 50: "Solidarity is often closely related to conceptions of personal identity, especially of personal honor and obligations, and it is evident that some, even if ambivalent, personal 'spiritual' attachment may exist between patrons and clients."

20.   Simkins, "Patronage and the Political Economy of Monarchic Israel," 128: "Patron-client relations are foremost personal bonds to which one's identity and honor are committed."

21.   Eisenstadt and Roniger, *Patrons, Clients and Friends*, 83. Eisenstadt and Roniger only discuss the client's acquisition of social standing through their identification with a powerful and highly reputed patron, though Campbell (*Honour, Family and Patronage*, 259) argues that the patron also gains honor from the relationship.

22.   Campbell, *Honour, Family and Patronage*, 259.

engage him as a patron. Likewise, disgrace for both is the result of being unable or unwilling to meet the commitments of the relationship. For the patron, there is loss of honor in choosing not to protect or support the client just as there is loss of honor in being unable to protect, implying that the patron did not actually control the resources that he claimed to control upon entering the relationship. There is also loss of honor for the client in not respecting or supporting the patron just as there is loss of honor for the client if the patron abandons the relationship. The failure of loyalty by either party means shame for both parties.

Loyalty, therefore, is the underpinning of the system, a central element of the relational ideology binding the committed parties. This particular brand of social relationship is often cemented by a powerful and compelling ideology of loyalty, in which the patron and client are bonded together through their commitment to faithfulness. In spite of the often heavily represented language of mutuality and solidarity that marks this relationship, this affiliation always remains a vertical one, between people of unequal social and economic status.

Moreover, despite the ideology of loyalty that often leads to a spiritual connection and the long-range nature of the relationship, a common facet of the relationship is that both parties participate voluntarily. In the ideological structure of the relationship, if not in the day-to-day functioning, both parties participate by choice. The patron and client do not, however, exhibit choice equally. Inherently a vertical relationship, the client's choices are always more limited than the patron's. This difference in power is central to the relationship and is a source of ambivalence, especially on the part of the client. The nature of the relationship as voluntary and hierarchical, as well as mutual and personal, leads to significant ambivalence that is often registered in the discourse of the relationship.[23]

The patron/client relational model has received limited but increasing attention in Hebrew Bible studies, drawing from ongoing discussions of patronage in the disciplines of anthropology and sociology.[24] Mario Liverani argues for the relevance of patronage and the "ideology of protection" in the ancient Near East,

---

23.   Eisenstadt and Roniger, *Patrons, Clients, and Friend*, 32: "In all human societies there develop different ways of interweaving trust and meaning with instrumental and power relations in special types of institutional formations; and yet it is such interweaving that permeates the very ambivalent attitudes which are at the roots of the basic development of interpersonal relations and the tensions inherent in them..." See also Halvor Moxnes, "Patron–Client Relations and the New Community," in Neyrey, ed., *The Social World of Luke–Acts*, 248.

24.   The most important are Campbell, *Honour, Family and Patronage*; Eisenstadt, "Ritualized Personal Relations"; S. N. Eisenstadt and René Lemarchand, eds., *Political Clientelism, Patronage and Development* (London: Sage, 1981); Eisenstadt and Roniger, "Patron–Client Relations," and *Patrons, Clients and Friends*; Ernest Gellner and John Waterbury, eds., *Patrons and Clients in Mediterranean Societies* (London: Duckworth, 1977); L. Roniger and Ayşe Güneş-Ayata, eds., *Democracy, Clientelism, and Civil Society* (London: Lynne Rienner, 1994); Saller, *Personal Patronage Under the Early Empire*; Bourne, *Patronage and Society*; Andrew Wallace-Hadrill, ed., *Patronage in Ancient Society* (London: Routledge, 1989); Eric R. Wolf, "Kinship, Friendship, and Patron–Client Relations in Complex Societies," in *The Social Anthropology of Complex Societies* (ed. M. Banton; London: Tavistock, 1966), 1–22.

and N. P. Lemche and Ronald Simkins both situate ancient Israel in the context of a general cultural familiarity with this kind of relationship.[25] The most relevant element in the work by Hebrew Bible scholars concerns patronage as a model of relationship in which to understand the social values of honor and shame. T. R. Hobbs's response to Saul Olyan's study of honor and shame language is instructive.[26] Olyan argues that the dynamics of honor and shame are best understood within the context of West Asian covenant relations. Hobbs's response is that the patron/client relationship is a closer, more readily apparent model of social relationship in which to investigate honor and shame language; he argues that patronage is a "more immediate social metaphor than political interactions between kings."[27] Covenant, therefore, is based upon the ideals of the patron/client relationship.[28] Shame in the context of patronage, he argues, is the result of publicly recognized inability or failure to maintain ideals of reciprocity and solidarity and is shared by the interconnected parties.[29] Dennis Tucker builds on this connection between shame and patronage in the Psalms, though he investigates honor and shame in the communal laments specifically.[30]

Hobbs's observation that the patron/client relationship may be a closer model of relationship than the ancient Near Eastern treaty practices is buttressed by the recognition among many who study patronage that it offers a nearly universally recognizable mode of affiliation. This kind of relationship was formerly understood to be a product of societies in transition from kinship-based to bureaucratically organized societies.[31] If this evolutional model were valid, however, one would not expect to find patronage in developed, bureaucratic societies. Most now recognize that while patronage may be more pronounced in societies in

---

25. N. P. Lemche, "Kings and Clients: On Loyalty between the Ruler and the Ruled in Ancient 'Israel,' " in *Ethics and Politics in the Hebrew Bible* (ed. D. A. Knight; Semeia 66; Atlanta: Scholars Press, 1995), 119–32; idem, "From Patronage Society to Patronage Society," in *The Origins of the Ancient Israelite State* (ed. Volkmar Fritz and Philip R. Davies; JSOTSup 228; Sheffield: Sheffield Academic Press, 1996), 106–20; Mario Liverani, *Prestige and Interest: International Relations in the Near East ca. 1600–1100 B.C.* (Padova: Sargon, 1990); idem, "Political Lexicon and Political Ideologies in the Amarna Letters," *Berytus* 31 (1983): 41–56; Simkins, "Patronage and the Political Economy." In addition to the work on patronage in the Hebrew Bible, see the following works regarding the New Testament: David A. de Silva, "Exchanging Favor for Wrath: Apostasy in Hebrew and Patron–Client Relationships," *JBL* 115 (1996): 91–116; idem, *Honor, Patronage, Kinship and Purity: Unlocking New Testament Culture* (Downers Grove, Ill.: InterVarsity, 2000); Malina, *The New Testament World*; Moxnes, "Patron–Client Relations."

26. Olyan, "Honor, Shame, and Covenant Relations"; T. R. Hobbs, "Reflections on Honor, Shame, and Covenant Relations," *JBL* 116 (1997): 501–3.

27. Hobbs, "Reflections on Honor, Shame, and Covenant Relations," 502.

28. Simkins ("Patronage and the Political Economy," 129) argues that patronage is a symbolic system, the "root metaphor" upon which covenant was founded. See also Lemche, "From Patronage Society to Patronage Society," 106–20.

29. Hobbs, "Reflections on Honor, Shame, and Covenant Relations," 502.

30. Tucker, "Is Shame a Matter of Patronage?"

31. Terry Johnson and Christopher Dandeker ("Patronage: Relation and System," in Wallace-Hadrill, ed., *Patronage in Ancient Society*, 219–20) challenge an evolutionary model of history in which one views patronage as a relational system that is part of a developing society, eventually overcome by bureaucracy.

transition, the core characteristics of this kind of relationship are commonly recognized; most societies are familiar with "powerful friends" and "obligated clients."[32]

Richard Saller, consequently, argues that simply designating a relationship as a patron/client affiliation is "of limited value, since they can be found in one form or another in most societies."[33] The question, then, is how the patron/client relational structure manifests itself in a particular time and place.[34] For present purposes, I do not take up the historical argument that ancient Israel was a patron/client culture in any sort of self-identified way. In fact, neither the laments nor the Hebrew Bible in general include terms that mean "patron" or "client."[35] While the psalmist may not have utilized this terminology, I will demonstrate that the language of the laments evidences the psalmist's familiarity with the dynamics of this kind of interpersonal relationship; this model of affiliation was part of a cultural repertoire of recognizable relational structures for interpersonal relationship between social unequals.[36] The assumptions of patronage shaped the God/human relationship and therefore also shaped the language an individual would use to address God in a time of need.

The question is, therefore, not whether or not ancient Israel was a patron/ client culture, but how that relational structure elucidates the laments' language particularly with regard to the psalmist/God interaction. There are specific roles assigned to parties in this relationship that provide a context in which to understand more fully how the psalmist perceives himself in relationship with God and upon what basis he claims entitlement to God's assistance during his period of suffering. The following categories of discursive elements organize elements of the language of the psalmist/God relationship in light of the relational dynamics of patronage.

---

32. Ibid., 220. Lemche also acknowledges the general familiarity of this relationship when he uses a scene from the 1972 movie, "The Godfather," to illustrate some characteristics of the patron/ client relationship. See Lemche, "Kings and Clients," 119–20.

33. Saller, *Personal Patronage Under the Early Empire*, 3. Patronage is not a static institution. Eisenstadt and Roniger, especially in *Patrons, Clients and Friends*, provide illustrative cross-cultural examples of patron/client relationships. A comparative analysis of the shape of patronage in ancient Israel and other manifestations of patronage, such as in Roman society, is outside the scope of this project. Nonetheless, it is important to recognize the diversity of patronage, even though there are certain core characteristics typical of this kind of affiliation.

34. See also Tucker, "Is Shame a Matter of Patronage?"

35. See also Simkins, "Patronage and the Political Economy of Monarchic Israel," 128, who observes that this terminology imposes *etic* categories of thought.

36. This study is not dependent on the presence of a specific ancient Israelite self-identification as part of a patronage system. See Gad Prudovsky, "Can We Ascribe to Past Thinkers Concepts They Had No Linguistic Means to Express?" *History and Theory* 36 (1997): 15–31. Prudovsky makes a compelling case for the appropriate use of anachronistic terminology to describe concepts that could not have been expressed in earlier historical periods. He argues that there is a chance of wrong and anachronistic historical ascription, but there is also danger in discarding historical descriptions of concepts simply because those in the past did not share the modern linguistic means of expressing them (p. 31).

b. *Language of Intimacy and Trust*

One primary way the psalmist constructs his relationship with God is in the use of historical discourse, narratives of the past that demonstrate God and the psalmist's long-standing connection and intimacy. These relational narratives not only reflect and construct the psalmist's memory of belongingness and trust inherent in his understanding of relationship with God, but also house expectations for future action, especially God's action on behalf of the suffering psalmist.

Significantly, narratives of intimacy and attachment are frequently part of the discourse of a patronage relationship. That narrative structure is often embedded in a fictive kinship or other similarly personal stories of the origin of the relationship that imply an enduring and unconditional connection. S. N. Eisenstadt and L. Rongier describe this narrative structure as creating a "realm of intimacy, trust or participation in a spiritual realm beyond the major institutionalized spheres of a society—particularly, but not only, that of kinship—in which trust is seemingly most fully articulated."[37] In this narrative of intimacy, the relationship is posited as long-lasting and meaningful, as opposed to bureaucratic and impersonal, based on a simple and instrumental exchange of goods. The fictive narrative structure creates a solidary community, a relational structure for the interaction of the joined parties that combines unconditionality with exchange of power resources.[38] The relational stories, therefore, are crucial to the patronage system because they afford the trust and the identity-forming past so important to the ideology of this relationship. Likewise, in the laments, these narratives contribute to the construction of an intimate relationship between the psalmist and God, offering each a formative role in their ongoing interactions.

In the laments, two main mini-narratives construct the relationship between the psalmist and God: historical mini-narratives and birth and nurture narratives. The elements of the historical narrative are found in the psalmist's invocation of God's past relationship with his ancestors in addition to God's previous actions on the psalmist's behalf. Narratives of relational history provide continuity, meaning, and security, all essential elements of the construction of identity. The psalmist's historical mini-narratives are focused on the historicity of his ancestor's special relationship with God, connecting himself to that relationship and thereby claiming entitlement to similar treatment by God.[39] In Ps 77:12–21, the psalmist refers to the redemption of the children of Jacob and Joseph (77:16) and then to the exodus story and the deliverance of Moses and Aaron (77:21). In Ps 39:13, he likens his own state of alienation and need to that of his ancestors, asking God to act on his behalf: "Hear my prayer, YHWH, listen to my cry, do not be silent to my tears. For like all my ancestors I am an alien, resident with you." This connection to the path of his ancestors is the psalmist's effort to link himself with a lineage that promises security and access to a God who is

---

37. Eisenstadt and Roniger, *Patrons, Clients, and Friends*, 29.
38. Ibid., 33.
39. Ps 44 is a communal lament, but it utilizes a similar narrative strategy: "We have heard, O God, our fathers have told us the deed you performed in their time, in days of old" (Ps 44:1).

available to a sufferer. His implicit assertion is that he should be treated like his ancestors were treated. The identity of the psalmist is based on a genealogy of trust and continuous relationship. In this case, historical discourse is a primary means of establishing the identity of the individual in an enduring relationship with God, emphasizing God's responsibility to this individual as well as aspects of God's character as merciful and beneficent, characteristics that may not be obvious to the psalmist in his time of suffering.

Psalm 22 establishes an overt connection between the historical mini-narrative and construction of the realm of trust. Evidenced by the repeated verb בטח, trust is a vital concept in Ps 22:5–6.[40] In these verses, the psalmist recalls the salvation of his ancestors. Though the circumstances of the rescue remain general, the actions of the ancestors and God are made abundantly clear, stated succinctly in two Hebrew words: בטחו ותפלטמו ("They trusted and you rescued them," Ps 22:5). The arrangement is depicted as simple and uncomplicated; the ancestors trusted and they were helped. A relationship of reciprocity is implied with this verb, in which the ancestors offered trust and God offered rescue. Likewise, the psalmist's trust implies expectation of God's actions of deliverance.

In another instance, the psalmist does not evoke his specifically genealogical connection to God's protection, but simply remembers, in a more general biographical fashion, earlier days when God demonstrated power and potency through action. For instance, in Ps 143:3–4, the psalmist depicts himself as crushed by the pursuing enemy, as having a "weakened spirit" (ותתעטף עלי רוחי) and a "numbed mind" (בתוכי ישתומם לבי). In his desperate state, he stops to remember God's actions of the past: "I remembered (זכר) earlier days, I told (הגה) of all your deeds, recounted (שיח) the works of your hands" (Ps 143:5). In his time of suffering, the psalmist casts God's passivity in a historical context of God's salvific action. The psalmist places his needs within that narrative characterization of God as capable, active, and effective. He finds meaning in remembering, in telling stories of God's historical actions of beneficence and power, and uses that memory to posit God as one who is capable and powerful. The memory of God's historical actions of trustworthiness is the basis for the psalmist's assertion of his own trust in God.

Biographical narratives in the laments not only express trust, but also communicate expectations for the present and future. The psalmist, in telling the past, assigns roles to himself and to God, conveying who he wants God to be (a

---

40. In the Psalms as whole, the root בטח is found most frequently in the individual laments, fourteen of the seventeen occurrences in the Psalms as whole, evidence of a special connection between lament and expressions of trust. (See Pss 13:6; 22:5 [×2], 6; 25:2; 26:1; 28:7; 31:7, 15; 41:10; 52:10; 56:5, 12; 143:8. Uses outside my designated individual laments are Pss 33:21; 78:22; 119:42.) Though the verb בטח is used three times in Ps 22, this usage of the root to describe the trust of others is actually unusual in the context of other uses in the laments. Most of the occurrences of this verb are, in fact, the individual's assertion of his trust in God, as opposed to the examples in Ps 22 where the psalmist discusses others' trust in God. Among those examples, there is direct address to God (Ps 31:15: "I trusted in you") and address of a third party (Ps 56:5: "In God I have put my trust"). The immediacy of second person address, such as in Ps 31:15, calls God to respond to the psalmist's trust.

protector) and who he desires himself to be in relationship with God (a protec-
tee).[41] The biographical narratives, like the genealogical ones, become biogra-
phy/expectation, as the psalmist implicitly articulates hopes that God will once
again become a God who acts so that the psalmist can recount those actions in
praise. The psalmist's memories of the past express his longing for the future,
for the attentive God to whom he stretched out his hands (Ps 143:6). Both kinds
of narratives of the past, genealogical and biographical, create a context of
intimacy in which the psalmist asserts trust in God's ability to act and a context
of expectation in which the psalmist appeals to those past actions as models for
the future.

The second narrative structure that affords a realm of trust/expectation for the
interpersonal psalmist/God relationship is embedded in references to and images
of the psalmist's conception, birth, and early nurturance. The birth narrative,
present in Pss 22:10–11; 51:7; 71:5–6, and 139:13–16, is a brief, storied account
of the psalmist's entry into the world.[42] I discussed these accounts in Chapter 2
in the context of the construction of the vulnerable body, but here I discuss them
in the context of relational construction. Imagery that involves God in the con-
ception, birth, and nurturance of the psalmist represents a personal relationship
that is the foundation for the assumptions of personal religion that Jacobsen
describes.[43] Jacobsen, in fact, notes a transition in the fundamental metaphor that
shaped the divine/human relationship with the rise of personal religion from that
of a master to a slave to that of a parent to a child.[44] This kind of birth imagery is
a fundamental means of relational identity construction, articulating clear under-
standings of self and God as interconnected and inseparable.

Narratives of birth and nurture accomplish two interrelated goals in creating
the realm of trust. First, they establish God's commitment to and responsibility

---

41.	See also Anthony Paul Kerby, *Narrative and the Self* (Bloomington: Indiana University
Press, 1991), 7: "in narrating the past we understand ourselves to be the implied subject generated by
the narrative."

42.	Birth imagery is complex and operates differently in each instance. In Ps 51:7, for instance,
it is used differently than any other instance. In Ps 51, God is not mentioned as explicitly involved in
the conception or birth of the psalmist, but the imagery nonetheless establishes God's responsibility
for the child who could not control the circumstances of his conception and birth: "Indeed, I was
born with iniquity, in guilt my mother conceived me." This language, and the rhetoric of the psalm
overall, portrays the psalmist as dependent on God for salvific and protective action. The vulne-
rability of the psalmist demands God's responsibility for him. In addition, see Brown, "*Creatio
Corporis,*" for analysis of how two different pericopes concerning birth imagery function distinctly
in their contexts.

43.	Jacobsen, *The Treasures of Darkness*, 158.

44.	See also Gerstenberger: "Faith is grounded in belongingness, and belongingness generates
the deepest kind of trust. Therefore, formulas of 'kinship' and expressions of confidence abound in
individual psalms of complaint and thanksgiving" (Erhard Gerstenberger, "Theologies in the Book
of Psalms," in *The Book of Psalms: Composition and Reception* [ed. Peter W. Flint and Patrick D.
Miller; Leiden: Brill, 2005], 610). The psalmist refers to God as the "father of the orphan" in Ps
68:6. Ps 103:13 likens God's compassion (רחם) to that of a father for his children. In Ps 89:27, God
says that David will speak of God as a father in his future words of praise: "You are my father, my
God, the rock of my deliverance."

for the psalmist's body and life. The psalmist represents himself and God as related through a sort of fictive kinship in that they are connected through the circumstances of birth. A better phrase than "fictive kinship," in this context, is "shared biography," a narrative of mutually meaningful and significant life events that imply long-term connection and obligation. The psalmist involves God in the earliest moments of his life and in the very construction of his body.[45] The psalmist defines his body and life as a site structured by and contingent upon relationship with God.

Second, birth mini-narratives provide a subject position for the psalmist of a dependent child, deeply in need of protection, and with extremely limited agency. In speaking of his birth and God's involvement in that birth in this context of request for action, the psalmist invites the hearer of the prayer to see him as a vulnerable infant in need of protection.[46] Rhetorically positioned as a child with no effective means of self-protection, the psalmist implicitly demands that God recognize God's obligation and accept the onus of responsibility for protection of a child in need.[47]

Indeed, for the psalmist, God's responsibility for his life is established in the womb. Creation language, as William Brown argues, implies a primordial commitment by God to the psalmist.[48] The womb is the generating habitat of this commitment that will, or should, according to the psalmist, endure throughout his life. The speaker consistently refers to the womb as the initiating place for the relationship with God to persuade God to action on behalf of the created. In Ps 71:6, the psalmist says he "leaned on [God] from the womb (בטן)." In Ps 139:13, the psalmist says that God "constructed me in my mother's womb (בטן)." The psalmist even depicts God as a midwife in Ps 22:10, saying that God "drew me from my mother's womb (בטן)," followed by the psalmist's declaration in Ps 22:11 that "from my mother's womb (בטן) you have been my God." In this psalm in particular, the psalmist establishes the most intimate of histories for the relationship between himself and God by repeatedly referring to the

---

45. The term "shared biography" is Ann Becker's, used to describe what she deems to be a difference between Western and Pacific Island views of the self (Ann Becker, *Body, Self, and Society: The View from Fiji* [Philadelphia: University of Pennsylvania Press, 1995], 4). Becker argues that the Western sense of self is anchored in the individual's discreet body, while Pacific Island societies view the body as a location of shared social relationship: "These elements of Fijan embodiment differ from Western folk models that posit the discreteness of embodied experience... and the sense of personal authorship of that body... [E]mbodied experience is quite contingent on how the self is situated in a relational matrix" (Becker, *Body, Self, and Society*, 127). Likewise, in these psalmic examples the body is a site of shared relationship, a shared site of creation and not a site of autonomous control and responsibility.

46. See also Lila Abu-Lughod's description (*Veiled Sentiments*, 113) of a similar dynamic in references to the speaker's childhood and infancy in Bedouin poetry, in which the speaker invites hearers to view her as helpless and dependent.

47. In Ps 131:2 the psalmist overtly refers to himself as a child calmed by his mother. Though I do not include Ps 131 in my list of individual laments, it shares some characteristics of a lament in that the psalmist positions himself as a child as an assertion of innocent powerlessness and need, thereby placing God in the position of obligated protector.

48. Brown, "*Creatio Corporis*," 124.

womb as the original location for that relationship, as opposed to the psalmist's current alienated position, far from God (Ps 22:12).

God's responsibility for the circumstances of the psalmist is particularly represented in Ps 22:10a: "For you burst me from the womb" (כי אתה גחי מבטן). God's responsibility is emphasized by the presence of the second person pronoun אתה. The action for which God is responsible is described by the word גחי,[49] an infrequent term used in the context of childbirth in Mic 4:10 and referring to water gushing from a womb in Job 38:8, though it refers to coursing water in Job 40:23. The image of powerful, flowing water is quite appropriate for a birth scene, but what is most significant is that it is God who initiates this forceful entry into the world, an introduction as insistent as coursing water. This is not a calm or mundane entrance, but one catalyzed by God's intervention. God is responsible for the psalmist's very entry into the world, for the gushing water that adamantly carries the psalmist into existence and his current distressed situation.

The psalmist conceives of his relationship with God as embedded in the very structure and emergence of his body and that intimate physical knowledge is the basis of the psalmist's address to God.[50] The psalmist even refers to the intimacy of the relationship as a secret in Ps 139:15, rhetorically stressing the special knowledge, and therefore, special power, that God has in the physical life of the psalmist: "My bones were not hidden from you. When I was created in secret (בסתר), I was intricately woven in the recess of the earth." Because God knows the psalmist from the very beginning and is, in fact, knowledgeable of the internal structure, the hidden bones, of the psalmist's body, God has a special power over and responsibility for the physical circumstances of that body in its present context as well.[51] In birth and nurture imagery, the psalmist reminds God of God's power over the psalmist, a power born of physical knowledge.

Extra-psalmic uses of personal creation imagery clarify the psalmist's assumption about God's protective role in his life. When Job asks twice why he was born, in Job 3:11 ("Why did I not die at birth, expire as I came out of the womb?") and in Job 10:18 ("Why did you let me come out of the womb?"), he accuses God of acting against the design of their relationship established in the protective environment of the womb. According to Job, for God to let him flourish in the womb, to (apparently) lovingly "shape and fashion" (Job 10:8, also 10:9) him in the womb only to destroy him in later life, is a hostile perversion of their relationship. The same is true for the psalmist. The psalmist shares

---

49.   גחי is a participle with a suffix from the root גיח, "burst forth."

50.   See also Brown, "*Creatio Corporis*," 114: "The psalmist's reflections upon his own genesis constitute the cornerstone of his appeal to God (and neighbor)."

51.   This connection between the body and secret knowledge helps to establish the power dynamics between God and the psalmist. Mark George notes how knowledge and power are related: "Knowledge of the body, the gaze on it which analyses its habits, workings, thoughts, feelings, behaviors, relationships, self-conceptions, and other aspects, is itself a form of power..." (Mark George, "Body Works: Power, the Construction of Identity, and Gender in the Discourse on Kingship" [Ph.D. diss., Princeton Theological Seminary, 1995], 18).

Job's assumption that God's creation of the body in the womb is evidence of God's commitment to that body and its life. His suffering body is, therefore, evidence of God's failure to respond adequately to that commitment and is against the design of the womb-initiated relationship between God and individual.

Moreover, God is implicated not only in the conception and birth of the psalmist, but also in nurturance of the child after birth, making the psalmist secure at his mother's breast (מבטיחי על שדי אמי) in Ps 22:10b. In this verse, not only did God determine the time of delivery (Ps 22:10a), God also saw to the nourishment and sustenance of this young life supplied by the mother's milk (Ps 22:10b). The significance of God's facilitation of this intimate nurturance relies on a general cultural association between nursing, dependence, and comfort. A nursing baby is an intimate image of warmth, protection, and bodily connection and one who nurses provides that comfort. For instance, in Isa 66:10–11 the image of a mother nursing her child expresses the joy and comfort to be experienced in the restoration of Jerusalem; all who mourned Jerusalem will find consolation and reassurance at her breast when she is restored. The image of nursing thus contributes to the construction of the realm of trust and intimacy that houses the psalmist and God.

Importantly, however, the image of nursing in Ps 22:10 generates ambivalence for the psalmist, as the image of intimacy in nursing contrasts starkly with the distance from God the psalmist currently experiences. The following verse begins a progression of images expressing that ambivalence and finally outright doubt about God as protector. In Ps 22:11, the psalmist describes being "thrown" (שלך) on God from birth. The psalmist's understanding is that he was not an agent in the creation of this relationship, but an infant who did not make decisions directly. The situation then, as now, was not in the psalmist's control. Directly ensuing are images of distance from God (v. 12) and then images of wild animals in pursuit of the psalmist (vv. 13–14). The progression of images, from God's role as caretaker in v. 10 to abandonment of the psalmist to wild animals in vv. 13–14, expresses God's failure to provide protection and nurturance and the urgent need for God to remember the commitment to the psalmist established in the womb. The implication of this progression of images is clarified by Job's question of God: "Why were there knees to receive me, or breasts for me to suck?" (Job 3:12). In his argument with God, Job implies that nursing that only perversely nourishes so that one may suffer later signifies a lack of compassion, a reversal of the natural assumptions that human beings have about the meaning of care. Likewise, the psalmist characterizes God as one who nurtures only later to abandon. Nursing in this context signifies the psalmist's radical dependence on God, an indication of trust and intimacy that is also a source of ambivalence because of the psalmist's utter exposure, lack of personal agency, and consequent vulnerability to failure of God's care.

In sum, relational narratives of historical and physical connection serve as a formative and identifying discourse in the laments that afford relational identity to God and the psalmist. The effect of these relational narratives is to establish long-term connection between God and the psalmist, constructing a rhetorical realm of intimacy, trust, and attachment. In these narratives, the psalmist's trust implies God's obligation, evident in God's past acts of deliverance and in the psalmist's own physical construction. Therefore, narrative accounts of interconnection and trust also articulate the psalmist's expectations about the present and future psalmist/God relationship, serving as the basis upon which the psalmist anticipates God's renewed acceptance of a historically and physically forged role of protection and deliverance.

c. *Language of Self-Abasement and Vertical Relationship*

Whereas language of trust and intimacy creates a solidary relationship between God and the psalmist, shaped by a shared history of attachment and connection, the God/psalmist relationship is also vertical, obvious in the psalmist's prevalent discourse of self-abasement. Importantly, the language of self-abasement is distinguishable from the language of bodily diminishment, though the distinction is not absolute, as the suffering body is also a way of positioning the psalmist socially. The language of self-abasement is different, however, in that it articulates the hierarchical social relationship between God and the psalmist. In the language of self-abasement, the psalmist overtly discusses himself in social categories, as powerless, poor, and in need, obviously in pain, but less in a physical way and more in social terms. In this section, I read self-abasing language through the lens of patronage, which facilitates more complete analysis of the implications of this self-representation. First, the patronage relational framework affords the psalmist and God an inherently hierarchical relationship in which God is the locus of relational power and the psalmist is consequently subservient, yet it also affords the psalmist the means by which to assert the honorability of his own deportment and to call God to account for God's own performance in the relationship. Second, the vertical psalmist/God relationship has implications for the structure of the laments' social vision, clarifying the psalmist's self-positioning in relation to others in his social world.

The psalmist repeatedly emphasizes his position of social abjection and subjugation to God. In this way, he constructs a vertical relationship with God by inhabiting a social and discursive position of powerlessness and inferiority and offering God a social position of power and superiority:

> Face me, have mercy on me,
> for I am alone (יחיד) and afflicted (עני). (Ps 25:16)

> But I am lowly (עני) and in pain;
> your help, YHWH, fortified me. (Ps 69:30)

> But I am poor (עני) and needy (אביון),
> O God, hurry to me!
> You are my help and my deliverer.
> YHWH, do not hesitate! (Ps 70:6)

> Incline your ear, Lord, and answer me,
> for I am poor (עני) and needy (אביון).
> Preserve my life, for I am devoted to you;
> save your servant (עבד) who trusts in you. (Ps 86:1–2)

The psalmist represents himself in a wide and varied vocabulary of social inferiority and need;[52] he is poor (אביון),[53] humble (עני),[54] afflicted (ענוים),[55] lowly (חלכה),[56] and oppressed (דך).[57] At times, these words appear in the combination "poor and needy" (עני ואביון),[58] emphasizing the psalmist's lowliness. In addition, he refers to himself as a servant (עבד),[59] placing himself in an obviously dependent and inferior social position and constructing an explicitly vertical relationship.

Not all of the references to social diminishment are self-designations. Even when the psalmist does not specifically identify himself as poor, oppressed, or needy, he may invoke this category of person in order to associate himself with social need and place himself under God's protection as one for whom God has special concern. For instance, in Ps 140:13 the psalmist states confidently, "I know that YHWH will act for the right of the poor (עני), the justice of the needy (אביון)." Further, the psalmist invokes the familiar social figures of powerlessness, the widow (עלמנה)[60] and the orphan (יתום),[61] to symbolize need and God's corresponding obligation to protect. While the psalmist does not self-identify as a widow or orphan, he does refer to these figures to indicate God's role as protector of the needy, as in Ps 10:14: "You have been the orphan's help" (יתום אתה היית עוזר). The rhetorical effect is to align the psalmist's situation of need with the need of recognized figures of social obligation and recipients of social protection. The psalmist simultaneously establishes his position of powerlessness and God's already established predisposition for protective and redeeming action on the part of the socially humble.

The self-abasing language of the laments is familiar to Psalms scholars. A brief overview of differing scholarly treatments helps to establish what is at stake in interpretation of the shape of selfhood implied. Many have attempted to identify the poor specifically or have discussed the language of poverty in the Psalms in terms of the Bible's larger understanding of wealth and poverty.

52. The word דל, "weak" or "poor," appears in one individual lament, though it is not used as a direct self-representation: "Blessed is he who considers the poor" (Ps 41:2). Other occurrences outside of the individual laments are in Pss 72:13; 82:3, 4; 113:7.

53. אביון is used ten times: Pss 9:19; 12:6; 35:10; 69:34; 70:6; 86:1 (superscription); 109:16, 22, 31; 140:13. This word occurs most often in the laments, but twenty-three times in the Psalter as whole.

54. עני is used nineteen times: Pss 9:13, 19; 10:2, 9, 12; 12:6; 22:25; 25:16; 35:10 (×2); 40:18; 69:30; 70:6; 86:1; 88:16; 102:1 (superscription); 109:16, 22; 140:13. It is used thirty-one times in the Psalter as whole (thirty Kethib and one Qere), and is the most represented word for "poor" in the psalms.

55. ענוים is used eight times: Pss 9:13, 19; 10:12, 17; 22:27; 25:9 (×2); 69:33. It occurs thirteen times in the Psalter as a whole.

56. חלכה only occurs in Ps 10:8, 10 (Kethib), 14.

57. דך is used in the Psalms only in 9:10; 10:18, and 74:21 (not an individual lament).

58. See Pss 9:19; 12:6; 35:10; 37:14; 40:18; 70:6; 72:4, 12; 82:3–4; 86:1; 109:16, 22; 140:13.

59. עבד is used in Pss 27:9; 31:17; 35:27; 69:18, 37; 86:2, 4, 16; 89:4, 21, 40, 51; 102:15, 29; 109:28; 143:2, 12.

60. See Pss 68:6; 78:64; 94:6; 109:9; 146:9.

61. See Pss 10:14, 18; 68:6; 82:3; 94:6; 109:9, 12; 146:9.

Often, scholars have focused on the type of poverty and need experienced by the psalmist, spiritual or material.[62] Recently, the psalmist's expression of poverty and oppression has made the language of poverty in the Psalms ripe material for liberation and materialist readings. For instance, in response to feminist and womanist theologies arguing that language emphasizing drastic differences in power between God and humanity inhibits the active pursuit of justice among oppressed people, Cynthia Rigby argues that language of human powerlessness and God's transcendent power in the Psalms is an empowering motivation in oppressed peoples' struggle for liberation.[63] Others see in this language an expression of specifically socio-economic oppression and understand the psalmist to be a materially poor individual. Gustavo Gutiérrez is the obvious name to mention in connection with this approach, as his liberation theology is rooted in biblical understandings of the injustice of poverty.[64] In addition, Leslie Hoppe argues that the laments are unique in the Hebrew Bible for including the voice of the oppressed, as opposed to words *about* the poor in wisdom literature.[65]

Jacobsen, in contrast, sees in the psalmist's humility and self-abasement personal religion run amok. His description of the psalmist's self-referential language of need is especially vivid:

> ...though this self-abasement and humility is arresting, it would be unwise to stop with it and not penetrate to its underlying presuppositions. Clearly, it would be pointless were it not for an underlying conviction in the penitent that God still cares deeply and personally about him and his fortunes. And the more we attend to this unspoken presumption, the more our first impression yields to something rather different, something which is not humility but unconscious self-importance and, considering that the attitude is an attitude to the Divine, self-importance almost without limits.[66]

62.   Richard J. Coggins, "The Old Testament and the Poor," *ExpTim* 99 (1987–88): 11–14; C. R. Dickson, "The Hebrew Terminology for the Poor in Psalm 82," *HvTSt* 51 (1995): 1029–45; Sue Gillingham, "The Poor in the Psalms," *ExpTim* 100 (1988): 15–19; Leslie J. Hoppe, *There Shall Be No Poor Among You: Poverty in the Bible* (Nashville, Tenn.: Abingdon, 2004); Hans-Joachim Kraus, *Theology of the Psalms* (trans. Keith Crim; Minneapolis: Augsburg, 1986), 150–54; J. David Pleins, *The Social Visions of the Hebrew Bible: A Theological Introduction* (Louisville, Ky.: Westminster John Knox, 2001), 420–37. For discussion of poverty language in Pss 2–89, see Dennis Tucker, "Democratization and the Language of the Poor in Psalms 2–89," *HBT* 25 (2003): 161–78.

63.   See also Cynthia L. Rigby, "Someone to Blame, Someone to Trust: Divine Power and the Self-Recovery of the Oppressed," in *Power, Powerlessness, and the Divine: New Inquiries in Bible and Theology* (ed. Cynthia L. Rigby; Atlanta: Scholars Press, 1997), 79–102. While not explicitly concerned with the language of poverty, others have found liberatory potential in the language of suffering in general. See especially Ulrike Bail, "'O God, Hear My Prayer': Ps 55 and Violence Against Women," in *Wisdom and Psalms: A Feminist Companion to the Bible* (2d Series; ed. Athalya Brenner and Carole Fontaine; Sheffield: Sheffield Academic Press, 1998), 242–63; Barbara A. Bozak, "Suffering and the Psalms of Lament: Speech for the Speechless, Power for the Powerless," *EgT* 23 (1992): 325–38.

64.   Gustavo Gutiérrez, *We Drink from Our Own Wells* (Maryknoll, N.Y.: Orbis, 1984). In his discussion of Pss 9 and 33, he says "the present experience of Latin American Christians is one that has been given profound expression in the Psalms" (p. 19). For further discussion of Gutiérrez's biblical interpretation, see Jeffrey S. Siker, "Uses of the Bible in the Theology of Gustavo Gutiérrez: Liberating Scriptures of the Poor," *BibInt* 4 (1996): 40–71.

65.   Hoppe, *There Shall Be No Poor Among You*, 126.

66.   Jacobsen, *The Treasures of Darkness*, 150.

According to Jacobsen, the psalmist's humility and meekness "swell to fill the whole picture."[67] This language, according to Jacobsen, may be arresting as an expression of pain and humility, but it implies presumptuous expectation of God's concern and intervention; despite the psalmist's language of servanthood to God, the psalmist assumes that God is a servant to the need of the individual.

These contrasting interpretations of the language of self-abasement render a conflicted portrait of the psalmist. Does this language offer a voice to the poor and powerless or does it reflect self-absorbed humility, deference that actually masks the assumption that God and the workings of the universe should bend to meet the psalmist's need? These scholarly approaches, though contradictory at times, make important contributions to understanding the significance of this language in the laments. There is a socio-economic component to the language, a forthright claim on God's attentions and sense of justice and entitlement to physical, material, and social restoration. There is also an unapologetic assumption that God should act to rescue one individual from personal suffering. What past treatments neglect is the nature of the laments as persuasive speech within a particular socio-rhetorical context. The relational framework of patronage as that which primarily shapes the psalmist's self-representation before God reconfigures the terms of the analysis. The structure of patronage provides the interpretive lens that enables the reader to see the full significance of this language within the particular relational and rhetorical world of the laments.

Most helpful in this endeavor is Mario Liverani's discussion of the rhetorical shape of the Amarna letters. The Amarna texts are a useful comparison because of the parallels with the laments in their usage of self-deprecating language and the relational model of patron/client political interaction evident in letters from a vassal state to the Egyptian overlords.[68] Liverani analyzes the rhetoric of the Amarna texts explicitly as political letters that are shaped language, "written by a specific author to a specific addressee with a specific aim."[69] Liverani contends that much of the rhetorical shape of the Amarna letters has been misunderstood because scholars have failed to consider their persuasive function. All letters, he argues, but especially political letters, are "written to convince the recipient to behave in a certain way or to lead him to think in a certain way."[70] Likewise, the laments are persuasive prayers.[71] Their fundamental intention is to convince God that the suffering of the psalmist merits God's intervention and enactment of the role of a just, protective patron. Again, the psalmist's (the client's) need implies God's (the patron's) obligation to act.

---

67. Ibid., 150.
68. See also Hobbs, "Reflections on Honor, Shame, and Covenant Relations," 503.
69. Liverani, "Political Lexicon and Political Ideologies," 42.
70. Ibid., 42.
71. Patrick D. Miller ("Prayer as Persuasion: The Rhetoric and Intention of Prayer," *WW* 13 [1993]: 356–62) addresses the laments as persuasive prayer and mentions the language of lowliness that is often part of lament: "His [the supplicant's] weakness and lowliness is the basis for appeal. All such pleas are grounded in an awareness that the God of Israel is, by nature, inclined toward the weak and the small and the powerless" (p. 359).

Further, Alex Weingrod, a scholar of patronage, characterizes the interaction between a patron and client as a performance of specific roles with concrete implications for the negotiation of relational power: "Encounters between patrons and clients...are highly stylized, ritualized performances, and hence patronage relationships can be conceptualized as ceremonies of a kind."[72] Likewise, in the figured world of the laments, the individual who desires alleviation from suffering posits himself in a stylized fashion, according to the roles of the relationship. Perceived in this light, the language of self-abasement and dependency is part of a performance of the role of dependence in the context of this type of relationship.[73] The language of self-abasement, then, is multivalent.[74] It could be an expression of material, socio-economic need *and* the language a client must assume in order to invoke the patron's obligation and achieve relief through the patron's intervention.[75] The language of self-abasement therefore works on several levels. Though materialist readings have stressed a socio-economic reading, the patronage relational framework enables one to see another co-existent aspect of this language as well. Deferential language signals the client's willingness to rely on the patron, to play the role of the client who is subject to the patron's power and authority. In the laments, therefore, the continual utterance of need and lesser status is an acceptance of dependence that reinforces God's power, but also God's obligation.

To be clear, to say that the language of self-abasement and humility is persuasive and performative speech is not to say that it is untrue speech. Arguing that this is speech shaped for persuasion according to preconceived relational roles should not be misunderstood to imply that the psalmist's articulation of pain is *merely* an enactment of a discursive role. Here, Liverani provides an important methodological clarification: "When we emphasize the persuasive character of the statements contained in a letter (particularly in a political letter), we often run the risk of being misunderstood as if we are automatically accusing its author of falsity and voluntary deception. But 'persuasive statement' is not the opposite of 'true statement.' "[76] In fact, as Liverani further argues, the facticity of the experience that gives rise to the persuasive form of address is helpful in the

---

72.   Alex Weingrod, "Patronage and Power," in Gellner and Waterbury, eds., *Patrons and Clients in Mediterranean Societies*, 50.

73.   So ibid., 50: "In these performances the various actors, patrons and clients, play particular roles, and their behavior can be seen to contain a variety of meanings and 'messages.' "

74.   See also Croft, *The Identity of the Individual in the Psalms*, 57, 71. Croft says that the self-designation as poor may be literal, but it could also be used metaphorically as a way of placing one's self in God's care.

75.   The observation that the language of poverty works on several levels may clarify why it is notoriously difficult to pinpoint what kind of poverty the psalmist endures. Poverty and want are certainly major themes in the laments, yet the precise circumstances of the need are often vague. Pleins argues that the vagueness of the experience of poverty lends credence to the idea that it is spiritualized in the Psalter, but I contend that the vagueness stems from the fact that the language sends multiple messages, not always serving a descriptive purpose so much as a rhetorical one (see J. David Pleins, "Poor, Poverty," *ABD* 5:413).

76.   Liverani, "Political Lexicon and Political Ideologies," 43.

composition of an effective, persuasive letter.[77] Truly persuasive speech relies upon real experience. Yet the language of social suffering is patterned and formulaic, not the spontaneous expressions of one individual's angst. Further, the psalmist represents himself in a particular way in order to seek change in the form of deliverance from suffering and dominance over those whom he holds accountable. That the psalmist's pain is real and that his pain is discursively shaped for persuasive and rhetorical effect must be held in tension.

One could argue that the divine/human relationship must always be vertical on some level. The noteworthy aspect of this self-representation, however, is not that the psalmist perceives his relationship with God to be a vertical one. What is significant is the particular way he frames this hierarchical relationship, placing emphasis on himself as abject, powerless, and dependent. The issue is one of emphasis and stress. By comparison, the suzerainty covenant language in Deuteronomy also constructs a thoroughly vertical relationship between God and Israel. Yet that language emphasizes God's role and the nature of the deity, not the characteristics of Israel as partner in the covenant. The laments' particular emphasis on the psalmist's abjection is further evident in comparison with Job. Job must also position himself as a certain kind of sufferer in order to achieve his rhetorical goals. He does not, however, represent himself in self-abasing language or address God with extreme humility. The discourse of self-abasement in the laments is unusually prominent, displaying the psalmist's ready and enthusiastic embrace of his dependency and need.

The relational model of patronage clarifies the significance of this self-presentation. This language of self-abasement reflects what sociologists of patronage Terry Johnson and Christopher Dandeker call a "commitment to deference," a highly articulated willingness to be subordinate to the patron.[78] Articulation of extreme need and lowliness is a way of communicating both the psalmist's acceptance of dependence and God's corresponding obligation to act on behalf of the dependent. In the laments, dependence implies obligation. The psalmist, representing himself as utterly needy and humble, emphasizes the dyadic, vertical relationship as his only recourse and places full responsibility for his survival and social restoration upon God.

The psalmist's enthusiastic acceptance of deference as a means of persuading God to act as a patron yields a conflicted portrait. As I described in the previous chapter, the psalmist fervently resists a position of social inferiority with regard to the hostile enemy by assuming a discourse of violence and dominance. Yet, in the context of the psalmist/God relationship, the psalmist eagerly embraces a position of deference and subjection. Especially in the context of a cultural predisposition toward expressions of social honor in terms of dominance and superiority, why does the psalmist so eagerly adopt a language of inferiority and lowliness here?

77. Ibid., 43.
78. Johnson and Dandeker, "Patronage: Relation and System," 240.

Campbell notes a similar point of tension in his study of patron/client rela-
tions; the language of self-abasement and need lies alongside the language of
dominance and violence as resistance to the position of inferiority.[79] The con-
straints of honor are quite different in the vertical psalmist/God relationship than
in the horizontal psalmist/enemy relationship, however. In the vertical psalmist/
God relationship, the psalmist's acceptance of deference is honorable because it
implies one's willingness faithfully to play one's role in the relationship.[80] The
patron, in turn, earns honor by faithfully playing his role as the protective patron.
The client's language of deference, therefore, is both an expression of relational
powerlessness and a language of honor, a means of being an agent by saving
face socially and stating publicly that he has not invited shame by abandoning
the relationship. The tension between the psalmist's self-representation as infe-
rior and dominant is a result of the multiple relational frameworks the psalmist
addresses in the context of the utterance.

Reading the psalmist's language of self-abasement as a means of establishing
honor within the psalmist/God relationship resonates with Margaret Odell's
ideas (discussed in Chapter 3) about the model of honor and shame relevant to
relationships where dependency is the goal, not the obstacle. Briefly, Odell's
observation is that within relationships where dependency rather than autonomy
is privileged, one's honor is derived from maintaining dependency upon the
relationship in spite of the other party's betrayal. Takeo Doi, a primary contribu-
tor to Odell's thought, notices in his studies of such relationships in Japan that a
common response to the shame of a failed relationship is to adopt a heightened
language of deference and dependency.[81] The language of deference is not only
a means of honorable self-presentation that protects the abandoned party's public
reputation, but also an expression of that individual's deep desire to re-establish
the relationship of dependence that afforded a strong sense of personal worth
and belongingness. The willingness to be dependent, then, is not only a means
of saving face and persuading the other individual to return to the relationship,
but also has an emotional and psychological role. This observation is highly

---

79.   Campbell notes the tension between social values when the concept of honor is defined in
terms of strength, yet dependence is the role of the client: "The role of patron is to give benefits; that
of the client is to honour the patron by accepting dependence. In a society where the concept of
honour is intimately connected with notions of individual strength and prepotence, to abdicate one's
independence, even to a person of power who is not a member of the community, is an act of
renunciation of some significance" (Campbell, *Honour, Family and Patronage*, 259).

80.   Though the psalmist's identification of himself as among the "righteous" (צדיק) does not
contribute to his construction of a position of dependency and need, it is worth mentioning here as
another way he asserts his worthiness of God's attentions. (See especially Pss 5:13; 7:10, 12; 11:3, 5;
31:19; 52:8; 55:23; 64:11; 69:29.) The psalmist, in claiming righteousness or association with the
righteous, clearly feels himself to be in accord with relational expectations. He does not understand
himself to have violated the terms of the relationship with God or community and therefore feels
justified in claiming social respect and the right to God's assistance. Language of righteousness is
therefore part of the psalmist's self-representation as honorable. For further discussion of the concept
of righteousness in the Psalms, see Gert Kwakkel, *"According to My Righteousness": Upright
Behavior as Grounds for Deliverance in Psalms 7, 17, 18, 26, and 44* (OTS 46; Leiden: Brill, 2002).

81.   Doi, *Anatomy of Dependence*, 57–59.

relevant for the laments. The psalmist's thorough acceptance of the position of inferiority in the laments is a means of self-positioning as honorable and a call for God to be honorable according to the patron's designated role as protector. Also embedded in this language of deference, however, is the psalmist's urgent hope that the relationship of substantial emotional interconnection and identity-forming significance will prevail. Honor as dominance is not the goal, but honor as relational interdependence. Though the psalmist clearly feels God should act to end his suffering, part of his loss is the sense of intimate belonging afforded in a relationship that is, at once, founded on personal attachment *and* the exchange of needed resources.

In this light, Jacobsen's understanding of the language of self-abasement as presumptuous and self-important misconstrues the significance of this self-representation. The patronage relationship is personal, and so the psalmist does assume God's commitment to his personal well-being. Self-abasement is a mode of persuasion that benefits the psalmist. Yet the psalmist's humility is not entirely about personal self-absorption, as Jacobsen describes, but also assertion of the psalmist's continued commitment to relationship with God. Self-abasement is a means of using the vertical nature of the relationship to achieve personal restoration, but it is also a means of achieving relational restoration.

The emphasis on the vertical relationship in the laments further illumines other aspects of the psalmist's self-representation in the social world of the laments, especially his representation of relationship with others in the figured world; the psalmist's rhetorical emphasis on the dyadic, vertical relationship between himself and God may clarify aspects of the psalmist's representation of his horizontal relationships. Johnson and Dandeker make a connection between the vertical relationship between the patron and the client and inhibited solidarity among social equals. They offer a somewhat different approach to the examination of patron/client relations that is more conducive to investigation of the kind of world signified by this relational language. Rather than asking what kind of social conditions produce patron/client relationships, they ask, "In what kind of society does the answer to the question 'Who are your friends?' become of decisive importance?"[82] Their question is about what kind of social world is reflected in and produced by the cultural privileging of vertical relationships.

In short, Johnson and Dandeker argue that vertical relational focus impedes horizontal solidarity and ideological identification with social equals.[83] In a

---

82. Johnson and Dandeker, "Patronage: Relation and System," 222.

83. This element of competition has been construed in different ways in the literature about patronage. Some, like Johnson and Dandeker (ibid., 223), emphasize the way competition for patronage weakens horizontal solidarity and emphasizes vertical relationship, which reinforces hierarchical social structures and debilitates unification among potential clienteles. Others have emphasized that the asymmetry of this relationship minimizes social hierarchies by creating vertical personal connections that would not otherwise have existed. In this understanding, patronage bridges social and economic gaps between the classes. Moreover, it provides a means of survival for the client, who is then empowered by his ability to lend status through deference to the patron, and is able to manipulate that power for his own good (see the discussion by Saller, *Personal Patronage Under the Early Empire*, 37–38).

situation where vertical relationships are seen as the only possibility for sur-
vival, agonistic relationships among social equals flourish. This discussion of
the psalmist/God vertical relationship, then, provides an important link to discus-
sion in the previous chapter of the hierarchical relationship implied in the honor
and shame relational framework that governs the psalmist's rhetorical construc-
tion of the hostile other, and indeed all other potential horizontal allies, including
family and friends. In terms of horizontal relationships, the psalmist represents
himself as utterly alone, placing more rhetorical stress on the vertical relation-
ship as the means of his deliverance and survival. In the mind of the psalmist, he
has no resources among his peers. From the perspective of the patron/client
relationship, this self-representation is easily understandable as part of the
performance of the role of the dependent client. The commitment to deference
embedded in these images of self-abasement and vertical relationship reflects the
psalmist's commitment to the hierarchical relationship not only between himself
and God, but possibly also between himself and others in his society.

d. *Language of Loyalty and Obligation*
Though the relationship between God and the psalmist is undoubtedly vertical,
implying God's greater power and the psalmist's subjection, it is also constructed
by a pronounced discourse of loyalty. Loyalty language endows the relationship
with a binding connection between God and the psalmist and serves as a bridge
between narratives of intimacy and trust that establish long-term attachment and
self-abasing language that clearly places the psalmist in a position of abjection
and inferiority in a vertical relationship. Rooted in the realm of trust created in
the narratives of intimate and enduring relationship, loyalty discourse signifies
mutual interdependence, personal connection, and solidarity. Also a prominent
facet of the patronage relationship, loyalty is a defining element, the legitimating
framework that serves as the "cement of the system."[84] When viewed through
the lens of patronage, the laments' concept of loyalty emerges as more than a
language of enduring interconnection, but one that implies God's obligation to
protect and the psalmist's entitlement to that protection. That implied sense of
entitlement in the laments' loyalty discourse endows the psalmist with relational
power.[85]

   That loyalty language is central to the relational framework that houses the
God/psalmist interaction is most obvious in the prevalence of specific vocabu-
lary: loyalty (חסד),[86] faithfulness (אמת),[87] gracious favor (חנן),[88] compassion

---

   84.   Johnson and Dandeker, "Patronage: Relation and System," 231.
   85.   See Eisenstadt and Roniger, *Patrons, Clients and Friends*, 49.
   86.   חסד occurs in Pss 5:8; 6:5; 13:6; 17:7; 25:6, 7, 10; 26:3; 31:8, 17, 22; 40:11, 12; 42:9; 51:3;
52:3, 10; 57:4, 11; 59:11, 17, 18; 61:8; 62:13; 63:4; 69:14, 17; 77:8; 86:5, 13, 15; 88:12; 89:2, 3, 15,
25, 29, 34, 50; 94:18; 109:12, 16, 21, 26; 130:7; 141:5; 143:8, 12.
   87.   אמת occurs in the laments in Pss 25:5, 10; 26:3; 31:6; 40:11, 12; 43:3; 51:8; 54:7; 57:4, 11;
61:8; 69:14; 71:22; 86:11, 15; 89:15.
   88.   חנן occurs in Pss 4:2; 6:3; 9:14; 25:16; 26:11; 27:7; 31:10; 41:5; 51:3; 57:2 (×2); 86:3, 16;
59:6; 109:12.

(רחם and רחמים),[89] love (אהב and אהבה),[90] constancy (אמונה),[91] and righteous-ness (צדקה).[92] All of these words convey the commitment between these parties and especially emphasize God's character as dependable. Yet, the most impor-tant of these words is הסד/ḥesed, here translated "loyalty," which is central to the psalms as a whole and particularly important in the laments.[93] This is not a surprise, since loyalty becomes more important in a time of distress, and the term is regularly used in situations of dire need, as Sakenfeld notes.[94] In the laments, חסד is, with the exception of one psalm, described as the desired action of God on the part of the psalmist.[95] The request for God's חסד, further, is not a general request for faithfulness, but a specific request for deliverance. The following examples reflect the direct connection between God's loyalty and the psalmist's desire for and expectation of the hostile others' destruction by God's hand:

> Deliver me according to your loyalty (חסד). (Ps 6:5)

> Show your face to your servant;
> deliver me in your loyalty (חסד). (Ps 31:17)

> He will return evil to my enemies'
> in your faithfulness (אמת), destroy them! (Ps 54:7)

> I will sing your strength (עז);
> in the morning I will shout out your loyalty (חסד). (Ps 59:17)

> Strength (עז) belongs to God;
> to you, my Lord, loyalty (חסד). (Ps 62:12b–13a)

---

89.   רחם occurs in Pss 18:2 and 102:14. רחמים occurs in Pss 25:6; 40:12; 51:3; 69:17; 77:10; 109:46.

90.   אהב occurs seventeen times in the Psalms. The following are usages in the laments: Pss 5:12; 11:5; 38:12; 40:17; 69:37; 70:5. אהבה only occurs in the laments, in Pss 109:4, 5.

91.   אמונה occurs in Pss 40:11; 88:12; 89:2, 3, 6, 8, 25, 34, 50; 143:1.

92.   צדקה as an attribute of God occurs in the laments in Pss 5:9; 22:32; 31:2; 40:11; 51:16; 69:28; 71:2, 15, 16, 19, 24; 88:13; 89:17; 143:1, 11.

93.   חסד occurs 245 times in the entire Hebrew Bible, 127 times in the Psalms, and 48 times in the laments designated in this project (see citations above). חסד, as commonly noted, is a rich and flexible term and its meaning is highly contingent upon context. Gordon Clark (*The Word Hesed in the Hebrew Bible* [JSOTSup 157; Sheffield: Sheffield Academic Press, 1993) does not even provide an English translation for the term in his monograph. (See also the fine review of Clark's book: Gary Long, *Journal of Near Eastern Studies* 58 [1999]: 67–69.) Sakenfeld (*The Meaning of Hesed in the Hebrew Bible*, 233) suggests the following definition, which she admits is too cumbersome for trans-lating: "deliverance or protection as a responsible keeping of faith with another with whom one is in a relationship." Even this definition, she avers, does not encompass the full sense of the term, espe-cially the concept of forgiveness that is sometimes implied. I translate חסד as "loyalty," though I recognize that it has a broader meaning. Because of the complexity of the term it is impossible to provide a full treatment of the concept here. In addition to those cited above, the following works provide further discussion: Nelson Glueck, *Hesed in the Bible* (trans. Alfred Gottschalk; Cincinnati, Ohio: The Hebrew Union College Press, 1967); Sakenfeld, *Faithfulness in Action*. See also Brueggemann, "Psalm 109," and Brian Britt, "Unexpected Attachments: A Literary Approach to the Term חסד in the Hebrew Bible," *JSOT* 27 (2003): 289–307.

94.   Sakenfeld, *The Meaning of Hesed in the Hebrew Bible*, 218.

95.   Ps 109:12 and 16 are the exception, the only instances of חסד described as a human attribute in the laments.

> And in your loyalty (חסד) annihilate my enemies,
> and destroy all who afflict my life,
> for I am your servant. (Ps 143:12)

The psalmist's connection of loyalty and deliverance is clearly articulated. Though God is asked to destroy through אמת and not חסד in Ps 54:7, the understanding is consistent. In the laments, the psalmist's plea for loyalty is a prayer for dominating deliverance.[96] As Sakenfeld argues, deliverance is the "concrete expression" of loyalty.[97]

Though the psalmist readily connects loyalty to concrete deliverance, scholars dispute the nature of the relational commitment embedded in the concept of loyalty and, by extension, the nature of the psalmist's entitlement. Is God obligated to the psalmist by loyalty, implying a position of entitlement to the psalmist? Or, is God responsible, but not obligated, giving the psalmist a position of earnest need and desire, but no basis for making a claim on God? The two contrasting views of Nelson Glueck and Katherine Doob Sakenfeld concerning God's role implied in חסד illustrate the issue.

Glueck understands חסד to imply God's obligation, the foundation for the individual's entitlement and claim on God.[98] Glueck maintains that the relationship implied in the concept of חסד is a mutual one of exchange between parties. For instance, in his discussion of Ps 44, Glueck argues: "A community faithful to God could *expect* its deliverance from dire need by Yahweh because of his *ḥesed*, his covenant-based conduct through which he renders loyal aid to his people."[99] חסד/*ḥesed* is a result of the covenant, according to Glueck. The original covenant may have been an act of generous kindness on God's part, but after the covenant was instituted, God was obligated and the human party was entitled: "While the *ḥesed* relationship between Yahweh and his people was regarded as having originated through this goodness, חסד itself remained the mutual relationship of rights and duties which Yahweh had obligated himself to show."[100] An individual to whom God has made commitment has claim on God's attention and therefore a degree of power in this relationship.

Sakenfeld challenges Glueck's argument. Sakenfeld rightly argues that while חסד may be related to covenant in some cases, one cannot assume that a covenant is implied in all uses of the term.[101] The word חסד is a relational term that

---

96. See also Sakenfeld, *The Meaning of Ḥesed in the Hebrew Bible*, 221: "Ps 143:12 brings together in succinct form what is typical of many psalms when the overall theme is considered."

97. Ibid., 218.

98. Glueck (*Ḥesed in the Bible*, 55) defines חסד as "conduct in accord with a mutual relationship of rights and duties, corresponding to a mutually obligatory relationship: reciprocity, mutual assistance, sincerity, friendliness, brotherliness, duty, loyalty and love."

99. Ibid., 80 (emphasis added).

100. Ibid., 81. Robin Routledge also emphasizes obligation, both God's and humans', as an essential characteristic of חסד (Robin Routledge, "*Ḥesed* as Obligation: A Re-Examination," *TynBul* 46 [1995]: 179–96).

101. Sakenfeld, *Faithfulness in Action*, 41 (emphasis original): "Loyalty is not restricted to any *one* kind of relationship, such as covenant, but conceptually it cannot be taken out of *some* context of relationship; it is shown within relationship." See also Sakenfeld, *The Meaning of Ḥesed in the Hebrew Bible*, 13 n. 31.

crosses many different types of relationships in the Hebrew Bible, though it is often related to covenant specifically.[102] Her observation is particularly relevant to the laments, in which the concept of covenant is not prevalent; though there is clearly a relationship of intimacy and long-term commitment, ברית is not a central concept in the mind of the psalmist of the laments.[103]

Sakenfeld also differs from Glueck in her understanding of God's obligation and the individual's entitlement to חסד. Though she does not deny elements of obligation, she stresses the more powerful party's uncoercibility and the unconditionality of חסד, arguing that חסד should not be understood in terms of duties or rights but as a "freely performed deed."[104] According to Sakenfeld, though the relationship implies responsibility, the powerful party (God) has no duties and the less powerful party (the psalmist) has no rights. The performance of חסד always involves incoercible willingness by a more powerful party on behalf of one who is in dire need, who has no other recourse for action.[105]

Though their theories appear to be in conflict with regard to the issue of human power afforded in the concept of loyalty, both Glueck and Sakenfeld have made plausible and important arguments about the quality of the divine/ human relationship implied in the concept of חסד. When looking at the issue through the lens of patronage, in fact, these theories are not mutually exclusive. Patronage contains both ideals of voluntariness and freedom (as Sakenfeld emphasizes) and the presence of expectation and entitlement, possibly even coercion (as Glueck emphasizes). Indeed, the tension that results from this apparent conflict, between a relationship that is ostensibly voluntary but also based in ideals of long-term interconnection and mutual dependency that imply the patron's obligation to the client, is a widely recognized element of the patron/client relationship. That tension often sparks significant ambivalence, especially on the part of the client, a topic I discuss in the next exegetical section.

Central to my analysis of the psalmist's power in the discourse of loyalty is the concept of voluntariness embedded in the patronage relationship. Whereas Sakenfeld emphasizes God's freedom to act or not act according to loyalty, a central ideal of the patronage relationship is that *both* parties participate voluntarily. Within patronage, the client's choices are more truncated than the patron's

102.   See Simkins, "Patronage and the Political Economy of Monarchic Israel," 129.

103.   The word ברית only occurs seven times in three laments: Pss 25:10, 14; 55:21; 89:4, 29, 35, 40.

104.   Sakenfeld, *The Meaning of Hesed in the Hebrew Bible*, 223. More recently, Sung-Hun Lee concludes similarly, arguing that the unconditionality and freedom of God's חסד (or grace) is the petitioner's dominant assumption, though there may be elements of mutuality and duty as well (Sung-Hun Lee, "Lament and the Joy of Salvation," in Flint and Miller, *The Book of Psalms*, 246, also 239.

105.   Sakenfeld, *The Meaning of Hesed in the Hebrew Bible*, 44: "…the circumstances are such that the person in need can have no control over the response of the person of whom assistance is asked. He cannot personally compel the desired response; and if he is turned down he either cannot…or will not be able…to appeal within the structure of formal or customary law." Sakenfeld, in this instance, describes acts of חסד in a secular context, though she later argues (p. 215) that the examples in the Psalms do not contradict any pervious arguments she made about חסד in other contexts.

because of the vertical nature of the affiliation; the possibility for exploitation of the other party always lies more with the patron.[106] Yet ostensibly, the client could choose to align himself with another patron. That possibility is a counterbalance to the patron's power because accumulation of clients is not simply the result of the patron's power, but often the means of his power.[107] Therefore, while the relationship is most obviously one in which power flows from the "top downwards," power also flows from the "bottom upwards."[108]

The mutual voluntariness that characterizes human patron/client relationships brings into focus the limits of the patronage model as it translates to the divine/human relationship represented in the laments. The psalmist does not explicitly or implicitly threaten to choose another God as a human client might exert power by threatening to choose another patron. The psalmist's exertion of power is significantly more passive than an overt threat to leave the relationship, yet the effect of the psalmist's particular mode of exertion of power is similar. Just as the human client positions himself beneficially by threatening to leave the patron, thereby impugning the patron's social status, the psalmist positions himself beneficially by articulating the many ways God's social status will be injured if God does not act according to loyalty. The basis of the psalmist's power is in his ability to affect God's social status in a similar way as in the human patronage model, in which the client's ability to choose another patron threatens the patron's social status. There are two connected but separable ways the psalmist articulates relational power with regard to God, both of which connect the psalmist's restoration with God's social status. First, the psalmist envisions God's diminished social honor should God abandon the commitment of loyalty. Second, the psalmist envisions God's enhanced social honor should God fulfill the commitment of loyalty.

The following examples illustrate the psalmist's assertion of relational power by imagining the potential loss of praise to God if God does not act according to loyalty and deliver the psalmist from danger. In these examples, the psalmist reminds God of God's potential loss of praise, a resource within the control of the psalmist that substantiates and reinforces God's social status:

---

106.   The issue of choice is complicated; if the client has a choice to leave the relationship he cannot be exploited by the patron. Exploitation of the less socially powerful party is always a possibility in this kind of relationship. Whether or not the client's choice is real or an ideal, however, choice is part of the ideology of the relationship, part of what justifies its existence and also what prompts tension and ambivalence in the relationship.

107.   Wallace-Hadrill, "Patronage in Roman Society," 82: "Clients promised absolute loyalty and allegiance to their patrons, yet the patron was well aware that his own ability to command the loyalty of a client depended on his political success. Clienteles evaporated at a whiff of failure."

108.   Ibid., 82. See also James Scott: "While a client is hardly on equal footing with his patron, neither is he entirely a pawn in a one-way relationship. If the patron could simply issue commands, he would have no reason to cultivate a clientele in the first place. His need for a personal following which can be mobilized on his behalf requires some level of reciprocity. Thus, patron–client exchange falls somewhere on the continuum between personal bonds joining equals and purely coercive bonds" (James Scott, "Patronage and Exploitation," in Gellner and Waterbury, eds., *Patrons and Clients in Mediterranean Societies*, 22).

Turn, YHWH, rescue my soul,
deliver me according to you loyalty (חסד).
For there is no remembering (זכר)[109] you among the dead.
In Sheol, who can praise (ידה) you? (Ps 6:5–6)

What is to be gained from my blood,
from my descent into the pit?
Can dust praise (ידה) you?
Can it tell (נגד) of your faithfulness (אמת)? (Ps 30:10)[110]

Do you work wonders for the dead?
Do the shades rise up to praise (ידה) you?
Is your loyalty (חסד) told in the grave,
your constancy (אמונה) in the realm of the dead?
Are your wonders praised (ידה) in the darkness,
your righteousness (צדקה) in the land of oblivion? (Ps 88:11–13)

In a conspicuous rhetorical move, the psalmist connects his loss of life resulting from God's failure of loyalty with loss of praise for God, his diminishment with God's diminishment. In this way, the psalmist represents himself as a significant asset to God's social status.

The examples above represent a passive threat to God of social diminishment, in which the psalmist does not actively disparage God for failing in loyalty, but simply does not (or cannot) actively praise. The psalmist, however, places words of active denigration and ridicule in the mouths of the hostile others. Therefore, the reported speech of the foe is a means of not only characterizing the psalmist's social diminishment, but God's as well, as is evident in the following quotations:

Many say to me,
"There is no deliverance of him through God." (Ps 3:3)

The wicked, arrogantly, thinks,
"God does not care. There is no God." (Ps 10:4)

He says in his heart, "He [God] forgets,
he hides his face, he does not see for eternity." (Ps 10:11)

They say to me all day, "Where is your God?" (Ps 42:11)

[My enemy] says, "God has abandoned him;
chase him and catch him, for no one will save him." (Ps 71:11)

The assumption underlying the psalmist's use of other's words is that God will feel the shame of their remarks just as the psalmist does. God's and the psalmist's social fortunes are connected. The failure of loyalty in abandonment that shames the psalmist casts shame upon God as well.

---

109. The LXX (ὁ μνημονεύων σου) suggests "no remembering you," which I believe fits better with the presence of אין. See also Kraus, *Psalms 1–59*, 160.

110. Ps 30 is not in my designated corpus of individual laments; it is a thanksgiving psalm. This example, however, comes from the psalmist's recollection of his lament, to which God responded positively. The lament is included in the larger context of thanksgiving.

Significantly, the contents of the reported speech do not address the behavior of the psalmist that sparks the foe's public disparagement; the hostile others do not scorn the psalmist for his failure of loyalty. Rather, God's failure of loyalty is the subject of their disdainful speech. Though the psalmist feels the social effects of God's failed loyalty, the rhetorical design is to place God in the position of having to respond to the others' characterization of God. If God does not act because God chooses not to, then God is shamed because of failure to be loyal. If God does not act because God does not have the resources to act, then God is shamed through claiming more strength than is actually possessed. In either case, God's social reputation is impugned. The element of rhetorical coercion is clear; if God will not act on behalf of the psalmist, God must surely act for the sake of restoring God's own lost honor, assuring the public that God is capable of strong deliverance, of being loyal.[111] The psalmist's rhetorical agency lies in situating God in a precarious social position, placing the burden on God to defend God's own honor and thereby restore the psalmist's honor.[112]

The second way the psalmist articulates relational power is by promising praise if God *does* act according to loyalty. In fact, a commonly recognized element of the lament is the promise of future praise.[113] Though there is not always a direct relationship established between God's deliverance of the psalmist and the psalmist's response of praise, the logic of exchange is implied in the promise of praise. Embedded in this rhetorical feature is the understanding that the psalmist's praise of God is contingent upon certain beneficial outcomes. The psalmist recognizes his praise, his public recognition of God's power and ability to act, to be a desirable resource to God:

> I trust in your loyalty (חסד),
> my heart exults in your deliverance.
> I will sing to YHWH,
> for (כי) he has been good to me. (Ps 13:6)
>
> I will praise (ידה) your name forever,
> for (כי) you have acted;

---

111.   Not acting on behalf of the psalmist amounts to God failing to defend God's honor in the public sphere, further incentive for public shame. According to Simkins, "Shame is the result of the failure to defend one's honor, or the public denial of one's claim to honor" (Simkins, "'Return to Yahweh,'" 50).

112.   See also Bechtel, "The Perception of Shame," 87: "Shame arose when people did not recognize or acknowledge YHWH's power or when YHWH was perceived as impotent. God's being shamed was usually manifested as a shameful reputation."

113.   Westermann notes the consistency of this motif. Even though there is much variation within the structure of a lament, the vow of praise nearly always comes at the end of the prayer (C. Westermann, *The Praise of God in the Psalms* [trans. Keith R. Crim; Richmond, Va.: John Knox, 1965], 75). Westermann argues that the transition from lament to praise indicates that praise is the foundation of the petition. During the course of the prayer, the psalmist knows that "God has heard and inclined himself to the one praying; God has had mercy on him" (p. 79). For Westermann, even if the material situation of the psalmist has not changed, the lament did not communicate the experience of God's abandonment, but was a "powerful witness to the experience of God's intervention" (p. 81).

I eagerly await (קוה) your name, for (כי) it is good,
in the presence of your faithful ones. (Ps 52:11)

See! God is my helper,
the Lord is the support of my life.
He will return the evil of my enemies.
In your loyalty (אמת), destroy them!
Then I will offer (בנדבה) you a sacrifice,
I will praise (ידה) your name, YHWH, for it is good,
for it has saved me from my foes,
and let me gaze triumphant on my enemies. (Ps 54:6–9)

The psalmist is not so bold as to threaten God with withheld praise if his needs
are not met; even when he implicitly threatens God with lost praise this is only a
result of his death and not his intentional refusal. Yet he understands his acts of
praise as connected to a positive response to his prayers for deliverance.

The exchange logic embedded in demonstrations of the psalmist's praise is
plain in Ps 40:10–13, in which the psalmist recounts his faithful declaration of
God's righteousness as justification for God's continued acts of חסד. The
psalmist, in v. 11, repeatedly and ardently tells of how he proclaimed God's
righteousness (צדק), declared God's faithful deliverance (אמונתך ותשועתך), and
told of God's faithful loyalty (חסד ואמת) to the great congregation (קהל רב).
The psalmist emphatically presses God to remember these acts of the psalmist's
loyalty, commitment, and deference: "YHWH, you know!" (Ps 40:10, יהוה אתה
ידעת). Because of the psalmist's current despair (v. 13), he feels sure that God
will act in compassion (רחם) and loyalty (חסד) to deliver again. The public
nature of his past recognition of God's power and loyalty are central to the
psalmist's petition. In the psalmist's mind, he has displayed his own loyalty,
publicly enhanced God's reputation as a strong deliverer, and on that basis has
expectations of God's continued assistance.

As a result of God's commitment to loyalty, the psalmist promises not just his
future praise, but also the praise and recognition of others, including foreign
nations, that will enhance God's social worth. For instance, in Ps 22:24–31, the
psalmist instructs all future generations to praise God because of God's benefi-
cence to the lowly. In a compelling strategy of persuasion, the psalmist promises
not just his own thanks and praise, but also public declarations of praise that are
persuasive to others:

He put a new song in my mouth,
a hymn to our God.
Many (רבים) see it and are awed,
and trust in YHWH. (Ps 40:4)

(After God shoots the enemy with arrows in Ps 64:8)
All humanity will be afraid.
They will tell of the work of God
and his deed which they saw.
The righteous will rejoice in YHWH
and take refuge in him;
all the upright of heart will exult. (Ps 64:10–11)

> There is none like you among the gods, Lord,
> and there are no works like yours.
> All the nations you have made[114]
> will come to bow down before you, Lord.
> They will honor (כבד) your name,
> for you are a great (גדול) worker of wonders.
> You alone are God. (Ps 86:8–10)

The psalmist subtly connects his deliverance through God's faithfulness to God's enhanced social reputation and honor. In Ps 86:10, the psalmist promises, in no uncertain terms, honor (כבד) to God as a result of God's salvific action. In essence, the psalmist promises increasing numbers of clients who know and acclaim God's power and ability to deliver. This is a powerful promise because, in the world of patronage, public acts of demonstrable power are crucial as the "basis of social credibility."[115] Public, demonstrable events are the means of maintaining honor, and also securing power for the future. The psalmist posits God as being quite interested in public declarations of honorability and presents himself as able to reinforce God's social worth.

The laments inherently afford God significant relational authority through the construction of vertical relations, implicitly acknowledging God's power to abandon the relationship. Simultaneously, the ideal of loyalty is one of mutuality and solidarity and therefore affords a limited degree of power to the psalmist. The result of the existence of choice and obligation, and therefore entitlement, within a single relational structure accounts for the rhetorical commitment to deference described in the previous section and the ways the psalmist also asserts power, makes claims, and even coerces God according to the obligations implied in God's loyalty. The language of loyalty signals this complicated web of interconnection, voluntariness, and obligation that can yield social honor or disgrace for both. The negotiation of relational power in the psalmist/God bond is not happily resolved and constitutes a provocative, live tension in the relationship. While the psalmist is always inferior, and, as described above, eagerly calls attention to his lowliness in the laments, the ideal of loyalty also affords the psalmist some rhetorical power in the interconnection of his social fate with God's social fate.

e. *Language of Relational Ambivalence*
Thus far, I have discussed the rhetorical construction of the relationship between God and the psalmist as one that affords the psalmist, simultaneously, a position of decided inferiority in a vertical relationship with God and a position of mutuality and entitlement. As I have also briefly discussed above, these overlapping subject positions are often a source of pronounced ambivalence and

---

114.   H. Bardtke, in the *BHS* apparatus, suggests transposing this phrase, עשר עשית, to v. 8b, rendering that line, "and nothing is like your works that you have done." Kraus follows this suggestion for reasons of meter (Kraus, *Psalms 60–150*, 179–80). I see no compelling need to emend the text, however.

115.   Wallace-Hadrill, "Patronage in Roman Society," 85.

instability within this kind of relationship. Ambivalence develops from several sources.[116] The most obvious catalyst that is relevant to the laments relates to the "rather peculiar combination of inequality and asymmetry in power with seemingly mutual solidarity expressed in terms of personal identity and interpersonal sentiments and obligations."[117] Parties with real differences in social and personal power are related in a language of mutual solidarity and trust.

There is little doubt that the dominant representation of God is as strong and potent, with the power to protect and act as a patron. Strength is an essential element of God's loyalty, especially evident in Ps 62:12b–13a: "Strength (עז) belongs to God. To you, my Lord, loyalty (חסד)." The connection between loyalty and strength is reinforced in the metaphorical descriptions of God that indicate forcefulness and might, particularly in military images. The psalmist depicts God as an army (צבאות),[118] a shield (מגן),[119] and as wielder of weaponry (כלי מות; חנית וסגר; חרב; חץ; קשת).[120]

God's strength and reliability is further evident in the many portrayals of God as a shelter (סתר),[121] a refuge (מחסה and משגב),[122] a tent (אהל),[123] a pavilion (סכה),[124] and in more architecturally prominent images of a strong tower (מגדל עז),[125] fortress (מצוד),[126] and stronghold (מעוז).[127] These images of God as a

116. The other major source of ambivalence in the patronage relationship stems from the ostensibly voluntary nature of the relationship. I discussed this element in the previous exegetical section, where I think it is most relevant, but I do not want overly to stress the element of voluntariness as heuristically helpful for the laments. The ambivalence connected with the ideal of voluntariness in a human patronage context cannot be mapped directly onto the God/psalmist relationship. Limits to the model should be respected.

117. Eisenstadt and Roniger, *Patrons, Clients, and Friends*, 49.

118. See Ps 59:6.

119. See Pss 3:4; 7:11; 28:7; 59:12; 89:19. See also Ps 35:2 (מגן וצנה). For a more thorough discussion of the shield as a metaphor, see Arne Wiig, *Promise, Protection, and Prosperity: Aspects of the "Shield" as a Religious Relational Metaphor in an Ancient Near Eastern Perspective; An Iconographical and Textual Analysis* (trans. Jennifer Evans; Lund: Novapress, 1999).

120. קשת appears in Ps 7:13; חץ appears in Pss 7:14; 38:3; 64:8; 77:18; חרב appears in Ps 7:13; 17:13; חנית וסגר appears in Ps 35:3; כלי מות appears in Ps 7:14. (Ps 7:13–14 is difficult to render; the main subject of the action is unclear. I interpret God to be the main subject, and therefore the wielder of the many weapons described in these verses, though others interpret differently. For instance, see NJPS and Kraus, *Psalms 1–59*, 167. I include weaponry vocabulary from Ps 7 as examples of God's military proficiency, but my overall argument is not dependent on these examples.)

121. See Pss 18:12; 27:5; 31:21; 32:7; 61:5; 81:8; 91:1; 101:5; 119:114; 139:15.

122. For other uses of מחסה, see Pss 61:4; 62:9; 71:7; 94:22; 142:6. See also Pss 14:6; 46:2; 73:28; 91:2, 9; 104:18, not individual laments. For other uses of משגב, literally, "high place of refuge," see Pss 9:10 (×2); 58:17; 59:10, 18; 62:3, 7; 94:22. See also Pss 18:3 and 144:2, not individual laments.

123. See Pss 27:5; 61:5.

124. See Pss 27:5; 31:21. See also Ps 18:12, though this is not an individual lament.

125. The only usage of this phrase, or מגדל alone, in the laments is in Ps 61:4. The only other occurrence of מגדל in the Psalms is in 48:13.

126. See Pss 31:3 (בית מצודות), 4, 22; 71:3. See also Pss 18:3; 91:2; 144:2, though these are not individual laments.

127. מעוז is used in Pss 27:1; 28:8; 31:3, 5; 43:2; 52:9. See also Pss 37:39; 60:9; 108:9, though these are not individual laments.

location of security and fortification, especially in the architectural images, portray God as one with the clear means to be loyal and protective. In fact, as Andrew Wallace-Hadrill notes, architectural representations of strength are often part of a patron's public persona. Stalwart structures concretize the patron's control of social and personal power as well as resources beneficial to current and prospective clients.[128] Importantly, God is not referred to as a cave or crevice, though these are also places of safety, escape, and refuge.[129] In the world of the laments, God's strength cannot be anything as hidden or concealed as a cave; God's loyalty must be articulated in visible, recognizable symbols that assert and reinforce the public appearance of readiness for defense and dominating power. The psalmist in Ps 31:22 praises God's strong loyalty through these images: "His loyalty (חסד) is wonderful, to me, (like) a fortified city (בעיר מצור)."[130]

Though the presence of loyalty language and trust imagery provides the appearance of stability and assurance, God's potential choice not to abide by loyalty generates a provocative tension in the relationship, a destabilizing factor that the psalmist feels acutely. A significant element of the laments, in fact, is the psalmist's experience of God's failed loyalty. At issue in the psalmist's representation of relationship with God is not so much God's ability to be a loyal patron (though he does allow the hostile other to voice questions about God's credibility as a protector), but God's *willingness* to be loyal. The major categories of ambivalence images fall into two categories: language of God's unavailability, and, in contrast, language of God's threatening presence. These representations evidence the tension between the enduring, loyal relationship and the failures of that ideal.

The psalmist's ambivalence is evident in images of God's unavailability. The often-discussed image of God's hidden face (פנים סתר) is a clear image of failed presence.[131] The psalmist's frequent entreaties of God not to hide God's face and to be present reflect the psalmist's real experience of God's unavailability and unresponsiveness. Ps 27:9 relates God's hidden face to God's angry rejection of the psalmist: "Do not hide your face from me; do not turn away (נטה) your

128.   Wallace-Hadrill discusses architecture in the Roman system of patronage. The homes of the patrons constructed the "domestic power base" and were meant to impress upon the public the patron's availability and control of desired resources ("Patronage in Roman Society," 83, see also 63).

129.   See also Keel, *The Symbolism of the Biblical World*, 181. In contrast, in Ps 22:8–9, the enemy is the one who lurks in covert places, as opposed to God's unconcealed and visible signs of power.

130.   Bardtke, in the *BHS* notes, suggests changing בעיר מצור to בעת מצור ("in the time of oppression") or בעת מצוק ("in the time of distress"). I see no reason to change the text here; God's loyalty portrayed as a fortified city is consonant with the military and structural imagery that symbolizes God's loyalty and strength.

131.   See Pss 10:11; 13:2; 22:25; 27:9; 51:11; 69:18; 88:15; 102:3; 143:7. Samuel Balentine's work on the theme of God's hiddennes is the most thorough and important on the subject (Samuel Balentine, *The Hidden God: The Hiding of the Face of God in the Old Testament* [Oxford: Oxford University Press, 1983]).

servant in anger (אַף); you have been my help. Do not disregard (נטשׁ) me and do not abandon (עזב) me, God of my salvation."[132] The significance of God's hidden face is made clear in Ps 22:25, when the psalmist praises God for *not* hiding God's face: "For he did not scorn, he did not spurn the plea of the lowly, he did not hide his face from him. When he cried out to him, he listened." This image of hiddenness implies the psalmist's sense that God sometimes intentionally chooses to be unresponsive. Though these images present God as sovereign and powerfully immutable, they are not images of consistent loyalty.

Related to images of God's hidden face is the language of the psalmist's experience of distance from God.[133] Proximity, again, is a measure of relational commitment and solidarity. The psalmist refers frequently to his spatial position with regard to God, the enemy, and the community, indicating the importance of spatial location in all relational frameworks in the laments. In direct contrast with assertions of God's loyalty and images of God's strength are references to the distance between the psalmist and God:

Why, YHWH, do you stand far away (רחוק)? (Ps 10:1)

You have seen, YHWH! Do not be still (חרשׁ).
My Lord, do not be far (רחוק) from me. (Ps 35:22)

Do not abandon (עזב) me, YHWH.
My Lord, do not be far (רחק) from me. (Ps 38:22)

God, do not be far (רחק) from me.
My God, hurry to help me. (Ps 71:12)

Psalm 22 is especially concerned with God's distance: "Why so far (רחק) from delivering me?" (Ps 22:2). Spatial proximity is invoked repeatedly in this psalm, which emphasizes the physical absence of God and the isolation of the speaker in vv. 2, 12, and 20.[134] The psalmist's ambivalence about relationship with God is therefore particularly emphasized in this psalm, which juxtaposes repeated assertions of the ancestor's trust (בטח: Ps 22:5–6) with repeated assertions of God's distance. The psalmist also expresses his sense of God's unavailability in the requests of God to come near: "Come near (קרב) to me and redeem me; because of my enemies, free me" (Ps 69:19). For the psalmist, relationship is, at least in part, a matter of proximity; identity has to do with the physical position of the self with regard to the other in space that is personalized and coded relationally. God cannot protect the supplicant from a distance, but must be near, showing solidarity through physical company.[135]

132. Ibid., 143, notes that the theme of God's hiddenness sometimes implies God's rejection. See also Ps 88:15.

133. See also ibid., 151–57.

134. The root רחק is used in all three instances. (See also Pss 35:22; 38:22; 71:12.) For further discussion, see Esther M. Menn, "No Ordinary Lament: Relecture and the Identity of the Distressed in Psalm 22," *HTR* 93 (2000): 305 n. 14.

135. Again, see Barbara Korte's discussion of "proxemics," or the cultural significance of space in the rhetorical and literary characterization of social affiliation (Korte, *Body Language in Literature*, 73–77).

Unavailability and distance is further indicated in the frequent pleas, "How long?" (see Pss 13:2–3; 35:17). In fact, as Samuel Balentine observes, questions of God are often related to the theme of God's aloofness and are a pronounced element in the laments.[136] Questions rhetorically denote a tone of uncertainty about God's commitment. The psalmist represents his sense of significant lag between his experience of need and God's response. The implication of this language is that the psalmist feels God does not act in an appropriately expedient manner to rescue him from suffering and must be motivated by urgent pleas.

Finally, the psalmist portrays God as asleep, a sign of unresponsiveness: "Wake (עור), rouse yourself for my cause!" (Ps 35:23).[137] The image implies not just unresponsiveness but intentional ignorance and casual dismissal of the psalmist's pain as the faithful protector rests in spite of the psalmist's urgent need. As Thomas McAlpine says of Ps 44: "…the problem is not simply that the god is 'sleeping,' but that this unresponsiveness is intentional."[138] God is pictured here as decidedly lacking in vigilance, a neglectful and careless protector.[139] The significance of God's sleep as a sign of unavailability and intentional unrespon-siveness is made clear by contrasting images of God's vigilant wakefulness. In Ps 121:3–4, the psalmist is assured of God's delivering power because he knows God does not sleep, but is dependable, alert, and ready for action.

A second way the psalmist expresses ambivalence about the God/psalmist relationship is in images of God's threatening presence. Though not as preva-lent, these images are significant. In these instances, the psalmist suffers because God is present, not because God is absent. The source of ambivalence is clear; in these instances, the psalmist says that it is not the hostile other who is the source of his suffering, but God:

> For your arrows have penetrated (נחת) me,
> your hand has descended (נחת) on me. (Ps 38:3)

> Remove your assault (נגע) from me,
> I perish from the might[140] of your hand. (Ps 39:11)

> You have put me at the bottom of the pit,
> in the darkest places, in the depths.
> Your rage (חמה) throws itself against me.
> You humble with all your breakers. (Ps 88:7–8)

136. Balentine, *The Hidden God*, 116–32, especially 116–24.

137. See also Pss 7:7; 35:22–23; 44:24–25; 59:5–6; 78:65; 121:3–4.

138. Thomas McAlpine, *Sleep, Divine and Human, in the Old Testament* (JSOTSup 38; Sheffield: JSOT Press, 1987), 198–99.

139. In contrast, Bernard Batto argues that the motif of the sleeping God connotes God's majes-tic power and control over the universe, his omnipotence, and not his inattention or passivity (Bernard Batto, "When God Sleeps," *BRev* 3 [Winter 1987]: 22). Undoubtedly, the resting god connotes divine power and sovereignty. The image is not univocal in the laments, however. In a time of need, the psalmist desires an active god as well as a powerful one.

140. The phrase תגרת ידך is difficult to render, as תגרה is not attested elsewhere. The LXX (ἀπὸ τῆς ἰσχύος) suggests מגבורת, "from the power of your hand." I follow the suggestion of the LXX because of the lack of attestation of תגרה elsewhere, but this translation issue is not settled. (See also Kraus, *Psalms 1–59*, 416.)

Psalm 88 is the most discussed of these examples because it is such a distressing and urgent depiction of the breach of loyal relationship between God and the psalmist.[141] In this psalm, God rejects, abandons, inflicts terror, alienates, and abuses. This depiction stands in sharp contrast to the ideology of loyalty that so pervades the laments' relational discourse and is witness to the psalmist's ambivalence resulting from God's simultaneous positions as protector and oppressor. The situation is succinctly summarized by Irene Nowell: "God is at once the only enemy and the only hope for rescue."[142]

God's active perpetration of suffering is not the only way the psalmist depicts God as threatening. In direct contrast to images of God's unavailability, Ps 139 portrays a God who does not actively abuse, but who is nonetheless ominous and inescapable. The psalm begins with a seemingly comforting description of God's intimate knowledge of the psalmist: "YHWH, you have investigated (חקר) me and know (ידע) me. You know (ידע) when I sit down and when I stand up. You understand (בין) my intentions from far away" (Ps 139:1–2). This depiction of God's intimate knowledge continues, until the tone changes in v. 7: "Where can I go (הלך) from your spirit? Where can I run (ברח) from your presence?" Here, the psalmist articulates his misgivings about God's unavoidable presence.[143] The psalmist would, in fact, welcome respite from God's presence, as he hopes for some cover in darkness only to realize in the next line that darkness is the same as light for God (Ps 139:11–12). The psalmist's famous description of God's knowledge of him even in the womb and God's careful participation in the construction of his body comes after the psalmist's question about where he can go to escape God. In light of the psalmist's description of inability to escape from God (vv. 7–12), the depiction of God's involvement in the womb is not a comforting vision of intimacy, but an ambivalent picture of suffocating and inevitable presence.[144] Moreover, God's inevitable presence still results in the psalmist's need to invoke God's help against the enemy (vv. 19–22). Though the psalmist cannot escape God, God's presence in this psalm is not protective, as the psalmist is still plagued by the hostile other.

Carolyn Pressler, who also recognizes the ambiguity in the implications of God's presence, argues that ambiguity ultimately transforms into trust over the

---

141. See especially David Blumenthal's discussion of Ps 88 in the context of his larger argument that a post-holocaust theology must acknowledge that "God is an abusing God, but not always" (David Blumenthal, *Facing the Abusing God: A Theology of Protest* [Louisville: Westminster John Knox, 1993], 248).

142. Irene Nowell, "Psalm 88: A Lesson in Lament," in *Imagery and Imagination in Biblical Literature: Essays in Honor of Aloysius Fitzgerald, F. S. C.* (ed. Lawrence Boadt and Mark S. Smith; Washington, D.C.: The Catholic Biblical Association of America, 2001), 105.

143. For more discussion of ambiguity about God's presence in Ps 139, see Carolyn Pressler, "Certainty, Ambiguity, and Trust: Psalm 139," in *A God So Near: Essays on Old Testament Theology in Honor of Patrick Miller* (ed. Brent A. Strawn and Nancy R. Bowen; Winona Lake, Ind.: Eisenbrauns, 2003), 93, and Walter Harrelson, "On God's Knowledge of the Self, Psalm 139." *CurTM* 2 (1975): 261–65.

144. Job 7:12–21 presents a particularly powerful depiction of God's unwelcome, oppressive. and pervasive presence.

course of Ps 139; remembering God's presence in the womb, the psalmist ends with assertions of assurance.[145] In fact, as Samuel Balentine points out, there is a tendency in Psalms scholarship to interpret images of hiddenness and unease about God's presence as subsidiary to expressions of thanks and confidence.[146] When viewed through the lens of patronage, however, the images of ambivalence in the laments are far from resolved by images, promises, or declarations of praise. The structure of the relationship itself prohibits resolution. Though Pressler correctly sees in Ps 139 an earnest desire to resolve the tension between a loyal God and a threatening God, the overall characterization of the relationship in the laments does not depict resolution.

Ambivalence is, in fact, an integral and irresolvable part of a relational structure that is based on both interdependence and hierarchy. Indeed, in a patron/client relationship, the presence of ambivalence often comes to be so recognized that it is accommodated in the discourse of the relationship, which reflects not only the ideals of loyalty, but also the failures of that ideal. As Johnson and Dandeker describe: "Tolerance of the discrepancy between the ideas and the reality is reflected in individual relations and becomes enshrined in the language itself. Paradoxically, without its 'failures' the system would degenerate. In short, tolerance of ambiguity is an adaptive feature of the system."[147] The discourse of ambivalence facilitates the space between the ideal of loyalty and the reality of distance and suffering. Ambivalence that is an intrinsic element in the structure of a patronage relationship brings into relief the discourse of ambivalence that is equally important to the psalmist's sense of positionality with regard to God.

The result of this inherent ambivalence is a relationship that is volatile and fluctuating, due to the anxiety inherent in the negotiation of relational positions according to the demands of mutuality and the prerogatives of power. While the dominant ideology of the relationship between a patron and a client may be one of enduring commitment and loyalty in spite of power differences, there is often a combination of representations of stability and instability.[148] The psalmist constantly negotiates relational positions of empowerment and dependence, assurance and profound unease. Ultimately, there is no reconciliation of ambivalence in the laments. What emerges from this representation of the relationship is not an image of a continuously stable relationship of solidarity, but one of unharmonized, unresolved representations of ambiguity and unease alongside a discourse of trust and loyalty.

3. *Conclusions*

The psalmist does not design the verbal shape of his address to God spontaneously, but according to specific culturally embedded assumptions that afford

---

145. Pressler, "Certainty, Ambiguity, and Trust: Psalm 139," 96.
146. Balentine, *The Hidden God*, 121–22, 166.
147. Johnson and Dandeker, "Patronage: Relation and System," 231.
148. See Eisenstadt and Roniger's ("Patron–Client Relations," 72–73) description of anthropologists' gradual recognition that this kind of relationship was not stable and continuous, but volatile.

particular modes of engagement and ways of asserting entitlement and negotiating relational power. Embedded in the laments' language is relational identity for the psalmist and God that is clarified when viewed through the lens of patronage. This relational model brings into relief important aspects of the psalmist/ God relationship and clarifies the importance of some familiar aspects of this relationship, like the psalmist's language of need and promises of praise. Moreover, the kind of power that the psalmist asserts is clarified within the patronage model of relationship. Though the element of exchange is featured in the laments and is a primary basis upon which the psalmist asserts God's obligation to act and restore his life, intimacy is another fundamental elements of the relationship. The psalmist, therefore, seeks his own restoration, but he also seeks renewed relationship with God, and tries, rhetorically, to construct a path for God's action that would achieve both his salvation from suffering and confirm a relationship with God that has provided him a strong sense of identity in the past.

In sum, the psalmist/God relationship is characterized by a mingling of ideologies that are in tension with one another. At once, their relationship is one of mutuality and familiarity, and also a vertical relationship that overtly preserves God's superior strength and the psalmist's relational dependence. The psalmist, in attempting to redress his situation of suffering, negotiates agency and articulates selfhood in a relational framework that results in a selfhood that is simultaneously assertive and dependent, trusting and ambivalent. The psalmist's is therefore an anxious selfhood, empowered and also submissive, according to the constraints of a relationship that is inherently unstable.

Chapter 5

RHETORICAL VIOLENCE AND CONSTRUCTION OF IDENTITY IN PSALM 109

1. *Introduction*

In previous chapters I have discussed the way the psalmist responds to his situation of suffering in a multifaceted rhetorical context in which he addresses God, the hostile other, his community, and himself. His rhetoric includes alternating expressions of powerlessness and assertions of rhetorical power that articulate his acute social and physical pain and also position him to become an effective agent. Though I cannot demonstrate in every lament the specific way these self-representational and relational dynamics combine, and to what effect, in this chapter I analyze one lament, Ps 109, demonstrating how the psalmist understands and represents himself, becomes a moral agent, and negotiates power within this figured world.

In Ps 109 the psalmist uses rhetorical violence to assert selfhood and then provides himself and others an interpretation that recasts the experience of imagined violence as a means to create restoration. Though Ps 109 is typical of lament psalms in some ways, the length and extremity of this psalm's curses against the enemy is unique, and offers a particularly clear opportunity to discuss the role of imagined violence in the psalmist's construction of identity. These verses exemplify the way the psalmist enacts a position of social worth and rejects a position of disdain and shame through a discourse of violence and aggression. The psalmist's agency lies in his verbalization, his rhetorical enactment, of the other's absolute and utter destruction.

The psalmist's agency also lies in his offer to others to join him in a powerful and persuasive rhetorical experience. A public utterance or a text is always an invitation into a specific set of values, and creators of texts make a claim on readers and hearers through the language they use. This is particularly true of texts that have an overt goal of persuasion. As James Boyd White observes, a text "offers the reader an experience of feeling and thought with a shape and meaning of its own and this experience enacts the values and attitudes the author wishes us to share."[1] In Ps 109, the psalmist's alternating assertions of anger and desire for revenge combined with expressions of utter powerlessness organize an emotionally, psychologically, and socially powerful rhetorical experience of

---

1. White, *When Words Lose Their Meaning*, 280–81.

imagined violence for all involved in the prayer—God, the enemy, the audience, and the psalmist. The psalmist asks the hearer to participate in the rhetorical obliteration of the hostile other and to understand that verbal eradication as an act of salvation, compassion, and redemption. By the end of the psalm, the violence itself is displaced as a positive means to restore selfhood and relationship with God and community.

2. *Entering the Figured World: Psalm 109:1–5*

1. למנצח לדוד מזמור
   אלהי תהלתי אל תחרש
2. כי פי רשע ופי מרמה עלי פתחו
   דברו אתי לשון שקר
3. ודברי שנאה סבבוני
   וילחמוני חנם
4. תחת אהבתי ישטנוני ואני תפלה
5. וישימו עלי רעה תחת טובה ושנאה תחת אהבתי

1. To the choirmaster. To David. A Psalm.
   Oh God of my praise, do not be silent.
2. For a mouth of wickedness,[2] a mouth of deceit,
   they have opened against me.
   They speak to me with a lying tongue.
3. Words of hate surround me.
   They war against me without cause.
4. Instead of my love, they accuse me,
   but I am prayer.[3]
5. They place upon me evil instead of good
   and hatred instead of love.[4]

The beginning of a story is important. In Ps 109, the entry point is the crucial place where the hearer will decide the legitimacy of the psalmist's claims.[5] Exegetical treatments have often slighted the first five verses of Ps 109 in favor

2. I accept Bardtke's proposed reading in the *BHS* apparatus of רָשָׁע for the MT's רֶשַׁע, which would read "the mouth of the wicked and a mouth of deceit."

3. This phrase has attracted many suggestions for emendation that seem unnecessary. The LXX (προσευχόμην) suggests אתפללה, "But I pray," and Syriac (ʿlijhwn) suggests ואני תפלתי להם, "I pray for them." Kraus (*Psalms 60–150*, 335–36) follows Syriac in his translation. The MT is plausible and the construction of the phrase is not altogether unfamiliar. Just as the psalmist says in Ps 120:7, "I am peace" (אני שלום), the psalmist says here that the totality of his existence is oriented to prayer.

4. Changing אהבתי ("my love"), as in the MT, to אהבה, as suggested by the Syriac version, accords well with the parallelism of the verse.

5. Karen Cerulo (*Deciphering Violence: The Cognitive Structure of Right and Wrong* [New York: Routledge, 1998], 7) argues that the entry point in a narrative that concerns violence is particularly important in the audience's determination of the legitimacy of the violent act. The sequencing of narrative events is a primary means by which the narrator imposes her perspective on the information and the hearer interprets the act of violence as legitimate or illegitimate. The sequencing of information in Ps 109 is what Cerulo would call a "victim sequence," in which the psalmist assumes the role of the victim and "serves as the audience's point of reference" (p. 40). This particular sequencing of events predisposes hearers to judge violent acts against the victim as illegitimate and violent acts perpetrated by the victim as legitimate.

of the more notorious imprecations in vv. 6–20, but these beginning verses contain essential language that establishes the psalmist's worldview. The psalmist issues a rhetorical invitation to this particular figured world, constructs the framework for his relationship with God and the enemy, and establishes the means by which others will grant the fundamental justice of his complaint.

The first words of the psalm, after the superscription, focus the hearer's attention on the psalmist's righteousness in relationship with God and God's failure to act on behalf of the psalmist. In four words, אלהי תהלתי אל תחרש ("God of my praise, do not be silent"), the psalmist demonstrates both his willingness to praise (to be a valuable client), and proclaims God's silence in the face of his suffering (a failure of loyalty). Importantly, the phrase "God of my praise" occurs only here in the Psalms, a unique rhetorical means of emphasizing the psalmist's sense of himself as one who has fulfilled his role in relationship with God.[6] In juxtaposition with the image of a silent patron, this verse establishes the psalmist's central question: Will God fulfill his role as the protective patron as the psalmist has fulfilled his role as the praising client?

The theme of silence and speech continues in v. 2 with description of the hostile other's loquacious and antagonistic speech about the psalmist. God's silence is effectively compared with three descriptions of the foe's inimical and fallacious speech: the mouth and tongue of the hostile other are wicked (פי רשע), deceitful (פי מרמה), and lying (לשון שקר). The enemy's mouth, open and intending to harm, is a ferocious image of predation. Though the hostile other is not directly described as a predatory animal, he behaves with his words like a ravenous beast of prey, voraciously seeking the psalmist's social destruction. The enemy's speech is further imbued with danger in v. 3, in which the psalmist describes the foe's words as warring against him with no justification (וילחמוני חנם). The psalmist posits himself as an innocent victim of a warring attacker. Effectively, the psalmist establishes his alienation from friend and foe. Through excessive silence *and* excessive speech, respectively, the psalmist is victimized by both God and enemy.

The agonistic imagery of predation and battle the psalmist uses to describe the enemy's speech reflects and creates, as I have discussed previously, a social world structured by the dichotomous categories of dominance and defeat. In vv. 4–5, that dichotomous worldview is articulated in three rhetorical binaries that characterize the psalmist's moral worldview. All three phrases turn on the use of the preposition תחת, "instead," to establish the comparison:

תחת אהבתי ישטנוני

Instead of my love, they accuse me. (v. 4a)

וישימו עלי רעה תחת טובה

They place upon me evil instead of good, (v. 5a)

---

6.   Gerstenberger (*Psalms, Part 2, and Lamentations*, 257) also notes the unusual nature of this initial address.

שנאה תחת אהבתי

and hatred instead of love. (v. 5b)

The simplicity of these comparisons, the assumption of the psalmist's total inno-cence and the enemy's total depravation, is taken for granted. There is no clear path for identification with the enemy. With this dualistic rhetorical world, the psalmist invites the hearer into clear, uncomplicated choices, simply articulated and powerfully paired. Indeed, the binary comparison of the hostile other's character to the psalmist's is an inviting rhetorical construction. Faced with the choice of supporting the entirely innocent psalmist, who *is* prayer (ואני תפלה, v. 4) or the wholly evil other, it is difficult to imagine any witness to these words voluntarily choosing to support the psalmist's enemy. Moreover, as an entryway to the psalmist's supplication and the preface to the extensive description of revenge that follows these verses, the clear guilt of the enemy justifies the psal-mist's desires. In fact, the enemy is the *initiator* of the violence. Anyone who triumphs over such a villain would emerge as a hero.

3. *Imagined Violence and Subjectivity; Psalm 109:6–20*

6. הפקד עליו רשע ושטן יעמד על ימינו
7. בהשפטו יצא רשע ותפלתו תהיה לחטאה
8. יהיו ימיו מעטים פקדתו יקח אחר
9. יהיו בניו יתומים ואשתו אלמנה
10. ונוע ינועו בניו ושאלו ודרשו מחרבותיהם
11. ינקש נושה לכל אשר לו ויבזו זרים יגיעו
12. אל יהי לו משך חסד ואל יהי חונן ליתומיו
13. יהי אחריתו להכרית בדור אחר ימח שמם
14. יזכר עון אבתיו אל יהוה והטאת אמו אל תמח
15. יהיו נגד יהוה תמיד ויכרת מארץ זכרם
16. יען אשר לא זכר עשות חסד
    וירדף איש עני ואביון ונכאה לבב למותת
17. ויאהב קללה ותבואהו ולא חפץ בברכה ותרחק ממנו
18. וילבש קללה כמדו ותבא כמים בקרבו וכשמן בעצמותיו
19. תהי לו כבגד יעטה ולמזח תמיד יחגרה
20. זאת פעלת שטני מאת יהוה והדברים רע על נפשי

6. Let a wicked man be appointed over him,
    let an adversary stand over his right hand.
7. From his judgment let him come forth guilty,
    and his prayer become offense.
8. May his days be few,
    let another take his position.
9. Let his children become orphans,
    and his wife a widow.
10. Let his children roam about and beg;
    let them seek from their ruins.[7]

---

7.   The problem with the second line of v. 10 is that ודרשו has no object. The LXX (ἐκβλη-θήτωσαν) suggests ינרשו, "let them be driven out," instead of the MT's ודרשו, "let them seek." Bardtke, in the *BHS* notes, suggests ודרשו is probable. This reading is plausible, though the previous

11. May the usurer lay snares[8] for all that is his;
     may strangers plunder his property.
12. May there not be anyone to give him faithfulness,
     let there be no one to show compassion to his orphan.
13. May his descendants fall to destruction,
     in another generation may his name[9] be annihilated.
14. May the guilt of his fathers be remembered to YHWH,[10]
     may the sin of his mother never be forgotten.
15. Let them be before YHWH continually,
     and he will cut their memory from the earth.
16. Because he did not remember to do loyalty;
     he pursued the poor and needy man,
     someone broken in heart, even to death.[11]
17. He loved the curse; let it come to him![12]
     He did not desire blessing; let it be far from him![13]

line contains imagery of begging and roaming about; the verb דרש therefore befits the theme of seeking in the verse. Further, no object is necessarily required, as the action of seeking in itself communicates the loss and poverty that the psalmist desires to impose upon the enemy's children. The line indicates that the children of the enemy should be in a position of extreme need, forced to seek food and adequate housing instead of the ruins (חרבות) that serve as the children's abode. For more discussion of this verse, see A. Guillaume, "A Note on Psalm CIX. 10," *JTS* 14 (1964): 92–93.

8.   The LXX (ἐξερευνησάτω) suggests יחפש, "may he search out," or יבקש, "let him seek," as Bardtke indicates in the *BHS* apparatus, instead of the MT's ינקש, "lay snares." The MT is to be preferred because it is consistent with the imagery of snares and traps used to describe the behavior of the psalmist's adversaries throughout the laments. That the psalmist desires his enemy experience the traps of a usurer, just as the psalmist has experienced the traps of the hostile other, is another example of the psalmist's desire for reversal of position.

9.   Here I read שמו, "his name," suggested by the Targum and the LXX (codex Veronensis), instead of the MT's שמם, "their name."

10. The Syriac version omits אל יהוה, "to YHWH," and Bardtke, in the *BHS* apparatus, suggests deletion as well. It is likely to be an explanatory addition and it is not necessary for intelligibility, but I include it because it clarifies the use of the passive verb יזכר. For further discussion, see Dahood, *Psalms*, 3:104–5.

11. The MT reads למותת, a rare Polel infinitive, "to deal the death blow." The Syriac version (*lmwt'*) suggests למות, "to death." The difference in tone is slight, but important. Dealing a "death blow" implies mercilessness, pursuit of the abuse of the wounded even when he is clearly already weakened and vulnerable. The use of this verb in all other instances (see also Judg 9:54; 1 Sam 14:13, 17:51; 2 Sam 1:9–10 and 16) depict situations in which the one to be killed is already exposed or defenseless. It is difficult to convey the full sense of this verb in translation, but למותת is to be preferred over למות.

12. The MT points the conjunction *waw* in ותבואהו as a *waw* consecutive, "and it came," and points the *waw* in ותרחק in the next line in the same manner. The LXX and some modern interpreters (see NJPS and Kraus, *Psalms 60–150*, 336) prefer to translate the *waw* as conjunctive, not consecutive, as an expression of wishes for the future. The LXX's "let it come to him" (καὶ ἥξει αὐτῷ) is preferable, especially when one considers the jussive form of תהי in v. 19, which implies that the verbs in the preceding verse might also be read as jussives. Dahood's translation, which maintains the MT, is also plausible, however: "Since he has loved cursing, it has come to him." (See Dahood's translation and discussion of this textual issue in *Psalms*, 3:106.)

13. The MT points the *waw* in ותרחק as a *waw* consecutive, "and it remained far away." (See note above for further discussion.) I follow the LXX's "let it be far from him" (καὶ μακρυνθήσεται ἀπ' αὐτοῦ). See NJPS and Kraus (*Psalms 60–150*, 336) for similar readings and Dahood (*Psalms*, 3:106) for a translation that maintains the MT.

18. He clothed himself in cursing like it was his garment.
    So, let it come[14] like water to his insides,
    like oil in his bones.
19. Let it be for him like a garment he covers himself with,
    (like) a belt he wears continually.
20. This is the reward of my accusers from YHWH[15]
    and those who speak evil against me.

The psalmist responds to the enemy's affronts with a heightened discourse of domination and violence. While they are intense, even vicious, words, the psalmist has prepared the hearer in the first verses for the necessity and justice of these desires. Given the agonistic world established in vv. 1–5, and the stark moral comparison of the psalmist's behavior with that of the enemy, the extensive desires for the other's destruction are not outrageous, but expected. In these verses, the psalmist constructs a revenge fantasy, a rhetorical situation of verbal aggression and imagined retaliation that usurps his position as diminished and attacked by the other. The issue I address here is the moral and aesthetic appeal of revenge fantasy and the kind of subjectivity that is afforded in such fantasy.

The identity of the speaker of these words, one of the central questions in past treatments of the psalm, must be clarified first: Are these the psalmist's words or the psalmist's quotation of the enemy's vitriolic speech, as many have concluded?[16] David Wright has helpfully and succinctly characterized the textual arguments that support the quotation theory, though I discuss only the two most compelling.[17] For instance, in vv. 6–20, the enemy is discussed using singular verbs, while the enemy in other parts of the psalm is referred to with plural verbs, a discrepancy that could indicate a change in speaker. Inconsistency in verbal number, however, is a feature of many psalms and cannot reliably indicate change in speaker.[18] More convincing is the argument that v. 5 and v. 20 form an *inclusio* in their references to the enemy's speech that brackets the quotation of the enemy's speech in vv. 6–19. In my opinion, however, it seems unlikely that such a prolonged quotation, so central to the psalm, would not be more directly identified as words belonging to someone other than the primary

---

14. For the sake of consistency with v. 17, I read "let it come," instead of the MT's "and it came." Again, this translation follows NJPS and Kraus, *Psalms 60–150*, 336.
15. Bardtke, in the *BHS* notes, suggests deleting מאת יהוה, "from YHWH." I choose to maintain the MT here, though I recognize that the phrase was probably added as clarification of God's agency, as I discuss in the body of the chapter.
16. Hans Schmidt (*Das Gebet der Angeklagten im Alten Testament* [BZAW 49; Giessen: Töpelmann, 1928], 40–45) was the first to make the argument that these are the words of the enemy. For similar interpretations, see also Harold L. Creager, "Note on Psalm 109," *JNES* 6 (1947): 121–23; Stephen Egwim, "Determining the Place of vv. 6–19 in Ps 109," *ETL* 80 (2004): 112–30; Kraus, *Psalms 60–150*, 338; Zenger, *A God of Vengeance?*, 59–61.
17. David P. Wright, "Ritual Analogy in Psalm 109," *JBL* 113 (1994): 393–94.
18. Examples of change of number within a single psalm are many, and Wright (ibid., 394 n. 22) offers a thorough list. See, for instance, Ps 35, where the enemy is plural in vv. 3–7, 11–13, 15–17, 19–21, and 24–26, but singular in vv. 8 and 10. See also Gerstenberger, *Psalms, Part 2, and Lamentations*, 259, for further discussion of this feature.

speaker.[19] Moreover, as Gerstenberger argues, quoting the enemy at such length would have been a "liturgical disaster," as "No worship service of any kind could stand such a quantity of foreign, hostile words within its agenda."[20]

When one considers the quality of the enemy's and the psalmist's speech in the rest of the laments, it is actually more likely that the psalmist would speak the most violent language. The words the psalmist attributes to the enemy throughout these prayers ridicule and mock the psalmist in painful ways, but they are not violent.[21] Further, when one considers the violent language of the rest of the laments, the psalmist is clearly capable of these desires against the hostile other.[22] While Ps 109 contains the most expansive list of such desires, those desires are not aberrant in tone, but only in length. In addition, this kind of rhetorically violent speech is a claim to honor in the context of the laments, as I have argued in Chapter 3. Rhetorical violence asserts culturally valued traits of strength and power, and is a central tool the psalmist uses to establish social worthiness. It would be counter to the psalmist's intention to represent the enemy as so rhetorically powerful, an implicit bestowal of respect upon the enemy.[23]

If one accepts my contention that the psalmist uses rhetorical violence to reject social diminishment and assert worth, then Ps 109 is surely a jewel in the psalmist's crown. In this vision of repayment (פעלה, v. 20), the psalmist envisions the hostile other's destruction through relentless, thorough, and methodical imposition of shame and the erasure of the enemy's ability to claim social respect, honorability, or connection.[24] Psalm 109 strikingly portrays this world of dominance, an unusually elaborate and specific description of the psalmist's desires for the enemy's eradication. The concept of revenge is noticeably social, concerning position, social protections, and public place. In 109:8, the psalmist requests that the other be removed from his position of prominence (פקדה) and social security and that he experience an early death. He next describes the social consequences associated with contemptibility and lack of social protection, honorability, and respect: loss of property and financial harassment (v. 11), inability to provide for family and children (vv. 9–10), social alienation (v. 12), loss of social respect attached to one's name or public reputation (v. 13), and the

---

19.   See also Wright, "Ritual Analogy in Psalm 109," 394.

20.   Gerstenberger, *Psalms, Part 2, and Lamentations*, 259.

21.   See Pss 3:3; 10:4; 22:9; 42:4, 11.

22.   See my discussion of the psalmist's discourse of violence and aggression in the previous chapter dedicated to the psalmist's relationship with the hostile other.

23.   In a challenge/riposte situation, the psalmist need only establish that he has been challenged and then move on to redeeming himself socially through vitriolic riposte. In his discussion of the dynamics of shame in Joel, Ronald Simkins describes the responsibility of one who is shamed. Shame demands a defense of honor and successful challenge must be made in order to regain honor: "Through successful challenge and riposte, one gains honor at the loss of another's honor. Shame is the result of the failure to defend one's honor, or the public denial of one's claim to honor" (Simkins, " 'Return to Yahweh,' " 50).

24.   See also Job 18 in which Bildad uses similar rhetorical elements to describe, at length, the destruction of the wicked. Bildad's words are a rhetorical erasure of the wicked, their property, family, physical vitality, and place in the world.

condemnation of one's whole family because of that contemptibility and social disgrace (vv. 13–15). This domino-effect of shame and disdain strikes at the very heart of patriarchal honorability, the ability to maintain one's respected name and care for dependents.

The horror of these verses is not in desires for the physical destruction of the enemy, but in the extensive way the psalmist imagines his social erasure. Ironically, though this psalm is frequently characterized as among the most disturbing of the imprecation psalms, the psalmist's desires for the enemy are less physically violent than in other psalms. The physical destruction of the enemy is not actually described; his annihilation is only indirectly represented in the creation of orphans and widows. If Ps 58, with its vision of wading in the blood of the slaughtered enemies, is the goriest depiction of the enemy's physical destruction, then Ps 109 is the most blatant depiction of social and psychological annihilation. This psalm is particularly potent as a rhetorical negation of every means by which the enemy creates his identity—social position, reputation, possession, family, and name. The psalmist undercuts every manner in which the enemy identifies himself, and every category, connection, or social role through which he might be known to others.

Only after he describes this social and psychological obliteration of the enemy does the psalmist turn to physical images of the enemy, images that envision the psalmist's control (rhetorical, if not physical) over the enemy's body. The psalmist imagines his curses becoming part of the enemy's physical constitution (v. 18), seeping like water or oil into his insides (קרב) and his bones (עצם), and thereby forcibly violating the boundaries of the enemy's corporal structure. The image of curses that cover like clothing (v. 19) is a different manifestation of the psalmist's negation of the enemy's identity. The shamed enemy covered in the psalmist's curses is forced to publicly display the psalmist's triumph and domination. This curse is primarily social, but it is also physically transforming, an unavoidable and enduring alteration to the enemy's identity that publicly marks him as condemned, and also witnesses to the psalmist's power to subvert his identity. The inability of the enemy to escape the psalmist's curses, the way they become part of his permanent physical existence and force him publicly to attest to the psalmist's control over him, is a powerful image of "intimate violence," a kind of violence that exhibits its power through "disorganization" of the self.[25] These images are about establishing control over the enemy, the way he thinks of himself and identifies himself socially through his body.

---

25. The concept of "intimate violence" is indebted to Laura Tanner's book, *Intimate Violence*. See especially the following quotation, which I think accurately describes the effect of these verses in this psalm: "Acts of intimate violence, then, transform human interaction into a struggle for power in which the victim is stripped of the ability to define and control his or her participation. The violator usurps the victim's body, forcing it to assume the configurations of the violator's decree; intimate violence thus results in what Bard and Sangrey describe as a physical and psychological 'disorganization of the [victim's] self'" (p. 3; Tanner refers to Morton Bard and Diana Sangrey, *The Crime Victim's Book* [New York: Basic, 1979], 35).

The psalmist's rhetorical subversion of the enemy's identity is nowhere clearer than in vv. 17–18. The psalmist imagines a simple reversal of position for the hostile other:

> He loved the curse; let it come to him!
> He did not desire blessing; let it be far from him! (v. 17)
> He clothed himself in cursing like it was his garment.
> So, let it come like water to his insides,
> like oil in his bones. (v. 18)

The structure of these verses articulates the satisfying simplicity of "turning the tables" on one's foes. This depiction has the ring of justice, a straightforward and uncomplicated reversal. The particular kind of justice envisioned here is so appealing because, in the psalmist's imagination, the enemy has established the contours of his own punishment. The enemy receives as his punishment only what he himself enacted in his own social dealings.

The moral, ethical, and theological implications of the psalmist's desire for revenge have been problematic for many exegetes.[26] One common way of dealing with this problem has been to emphasize, rightly, that the psalmist positions God as the agent of revenge. In v. 15, the psalmist says that God will "cut their memory from the earth." Again in v. 20, the psalmist explicitly states that his wishes are the "reward of my accusers from YHWH." Though the phrase "from YHWH," is awkward and could easily be a later addition intended to clarify the means by which the "reward" will be distributed, God is clearly depicted as the agent.[27] Some scholars understand this to be evidence of the psalmist's beneficial means of dealing with anger through prayer in a way that diminishes the human impulse toward violence. As Walter Brueggemann says, "such rage is not only brought into Yahweh's presence. It is *submitted* to Yahweh and *relinquished* to him."[28] Similarly, Erich Zenger argues that a transfer occurs in this psalm that implies "renouncing one's own revenge."[29]

Paradoxically, these quotations assert that the psalmist might become less violent, or at least release vengeful desires, through praying for violence. This idea has a long history, most recognizably articulated in Aristotle's idea of catharsis that occurs in the dramatic imitation of events that would normally cause pain, but which lead to a purgation of undesirable emotions when one is brought to a place of "pity and fear."[30] Aristotle's idea of catharsis relies upon

---

26.   See also Kraus, *Psalms 60–150*, 341–42.

27.   See also Kraus (ibid., 337), who describes the phrase מֵאֵת יהוה in v. 20, and the similar phrase אֶל יהוה in v. 14, as "probably an explanatory accretion."

28.   Walter Brueggemann, *The Message of the Psalms: A Theological Commentary* (Minneapolis: Augsburg, 1984), 85 (emphasis original). See also Brueggemann, "Psalm 109," 152. Firth ("Context and Violence") offers a similar argument, though he does not address Ps 109 directly, but refers to other psalms (Pss 3; 27; 35; 55; 56; 64; 143) in which violent acts of revenge are ultimately assigned to God.

29.   See especially Zenger, *A God of Vengeance?*, 92.

30.   Aristotle, *Poetics* (ed. and trans. Stephen Halliwell; LCL; Cambridge, Mass.: Harvard University Press, 1995), 48–49.

the idea that one develops a more profound understanding of human life through the artistic representation of even very painful and violent events.[31] Brueggemann and Zenger, similarly, might argue that in turning over violent or aggressive desires for vengeance to God, the psalmist learns to perceive himself, others, and God more fully, that this transference of agency liturgically leads to wise and socially beneficial acknowledgment and adjudication of aggressive thoughts and feelings. Brueggemann and Zenger do not deal in a simplistic or depleted idea of catharsis as simply "letting off steam."[32] Though I do not discount the idea that there may be some significant and theologically important release of emotion in the experience of praying these words, the assumption that the psalmist rids himself of the impulse to revenge overlooks the way that a certain sense of agency is also conceptualized, articulated, and authorized in this violent rhetoric. Words have power and violent words have violent power.[33] The psalmist experiences and offers his audience a certain kind of power in this language, the investigation of which requires recognition of rhetorical violence as an act of violence.[34] That the psalmist does not see himself as a direct agent of

31. Aristotle, *Poetics*, 37–38 (Halliwell, LCL): "A common occurrence indicates this: we enjoy contemplating the most precise images of things whose actual sight is painful to us, such as the forms of the vilest animals and of corpses. The explanation of this too is that understanding gives great pleasure not only to philosophers but likewise to others too, though the latter have a smaller share in it. This is why people enjoy looking at images, because through contemplating them it comes about that they understand and infer what each element means, for instance that 'this person is so-and-so.' "

32. The idea of "venting" emotions as a mode of catharsis is sometimes employed by those who defend the role of violence in the media. Jib Fowles (*Why Viewers Watch: A Reappraisal of Television's Effects* [Newbury Park, Calif.: Sage, 1992], 229, 254) writes, "Gory programs usher children into an otherwise forbidden world, where they can vicariously vent their frustrations and hostilities. Seething resentments and impulses toward unspeakable cruelties can be spent in a way that is not absolutely chastised by society, one that is—more important, from the small child's point of view—totally free of any chance for hurtful retaliation…" (For further discussion of Fowles's ideas, see Sissela Bok, *Mayhem: Violence as Public Entertainment* [Reading, Mass.: Addison-Wesley, 1998], 45, 48.) Most studies do not support such positive emotional benefits to viewing violent media. In fact, most studies support a correlation between witnessing violence and increased aggression (physical and verbal), desensitization to violence, disinhibition, and fear. See, for instance, W. James Potter, *On Media Violence* (Thousand Oaks, Calif.: Sage, 1999), 25–42, and *The 11 Myths of Media Violence* (Thousand Oaks, Calif.: Sage, 2003), 29–30; Richard B. Felson, "Mass Media Effects on Violent Behavior," *Annual Review of Sociology* 22 (1996): 103–28. For discussion of the moral and aesthetic effects of exposure to media violence, see Arthur Kleinman, "The Violences of Everyday Life: The Multiple Forms and Dynamics of Social Violence," in *Violence and Subjectivity* (ed. Veena Das et al.; Berkeley, Calif,: University of California Press, 2000), 226–41, esp. 231–33.

33. For a different interpretation of verbal violence, see Brueggemann, *The Message of the Psalms*, 175: "In the Psalms we do not have violent acts, but only violent speech." Similarly, David Blumenthal ("Liturgies of Anger," *Cross Currents* 52 [2002]: 186) argues, "A curse is performative speech, speaking is doing… And yet, a curse is not performative action; it is not accomplishing one's rage in social deed. The text acknowledges the power of the curse, but shies away from turning it into action—perhaps in modesty, perhaps for ethical reasons."

34. Nancy Armstrong and Leonard Tennenhouse, in the introduction to their edited volume (*The Violence of Representation*, 9), argue for continuity between material and representational violence: "We have offered a crude distinction between two modalities of violence: that which is

revenge does not minimize the other complex and subtle ways he constructs subjectivity for himself and those who witness his words through rhetorical violence and imagined revenge.

The appealing emotional and psychological power of revenge fantasy is evident in a great number of literary works.[35] Imagined violence produces another version of reality, a means of undermining an undesirable, oppressive, or enraging situation.[36] Revenge fantasy mobilizes an alternate selfhood in relation to a specified enemy, one that reverses the structures of power. Likewise, in Ps 109, it creates a mode of agency for the psalmist and also for the witness to this language who identifies with the psalmist's suffering and agrees to be represented by his language.

The aesthetic experience, both for the psalmist and for the hearer or reader, also contributes to the functioning of rhetorical violence.[37] Over the course of fifteen verses, the psalmist draws from a repertoire of available methods of humiliating his enemy and brings them together in a masterful and relentless visualization of the enemy's social and physical eradication. David Blumenthal recognizes the aesthetic appeal of this psalm in his assertion that moderns have lost the "art of imprecation" that Ps 109 evidences.[38] Though this flood of ill-wishes is aggressive and violent, it is not, as Blumenthal says, "pornographic."[39] The completeness with which the psalmist accomplishes this rhetorical eradication is a performance of sorts, an impassioned, yet controlled, demonstration of skill. The thoroughness of the proliferating images of dominance and aggression against the enemy invites witnesses to respect, appreciate, and even enjoy the rhetorical expertise with which the psalmist dispatches his foe.

For the psalmist, to be powerful is to be able to use aggressive language in a way that induces respect, appreciation, and fear, even from his sympathizers.

'out there' in the world, as opposed to that which is exercised through words upon things in the world... But our ultimate goal is to demonstrate that the two cannot in fact be distinguished..." I think the two modalities of violence these authors describe can and should be distinguished, though the violence of representation should be attributed significantly more formative power than it has been, at least with regard to this psalm. This kind of empowerment may not have resulted in immediate acts of violence against the psalmist's enemy, but it no doubt contributed to the moral and ethical imagination of those who participated in the liturgical context in which these words were prayed.

35. Revenge is a pervasive theme in Western literature. See also Susan Jacoby, *Wild Justice: The Evolution of Revenge* (New York: Harper & Row, 1983), 14, and Linda Anderson, *A Kind of Wild Justice: Revenge in Shakespeare's Comedies* (Cranbury, N.J.: Associated University Presses, 1987), 13.

36. See also Judith Halberstam, "Imagined Violence/Queer Violence: Representation, Rage, and Resistance," *Social Text* 37 (Winter 1993): 189.

37. See also Richard Brucher ("Fantasies of Violence: *Hamlet* and *The Revenger's Tragedy*," *Studies in English Literature, 1500–1900* 21, no. 2 [1981]: 257–70) for discussion of the role of aesthetics in revenge fantasies.

38. Blumenthal, "Liturgies of Anger," 186: "Indeed, there is the art of imprecation; the tailored, almost restrained, language of execration; the carefully considered malediction. Not the ladylike demur or gentlemanly protest, but the well-placed curse. A lost art in our day."

39. Ibid.

The rhetorical skill with which the psalmist imagines the enemy's destruction creates tension and heightens anxiety. As literary critic Sidney Sondergard describes, "rhetorical violence is applied to confer an immediacy to textual arguments. Even when employed to support arguments conceived as beneficial to the reader, it functions as a threat, a suggestion of what can happen to the reader if the writer's message is ignored or rejected."[40] Psalm 109 fosters tension and anxiety that is not just intended to intimidate the enemy, but also anyone who witnesses this prayer enacted in a public context.[41] To witness these violent words being prayed in the kind of public ritual in which I imagine the laments were originally used is to feel one's self threatened on some level.[42] By placing the hearer or reader in a position both to appreciate his skill as rhetorician of violence and be fearful of that skill and the anger that fuels it, the psalmist positions his audience as vulnerable. The witness is simultaneously invited to see the legitimacy of the psalmist's anger and also experience the urgency and force of his rage in a way that places everyone, not just the enemy, at risk. The psalmist negotiates power by rhetorically "undoing" the emotional and physical security enjoyed even by those he does not directly hold responsible for his own suffering.[43]

In these verses, the psalmist offers himself an emotionally and socially power-ful rhetorical experience. In an act of persuasion, however, the "site of meaning" is not only in the characteristics of a text, but also in its reception.[44] Again, the issue I am concerned with is not whether this prayer resulted in physical violence, though I do not discount the possibility that such liturgical language contributed to and reinforced a more general culture of agonistic violence.[45] We

40.   Sidney L. Sondergard, *Sharpening Her Pen: Strategies of Rhetorical Violence by Early Modern English Writers* (London: Associated University Presses, 2002), 18.

41.   The representation of violence conceptualizes possibilities for violence in a way that can become part of one's enduring experience in the world. Tanner (*Intimate Violence*, iv) discusses this anecdotally as part of her own motivation to examine how witnessing even fictional violence can effect one's sense of personal safety, but an increased sense of fear and endangerment is a widely acknowledged repercussion of reading or viewing acts of violence. See, for example, Bok, *Mayhem*, 61–66; Potter, *On Media Violence*, 36–39, 125–26. Though there are undoubtedly differences in the extremity of the effect between witnessing the psalmist's words in Ps 109 and watching extreme film violence, for instance, verbal and visual violence both contribute to heightened tension and anxiety in the witness.

42.   For further discussion of this effect of represented violence, see Cynthia Marshall, *The Shattering of the Self: Violence, Subjectivity, and Early Modern Texts* (Baltimore: The Johns Hopkins University Press, 2002), 1.

43.   See also ibid., 2.

44.   Ibid., 1.

45.   Many scholars are currently studying violence in biblical texts. See especially Jonneke Bekkenkamp and Yvonne Sherwood, eds., *Sanctified Aggression: Legacies of Biblical and Post-Biblical Vocabularies of Violence* (JSOTSup 400; London: T&T Clark, 2003); Collins, "The Zeal of Phinehas"; Terence Fretheim, "God and Violence in the Old Testament," *Word and World* 24 (2004): 18–28; James G. Williams, *The Bible, Violence, and the Sacred: Liberation from the Myth of Sanctified Violence* (New York: HarperCollins, 1991). There are important counter-voices to an ethic of violence and dominance in the Hebrew Bible as well that reflect cultural awareness of the need for care in the use of violence. An obvious example is the lion lying down with the lamb in Isa

have no way of knowing how the audience responded to this prayer in its original context. What we do have is evidence within the following verses about how the psalmist understands these violent desires, an interpretation that the psalmist invites the hearer or reader to share. In these verses, a sudden transition to a discourse of powerlessness, the psalmist offers another "site of meaning" for his violent imaginings.

4. *Powerlessness and Subjectivity: Psalm 109:21–31*

21. ואתה יהוה אדני עשה אתי למען שמך
    כי טוב חסדך הצילני
22. כי אני ואביון אנכי ולבי חלל בקרבי
23. כצל כנטותו נהלכתי ננערתי כארבה
24. ברכי כשלו מצום ובשרי כחש משמן
25. ואני הייתי חרפה להם יראוני יניעון ראשם
26. עזרני יהוה אלהי הושיעני כחסדך
27. וידעו כי ידך זאת אתה יהוה עשיתה
28. יקללו המה ואתה תברך קמו ויבשו ועבדך ישמח
29. ילבשו שוטני כלמה ויעטו כמעיל בשתם
30. אודה יהוה מאד בפי ובתוך רבים אהללנו
31. כי יעמד לימין אביון להושיע משפטי נפשו

21. You, Yahweh, my lord,
    deal with me according to your name,
    for good is your loyalty. Save me!
22. For I am poor and needy,
    my heart convulses[46] within me.
23. Like a shadow when it spreads out, I am made to disappear.[47]
    I am shaken off like a locust.
24. My knees tremble from fasting,
    my flesh is emaciated from fat.
25. I have become a disgrace for them,
    they see me and shake their heads.
26. Help me, YHWH, my God,
    save me according to your loyalty.
27. They will know that this was your hand,
    you, YHWH, did it.

11:6–7, a vision of social harmony that stands in tension with visions of social dominance and competitive challenges for honor through rhetorical expressions of strength.

46.　In the MT, חלל is pointed as a Qal active verb and would require repointing to indicate the passive sense required for the translation, "my heart is wounded within me," as Dahood (*Psalms 101–150*, 107) explains. Dahood supports that reading, as does the NJPS, though the LXX and the Syriac version suggest the preferable reading of חולל, a Polal form from חיל, "my heart convulses within me" (*HALOT* supports this suggestion as does Kraus, *Psalms 60–150*, 336). See also Ps 55:5.

47.　This is the only example of הלך in the Niphal in the Hebrew Bible. Though my translation, "I am made to disappear," is awkward, I want to convey the passive sense of this verb, which is carried over into the next line with another Niphal, ננערתי. Kraus (*Psalms 60–150*, 336) translates the line, "Like a shadow when it vanishes do I depart," and the NJPS translates, "I fade away like a lengthening shadow," neither of which capture the passive sense of the verb. The passive verbal form indicates the psalmist's sense of powerlessness and lack of agency.

28. They will curse and you will bless,
    let them rise up and be shamed,[48]
    and let your servant rejoice.
29. My accusers will be clothed in shame,
    let them wrap themselves with their shame like a robe.
30. I will thank YHWH profusely with my mouth,
    amidst the multitudes I will praise him.
31. For he stands at the right hand of the needy,
    to save from the judges[49] of his life.

The psalmist's self-representation changes abruptly in vv. 21–31. The psalmist moves from a self-representation as forceful and dominating to one of submission: "You, Yahweh, my lord... Save me!" (Ps 109:21). He exchanges his aggressive rhetorical position for one of dissolution: "Like a shadow when it spreads out, I am made to disappear" (Ps 109:23). Combining many elements discussed in previous chapters, the psalmist represents himself as socially and physically diminished in language of bodily suffering (vv. 21–24), imagery of extreme social alienation and rejection (v. 25), and finally, language of dependence and need related directly to the psalmist/God relationship (vv. 26–31).

As I discussed in previous chapters, that language of powerlessness enables the psalmist to claim authority according to different relational frameworks that co-exist in the psalmist's imagination and mingle in the construction of the psalm itself. What further empowers the psalmist, as Kleinman suggests, is that this language organizes others' responses to his suffering, providing those addressed a culturally valued way of responding to his pain.[50] Language of powerlessness is central to the goal of persuasion. In Ps 109, the representation of the endangered self positions both the psalmist and his witnesses to the rhetoric of violence in the previous verses. It is rhetorically (and emotionally) significant that this psalm represents the psalmist's diminishment as fully as the psalmist asserts rhetorical rage. The psalm offers all involved in this speech act a powerful, aestheticized experience of rhetorical violence and a means to interpret that experience as one of solidarity with one who suffers. This interpretation casts violence and aggression as redemptive and salvific, and the sympathetic witness as one who seeks justice for the powerless and wounded. That the psalmist suddenly inhabits a subject position of powerlessness emerges as the hermeneutical key to the psalmist's self-understanding, his probably unacknowledged assumptions about the validity of his violent desires, and his hopes about how others will understand and affirm those desires as just and necessary.

The literary concepts of comedy and tragedy, used as heuristic devices, elucidate the trajectory and embedded worldview of Ps 109. In using these concepts,

---

48. Instead of the MT's "let them rise up and be shamed," the LXX reads οἱ ἐπανιστανόμενοί μοι αἰσχυνθήτωσαν ("let my opponents be shamed"). I maintain the MT in this instance, as the significance of the change seems minimal, but see Kraus (*Psalms 60–150*, 337) for brief discussion of his preference for the LXX.

49. The LXX reads ἐκ τῶν καταδιωκόντων, suggesting מֵרֹדְפִים.

50. Kleinman, *Social Origins of Distress and Disease*, 151, 178.

my intention is narrowly defined, restricted to how violence and revenge are treated within the tragic and comic visions.[51] I do not use these concepts to explore issues of form or genre, but to isolate the point of view of the psalmist in Ps 109 with regard to the assertion of aggression and its implications.[52]

The difference between comedy and tragedy is not that tragedy is violent and comedy is not, but lies in the overall narrative worldview in which violence functions.[53] Both the comic and tragic visions recognize the appeal and the emotional attraction of violent revenge perpetrated upon an enemy. The tragic vision, however, often highlights the hideous, dehumanizing, and reprehensible aspects of such revenge. *Hamlet*, for instance, presents a tragic hero who is compelled to commit a violent act, and Shakespeare's treatment of violence leads the audience to the "horror of real murder and revenge."[54] In contrast, a comic structure presents even violent revenge as a fundamentally positive, or at least necessary, display of force that leads to social restoration.[55] The violence of revenge is not morally compromising within the comic vision, but leads to reintegration.[56]

Importantly, the comic structure may not lead to restoration for every character. A comedy may achieve restoration agonistically and may require the ultimate exclusion of an antagonist through punitive measures.[57] In this scenario,

51. Exum helpfully describes the methodological approach of using a fairly contested and broad literary category as a heuristic device: "the term 'tragedy'…provides a way of looking at texts that brings to the foreground neglected and unsettling aspects…" (J. Cheryl Exum, *Tragedy and Biblical Narrative: Arrows of the Almighty* [Cambridge: Cambridge University Press, 1992], 2). My intention is similar to Exum's in that I do not provide a comprehensive theory of tragedy or comedy. They are highly disputed concepts, yet as Exum observes, "most people have a general idea of what tragedy is about" (p. 4). My use of these concepts relies on the "general" recognition that there is a fundamentally different worldview in tragedy that leads to a dramatically different interpretation of violence as a thematic issue. I use comedy and tragedy only as an entryway into discussion of violence in Ps 109 in particular.

52. The literary critic Robert Corrigan (*Comedy, Meaning and Form* [2d ed.; New York: Harper & Row, 1981], 6–7) discusses comedy as a worldview, as opposed to a form.

53. G. Beiner (*Shakespeare's Agonistic Comedy: Poetics, Analysis, Criticism* [Cranbury, N.J.: Associated University Presses, 1993]) notes that Shakespeare, whose works are often discussed in literary-critical treatments pertaining to fictional representations of violence and revenge did not conceive of violence and revenge as inimical to the comic literary structure.

54. Brucher, "Fantasies of Violence," 270.

55. Literary critics have fruitfully discussed the implications of violence that occurs within a tragic or comic narrative structure with regard to Shakespeare's plays because of the obvious importance of the theme of revenge in all genres of his work. Most helpful to this study have been Anderson, *A Kind of Wild Justice*; Beiner, *Shakespeare's Agonistic Comedy*; Brucher, "Fantasies of Violence," 257–70; Harry Keyishian, *The Shapes of Revenge: Victimization, Vengeance, and Vindictiveness in Shakespeare* (Atlantic Highlands, N.J.: Humanities, 1995).

56. The appeal of comic revenge is also evident in the Samson narrative (Judg 13–16), as Exum (*Tragedy and Biblical Narrative*, 42–44) has argued. Though I do not concur with Exum in her argument that Samson's story is ultimately comic, there are certainly comic elements, especially in the narrative's implicit appreciation of violence as a means of turning the tables.

57. See Beiner, *Shakespeare's Agonistic Comedy*, 13: "Comedy of love is essentially reparative and directed toward resolution, though it proceeds via release, which reveals underlying causes of

restoration is purchased at the cost of the eradication of the antagonist, but the fate of the antagonist does not in any way impugn the protagonist, with whom the sympathies of the audience are fully entrusted. When revenge is portrayed in an agonistic comedy, it has the appeal of exposing social transgressors and empowering a heroic imagination in which a virtuous character triumphs through superior strength or wit.[58] The subversive quality of violence in the agonistic comedy attracts because it entertains through humiliation of the antagonist and asserts the authority of the protagonist. The reader or hearer is not invited to view the "squalor of violence," its brutalizing effects or the complex psychological and social aftermath of revenge or violence, as in a tragic portrayal of revenge.[59]

The violence in Ps 109 is best conceived of as an essential ingredient in the overall comic vision of the psalm. That is, in the transition from imprecation to description of distress and endangerment, the psalmist does not invite the hearing audience to scrutinize the desires of vv. 6–20, but rather to assume that these images represent a just response to the suffering and need described in vv. 21–31. The psalmist places the experience of rhetorical aggression and violence within a fundamentally restorative and positive trajectory. The violence that eradicates the foe aids one who is suffering and alienated from society. The result, especially in vv. 30–31, is socially and relationally restorative; the psalmist ends his prayer with praises to God amidst the multitudes, and a declaration of confidence and assurance that God is indeed the support of the needy. God and the psalmist are aligned through the destruction of the enemy. This image of reconciliation contrasts sharply with the alienation of God's silence with which the psalmist begins the prayer. The psalmist's honor is restored, as he is included among the multitudes and no longer socially disdained. God has restored, even increased, God's own honor by buttressing God's reputation as an effective help to those who are dependent, and consequently receives beneficial public affirmation. The psalm has a comic vision because violence is simply a necessary means of eradicating the source of distress that impedes restoration, peace, and wholeness. Nowhere does any figure in this psalm examine the means of achieving restoration or problematize the dehumanizing desires for the humiliation and destruction of the enemy and his family.

The sudden shift in the psalmist's self-representation in v. 21 subverts any meaningful consideration of the enemy as sympathetic, as he is replaced by the

---

problems and errors. Resolutions need not represent perfection, and the resolution to a given comedy may be stratified, distinguishing between more profound and more shallow levels. But they do complete a reparative trajectory, whether the solutions emerge through a process of correction or as comic fiat (or a combination of the two). Agonistic comedy is essentially punitive, though it may qualify the antagonist's fundamental negativity, and leads to his effective exclusion. This basic difference has radical implications for structure, perspective, response, the function of the main characters, and the function of the respective comic levels within the totality of the play. It derives from distinctive comic traditions, though Shakespeare combines the two strategies in his plays."

58. Anderson, *A Kind of Wild Justice*, 171.

59. The phrase "squalor of violence" is borrowed from Brucher, "Fantasies of Violence," 270.

magnitude of the psalmist's dissolution, pain, and need. The psalmist's own physical boundaries are threatened in vv. 21–24, in contrast to vv. 18–19 in which the psalmist envisions aggressively breaching the boundaries of the enemy's body. The abrupt shift in self-representation defines for the hearer who the "real" victim is. Throughout this psalm, in fact, the psalmist's body is much more present than the enemy's as material proof of suffering. When the psalmist does refer to the body of the enemy (vv. 18–19), it is portrayed in images that demonstrate the psalmist's victorious control; the enemy's body in pain is not present in this psalm. The psalmist's pain replaces any pain a hearer might attribute to the enemy, or any pain his family and friends might endure as a result of the psalmist's rage.

In fact, the violence itself is defined as something other than violence. Because of the psalmist's powerful suffering, any violent desires of sympathetic witnesses are reinscribed as compassion and justice, and with regard to God, as assistance to the needy that demonstrates חסד.[60] The effects of the violence itself are displaced.[61] Any aggressive act by the psalmist, the clear victim, is conceptualized as an act necessary for positive restoration. Further, responding positively to the psalmist's rhetoric of violence is not delight in or support of crafted, thorough, and structured violence, but sympathy with the powerless and the diminished.

To say that the comic moral vision best elucidates the trajectory of violence in Ps 109 is not to say that all elements of tension and anxiety are resolved. As I discussed above, the psalmist's violent discourse in vv. 6–20 heightens anxiety and unease about the psalmist's anger, an effect the psalmist directly intends for the enemy, but one that indirectly affects all witnesses. Similarly, the psalmist's promise to praise God, and the lofty confidence with which he speaks of God's assistance to the needy, also establishes unease. The psalmist's promise is contingent upon God's successful diminishment of the enemy (see vv. 28–30).[62]

---

60. The fact that God's destruction of the enemy is the necessary demonstration of loyalty is also brought into the foreground when viewed though the comic lens. God's destructive agency is not scrutinized as it might be in a tragic context (see Exum's discussion of the hostility of God in the Saul story; *Tragedy and Biblical Narrative*, 16–42). This is explained, in part, by the relational framework of patronage that shapes the psalmist's representation of God. As L. Roniger describes, in some manifestations of patronage it is not the moral character of the patron that is the source of honor, but his power to act. He argues, for instance, that moral honor is not as important in Brazil and Mexico as honor earned through strength and domination (Roniger, *Hierarchy and Trust in Mexico and Brazil*, 189). Likewise, the issue of God's violence as a moral issue is not as much a concern in the laments' construction of honor (God's and the psalmist's) as the shame of *not* acting with strength and aggression.

61. Literary critic David Forgacs describes this process of displacement in the discourse of fascism in Italian texts written between World Wars I and II. Acts of violence "are not really visible…as real acts of violence, since in their imaginary the relation between aggressor and victim becomes inverted or otherwise displaced" (David Forgacs, "Fascism, Violence, and Modernity," in Howlett and Mengham, eds., *The Violent Muse*, 11).

62. See also Tony W. Cartledge, "Conditional Vows in the Psalms of Lament: A New Approach to an Old Problem," in *The Listening Heart: Essays in Wisdom and the Psalms in Honor of Roland E. Murphy* (ed. Kenneth G. Hoglund et al.; JSOTSup 58; Sheffield: JSOT Press, 1987), 87.

The psalmist implies that if God does not act, all will know that God could not or did not act to save the psalmist, a failure of loyalty that would make God's status as a strong deliverer dubious.[63] Even when he effusively asserts power-lessness and inferiority in relation to God, the psalmist also asserts relational power coercively by connecting God's social fate to his own social restoration.[64] The threat to God's reputation and status posed by the psalmist may be minor, yet it is an important aspect of the psalmist's particular brand of moral agency in Ps 109 that mixes supplication with coercion and appeals for sympathy with elements intended to heighten anxiety—God's, the enemy's, and the hearer's.

5. Conclusions

In Ps 109, the psalmist negotiates agency through a combined rhetoric of power-lessness and violence. This chapter has illustrated how the psalmist, through differing modes of self and other representation, guides himself and others to view his desires for violence as unproblematic, uncomplicated, and ultimately positive. I have attempted to demonstrate what kind of world one accepts, and what kind of desires one embraces or affirms, in order to let these words represent one's own desires in a situation of suffering. The kind of agency the psalmist claims in this psalm is a powerful and compelling form of selfhood. Literary critic Harry Keyishian's treatment of revenge in Shakespeare's plays astutely describes the potentially restorative work of violent revenge fantasy in the reconstruction of personhood:

> The impulse to revenge derives not only from such destructive feelings as hatred, rage, pride, and vindictiveness, but also from many that are heroic and essential to individual and social existence, like indignation, gratitude, compassion, loyalty, appropriate self-regard, a sense of integrity, and a passion for justice.[65]

Revenge fantasy appeals to a strong, decisive, and clear kind of justice that addresses the depth of suffering the psalmist feels. The enactment of heroic, triumphant, and violent revenge through fantasy empowers one in a situation of acute suffering or oppression.[66] I do not discount, nor do I desire to trivialize, the effect of such language as a means of mobilizing assertive personhood and emboldened agency.

63. The strong second person pronoun (אתה) in v. 27 emphasizes God's role as the potential strong deliverer: "They will know that this was your hand, you, YHWH, did it." The psalmist articulates in a culturally potent way the consequences of failed loyalty, which result in diminishment not only for the psalmist but also for God.

64. John Shepherd recognizes that God's honor is at stake in these verses, that the psalmist's desire is for God to be vindicated: "The Psalmist's primary desire is not the destruction of his enemies, but the glory of God" (Shepherd, "The Place of the Imprecatory Psalms," 41). In contrast, I argue that, for the psalmist, God's restored honor is attained by the destruction of the enemy. The two outcomes are mutually dependent.

65. Keyishian, *The Shapes of Revenge*, 9.

66. See, for instance, Blumenthal's powerful and horrifying description of the kind of abuse victims endure that might motivate such rage and make the words of Ps 109 particularly relevant as prayer (Blumenthal, "Liturgies of Anger," 184–85).

Yet critical implications of violence—for the psalmist, enemy, God, and wit-
ness—are not portrayed in this psalm, nor are witnesses guided toward scrutiny
of this agonistic world or the punitive means by which restoration is imagined.[67]
It is not my intention to argue that only a tragic vision of violent revenge can
capture the "truth" about violence, but to isolate what a comic vision of violence
does not lead one to consider. As Kenneth Burke says, "A way of seeing is also
a way of not seeing."[68] What sort of moral imagination is both expressed *and*
suppressed by these words? Psalm 109 empowers in specific ways, primarily in
an aesthetic representation of revenge that reflects only the recuperative effects.
What this psalm does not portray about real violence and revenge is important to
hold in tension with the positive kind of agency that might be afforded a sufferer
in this language. My reading attempts to explain what one does not see about the
experience of these words unless one assumes some degree of sympathetic dis-
tance from the psalmist's rage, which allows for scrutiny of his desires and the
way his desires potentially shape the reader's desires.

---

67. Though Serene Jones's primary concern is with the potential paths for healing from trauma
offered in the Psalms, she also acknowledges other elements in the Psalms that might lead to the
reinforcement of violence: "If this is true—if people who have suffered traumatic events can become
caught in a time warp where the violence done to them is constantly reenacted in the present, often
in a manner unknown to them or in ways that pass as 'normal'—it may well be that a community
could use the often vengeful rhetoric of the psalms to fuel hate rather than transform it into healing
praise of God" (Jones, "'Soul Anatomy,'" 284).

68. Kenneth Burke, *Permanence and Change: An Anatomy of Purpose* (3d ed.; Berkeley,
Calif.: University of California Press, 1984), 49.

Chapter 6

CONCLUSION

1. *Summary*

Because the laments are prayers, the psalmist's primary addressee is God, and the psalmist's relationship with God governs the contours of this language. A chief purpose of this utterance is to induce God to act, to make something happen on behalf of the suffering psalmist. In the course of the prayer, however, the psalmist also positions himself rhetorically to other participants in this figured world—the enemy, the community, and his own body—and so draws on other relational structures in order to define himself. My analysis explicates how these relational structures afford the psalmist and others roles that both reflect and create the figured world of the laments and provide the psalmist a means to negotiate power in the context of these overlapping relational discourses and self-representative languages.

The concept of the figured world, a culturally constructed location of interpretation, is a way of entering and exploring the particularity of the language used by the psalmist to represent his pain to himself and others, and the assumptions about relationship, selfhood, and restoration embedded therein. The laments are here understood as artifacts that were produced by and sustained a cultural world into which the psalmist entered when he assumed the subject position of the "I." This cultural world is populated by stable figures and characterized by formulaic imagery and an expected plot line, rhetorical elements that offer a means of apprehending and acting within a specific cultural interpretation of personhood in the context of acute suffering. The language of this figured world gave form and meaning to the psalmist's experience, and within this discourse, the psalmist became a particular kind of sufferer.

The psalmist's dominant self-representation is as a powerless and needy individual. This language of powerlessness posits him as embattled, vulnerable to attack and physical incapacitation, and utterly dependent upon God for salvation. Though the dominant representation of the self is as endangered, this language is simultaneously a means of claiming authority and making demands, both modes of empowerment for the psalmist. Further, it organizes the psalmist's experience of suffering for others, casting his plight in a culturally valued discourse that also offers a recognized mode of response to witnesses. As the psalmist inhabits the role of the sufferer in the language of the laments, he also makes claims about how others—the hearing audience and God—should respond to his pain by assuming the role of the sympathetic protector.

To focus on the psalmist's representation of his powerlessness is to overlook another equally important articulation of identity in the laments, found in the psalmist's discourse of aggression. Through the discourse of aggression and imagined violence, the psalmist asserts a rhetorical identity of strength, power, and honor. In this language he appeals to the dominant cultural values of agonistic strength and dominance as a way of enacting a position of social worth. This language is also a compelling kind of moral agency to the psalmist, who uses rhetorical violence to defend and sustain a sense of personhood. Especially in his construction of revenge fantasy, the psalmist insistently invites the hearing audience into a world of agonistic justice and aesthetically shaped violence to effect a radical psychological and emotional reaction. The hearer is invited to appreciate the completeness of the other's destruction, to grant the justice and righteousness of that obliteration, and feel the strength and power in the desires for that (rhetorical?) harm of another. The particular worldview of the psalmist is evident in his use of rhetorical violence to humiliate the enemy and establish his social worth *and* in his subsequent displacement of that violence as an act that results in restoration.

What emerges from this complex of unmerged self-representations is not a portrait of unified self, but one that is fluid and volatile. Identity is afforded the psalmist through different and sometimes contradictory discourses. Though this combination of elements yields a conflicted portrait of the psalmist, the multifaceted nature of the psalmist's rhetorical identity *defines* the subjectivity of the psalmist. The question of the rhetorical construction of identity in the laments, therefore, requires a concept of the self that is not consolidated, unitary, and coherent, but dispersed, contingent, and volatile. The psalmist's negotiation of identity and vision of restoration in this psalm rests upon the subtle, yet probably unacknowledged, combination of self-representations of domination and powerlessness, assertion and dissolution.

While I have focused on the psalmist's negotiation of social and relational power, I do not imagine the psalmist was conscious of the complex relational texture of his utterance. The figured world of the laments is a web of assumptions and presuppositions within which the psalmist constructed his identity that was probably, for the most part, taken for granted by the psalmist and those who witnessed the prayer. That is, I do not understand the discourse of the laments to be unique personal expression, but a pre-existent cultural artifact that the psalmist entered into, even as he adapted it according to his individual needs. The language of the laments was not determinative of every aspect of the psalmist's selfhood, but afforded a subject position for the speaker of the psalms to manipulate creatively according to the needs of the particular lived moment. I do not believe that the psalmist was inherently aggressive or innately submissive, but that he used every discourse of selfhood available to him to put meaningful words to his pain and create a supplication that was emotionally persuasive for himself and those in his immediate and imagined audience. The kind of relational claims, accepted modes of self-assertion and self-representation, and the trajectory of his desired path for restoration, I believe, were afforded by a deeply embedded liturgical tradition that simply "felt right" to one who was in a situation of severe pain, as it does to many who pray these psalms today. Yet the laments bear evidence of the psalmist's intention to invoke different relational frameworks in an utterance that he constructs in a culturally valued and persuasive language of supplication. This language was a powerful means of organizing the experience of suffering, for the psalmist and for others who witnessed his prayer, and also functioned as a mode of agency through which to seek change.

2. *Further Considerations*

Israeli poet Yehuda Amichai wrote the following poem, entitled "Psalms":

> I wish everyone
> in the world
> would begin to read
> the names
> in this phone book
> more than Psalms.[1]

Amichai's poetic comparison of the Psalms with a phone book is provocative. The absurdity of juxtaposing these radically different textual genres invites the obvious question: What, in Amichai's opinion, does the phone book have that the Psalms do not? One answer is that the phone book has names of individuals. Indeed, reading the phone book inundates the reader in concrete and personal evidence of humanity. The Psalms, in contrast, deal in broad and non-specific categories of people ("enemy," "evildoer," even "I" and "We"). Amichai's poem invites comparison of the way these texts deal with generality and particularity. As I have argued, the laments *are* particular in that they reflect and create a specific worldview. Moreover, they become an individual's personal prayer if one allows the laments to articulate one's suffering and desires. Amichai calls his reader's attention to an aspect of particularity lacking in the Psalms. One plausible interpretation of this poem is that Amichai's wish that people read the phone book *more* than the Psalms indicts psalmic language that invites supplicants into a world without names, yet one that provides such powerful language for rhetorical violence and potent imagery for imagining the obliteration of the very individuals listed in the phone book, all authorized and rendered normative by the agonistic assumptions of the psalmic cultural world.

This poet privileges a textual worldview that values particularity, though Amichai does not encourage readers to disregard the Psalms. Yet Amichai's assertion of the value of the phone book implies limitation, even danger, in the worldview of the Psalms. The danger to which Amichai alludes, I believe, lies at least in part in the ability of the psalmist to obscure the humanity of the one he

---

1. Yehuda Amichai, "Psalms," translated by Leon Wieseltier, *The New Republic* (December 13, 2004): 42.

prays against, the target of his ill-wishes and imprecations, and to escape the responsibility of praying explicitly for the downfall of a named individual. Amichai's succinct poem suggests that it is not a question of choosing one worldview over another, but of placing these texts with radically different textual perspectives in a relationship that evokes comparison and dialogue.

Amichai's allusion to the possible limitations of the Psalms differs in tone from some modern interpreters' attempts to reclaim the laments for theological and liturgical use. These efforts exhibit passionate sensitivity about the need for wounded individuals to express pain and for faith communities to have a language for dealing with suffering.[2] The basic argument, in brief, is that the individual laments are an important resource for those who suffer and that the totality of the human experience can and should be brought before God in prayer; God is fully present in the dialogical act of prayer. I fully agree with the theological value of this mode of prayer that provides acknowledgment of the individual's suffering. The laments are a powerful resource for those who suffer. This mode of address to God and community is a potential path to healing for wounded individuals and recuperation of selfhood in a situation of dehumanizing distress, and the biblical tradition provides important resources for that.[3]

There is, however, another story to tell about the laments that is equally important. If one is to ask what one is able to see about the expression of pain before God in the context of the laments, one must also ask what is obscured, or even invisible, when one adopts the laments' viewpoint. While these texts are a liturgical resource with liberative potential, they also construct social conflict in an agonistic framework that requires the suffering of others as a means of relieving the suffering of the psalmist. They are dangerous in their desire to enlist God as a personal champion in order to relieve suffering by imposing suffering. The laments are both prayers for liberation and redemption as well as prayers for domination and violence.

Recognition of the laments' oppressive potential does not invalidate their liberative potential, however. In order for the laments to be theologically relevant today, and possibly more importantly, for individuals to be in solidarity with those who suffer, one need not uncritically affirm the worldview of the psalmist. I propose a reading of the laments that stands strongly with the sufferer but also challenges a worldview based on values of overwhelming strength and the necessity of social dominance as a means to restored social worth. As Amichai suggests, placing the laments in conversation with other texts that provide a

---

2. See, for instance, Walter Brueggemann, "The Costly Loss of Lament," *JSOT* 36 (1986): 57–71; idem, "The Formfulness of Grief," *Int* 31 (July 1977): 263–75; Sally A. Brown and Patrick D. Miller, eds., *Lament: Reclaiming Practices in Pulpit, Pew, and Public Square* (Louisville, Ky.: Westminster John Knox, 2005); Swenson, *Living Through Pain*; Blumenthal, "Liturgies of Anger." See also Ee Kon Kim, "'Outcry': Its Context in Biblical Theology," *Int* 42 (1988): 229–39; Matthew Boulton, "Forsaking God: A Theological Argument for Christian Lamentation," *SJT* 55 (2002): 58–78.

3. See especially Swenson's sensitive discussion of "living through" suffering with the Psalms as a resource in her recent work, *Living Through Pain*, 2005.

different construction of selfhood in the context of acute suffering, and describe other paths to social and personal restoration for sufferers, may be a helpful way to further clarify the benefits *and* limitations of the worldview of the laments. Though I cannot attempt such a project here, the value of that conversation would, in my opinion, be an essential part of the modern conversation about the ethical, moral, and theological vision of the laments and their appropriation for theological use in liturgical contexts.

BIBLIOGRAPHY

Abu-Lughod, Lila. *Veiled Sentiments: Honor and Poetry in a Bedouin Society*. Berkeley, Calif.: University of California Press, 1986.

Aho, James A. *This Thing of Darkness: A Sociology of the Enemy*. Seattle, Wash.: University of Washington Press, 1994.

Amichai, Yehuda. "Psalms." Translated by Leon Wieseltier. *The New Republic* (December 13, 2004): 42.

Anderson, G. W. "Enemies and Evildoers in the Book of Psalms." *Bulletin of the John Rylands University Library of Manchester* 48 (1965–66): 18–29.

Anderson, Linda. *A Kind of Wild Justice: Revenge in Shakespeare's Comedies*. Cranbury, N.J.: Associated University Presses, 1987.

Argyle, Michael. *Bodily Communication*. 2d ed. London: Methuen: 1988.

Aristotle. *Poetics*. Translated by Stephen Halliwell. Loeb Classical Library. Cambridge: Harvard University Press, 1995.

Armstrong, Nancy, and Leonard Tennenhouse, eds. *The Violence of Representation: Literature and the History of Violence*. New York: Routledge, 1989.

Bail, Ulrike. "'O God, Hear My Prayer': Psalm 55 and Violence Against Women." Pages 242–263 in *Wisdom and Psalms: A Feminist Companion to the Bible*. 2d Series. Edited by Athalya Brenner and Carole Fontaine. Translated by Charlotte Methuen. Sheffield: Sheffield Academic Press, 1998. Repr. from "'Vernimm, Gott, mein Gebet.' Ps 55 und Gewalt gegen Frauen." Pages 67–84 in *Feministische Hermeneutik und Erstes Testament*. Edited by Hedwig Jahnow. Stuttgart: Kohlhammer, 1994.

Bailey, F. G. *The Need for Enemies: A Bestiary of Political Forms*. Ithaca, N.Y.: Cornell University Press: 1998.

Bakhtin, Mikhail. *The Dialogic Imagination: Four Essays*. Edited by M. E. Holquist. Translated by Caryl Emerson and Michael Holquist. Austin: University of Texas Press, 1981.

———. *Problems of Dostoevsky's Poetics*. Edited and translated by Caryl Emerson. Theory and History of Literature 8. Minneapolis: University of Minnesota Press, 1984.

Balentine, Samuel E. *The Hidden God: The Hiding of the Face of God in the Old Testament*. Oxford: Oxford University Press, 1983.

Bard, Morton, and Diana Sangrey. *The Crime Victim's Book*. New York: Basic, 1979.

Batto, Bernard F. "When God Sleeps." *Bible Review* 3 (Winter 1987): 16–23.

Becker, Ann E. *Body, Self, and Society: The View from Fiji*. Philadelphia: University of Pennsylvania Press, 1995.

Bechtel, Lyn M. "The Perception of Shame Within the Divine–Human Relationship in Biblical Israel." Pages 79–92 in *Uncovering Stones: Essays in Memory of H. Neil Richardson*. Edited by Lewis M. Hopfe. Winona Lake, Ind.: Eisenbrauns, 1994.

———. "Shame as Sanction of Social Control in Biblical Israel: Judicial, Political, and Social Shaming." Pages 232–258 in *Social-Scientific Old Testament Criticism*. Edited by David J. Chalcraft. The Biblical Seminar 47. Sheffield; Sheffield Academic Press, 1997. Repr. from *Journal for the Study of the Old Testament* 49 (1991): 47–76.

Beiner, G. *Shakespeare's Agonistic Comedy: Poetics, Analysis, Criticism*. Cranbury, N.J.: Associated University Presses, 1993.

Bekkenkamp, Jonneke, and Yvonne Sherwood, eds. *Sanctified Aggression: Legacies of Biblical and Post-Biblical Vocabularies of Violence*. Journal for the Study of the Old Testament: Supplement Series 400. London: T&T Clark, 2003.

Bending, Lucy. *The Representation of Bodily Pain in Late Nineteenth-Century English Culture*. Oxford: Clarendon, 2000.

Benthien, Claudia. *Skin: On the Cultural Border Between Self and the World*. Translated by Thomas Dunlap. New York: Columbia University Press, 2002.

Benveniste, Emile. *Problems in General Linguistics*. Translated by Mary Elizabeth Meek. Miami, Fla.: University of Miami Press, 1971.

Bergant, Dianne. "The Song of Songs and Honor and Shame." *Semeia* 68 (1994): 23–40.

Beyerlin, Walter. *Die Rettung der Bedrängten in den Feindpsalmen der Einzelnen auf institutionelle Zusammenhänge untersucht*. Göttingen: Vandenhoeck & Ruprecht, 1970.

Birkeland, Harris. *The Evildoers in the Book of Psalms*. Oslo: Jacob Dybwad, 1955.

———. *Die feinde des individuums in der israelitischen Psalmenliteratur*. Oslo: Grøndahl & Sons, 1933.

Blumenthal, David R. "Liturgies of Anger." *Cross Currents* 52 (2002): 178–99.

———. *Facing the Abusing God: A Theology of Protest*. Louisville, Ky.: Westminster John Knox, 1993.

Bok, Sissela. *Mayhem: Violence as Public Entertainment*. Reading, Mass.: Addison-Wesley, 1998.

Botha, Phil J. "The 'Enthronement Psalms': A Claim to the World-Wide Honour of Yahweh." *Old Testament Essays* 11 (1998): 24–39.

———. "'The Honour of the Righteous Will Be Restored': Psalm 75 in Its Social Context." *Old Testament Essays* 15 (2002): 320–34.

———. "Shame and the Social Setting of Psalm 119." *Old Testament Essays* 12 (1999): 389–400.

Boulton, Matthew. "Forsaking God: A Theological Argument for Christian Lamentation," *Scottish Journal of Theology* 55 (2002): 58–78.

Bourne, J. M. *Patronage and Society in Nineteenth-Century England*. Baltimore, Md.: Edward Arnold, 1986.

Bowen, Nancy R. "Damage and Healing: Shame and Honor in the Old Testament." *Koinonia* 3 (1991): 29–36.

Bozak, Barbara A. "Suffering and the Psalms of Lament: Speech for the Speechless, Power for the Powerless." *Église et Théologie* 23 (1992): 325–38.

Brettler, Marc Zvi. "Images of YHWH the Warrior in Psalms." *Semeia* 61 (1993): 135–65.

———. "Women and Psalms: Toward an Understanding of the Role of Women's Prayer in the Israelite Cult." Pages 25–56 in *Gender and Law in the Hebrew Bible and the Ancient Near East*. Edited by Victor H. Matthews, Bernard M. Levinson, and Tikva Simone Frymer-Kensky. Journal for the Study of the Old Testament: Supplement Series 262. Sheffield: Sheffield Academic Press, 1998.

Britt, Brian. "Unexpected Attachments: A Literary Approach to the Term חסד in the Hebrew Bible." *Journal for the Study of the Old Testament* 27 (2003): 289–307.

Brodwin, Paul E. "Symptoms and Social Performances: The Case of Diane Reden." Pages 77–99 in DelVecchio Good et al., eds., *Pain as Human Experience*.

Brown, Sally A., and Patrick D. Miller, eds. *Lament: Reclaiming Practices in Pulpit, Pew, and Public Square*. Louisville, Ky.: Westminster John Knox, 2005.

Brown, William P. "'Come, O Children...I Will Teach You the Fear of the Lord' (Psalm 34:12): Comparing Psalms and Proverbs." Pages 85–102 in *Seeking Out the Wisdom of the Ancients: Essays Offered to Honor Michael V. Fox on the Occasion of His Sixty-Fifth Birthday*. Edited by Ronald L. Troxel, Kelvin G. Friebel, and Dennis R. Magary. Winona Lake, Ind.: Eisenbrauns, 2005.

————. "Creatio Corporis and the Rhetoric of Defense in Job 10 and Psalm 139." Pages 107–24 in *God Who Creates: Essays in Honor of W. Sibley Towner*. Edited by William P. Brown and S. Dean McBride. Grand Rapids: Eerdmans, 2000.

————. "The Psalms and 'I': The Dialogical Self and the Disappearing Psalmist." Paper presented at the Baylor University Psalms Symposium. Waco, Tex., May 19, 2006.

————. Review of Sigmund Mowinckel, *The Psalms in Israel's Worship. Review of Biblical Literature*, available online http://www.bookreviews.org (16 July 2005).

————. *Seeing the Psalms: A Theology of Metaphor*. Louisville, Ky.: Westminster John Knox, 2002.

Brucher, Richard T. "Fantasies of Violence: *Hamlet* and *The Revenger's Tragedy.*" *Studies in English Literature, 1500–1900* 21, no. 2 (Spring 1981): 257–70.

Brueggemann, Walter. "The Costly Loss of Lament." *Journal for the Study of the Old Testament* 36 (1986): 57–71.

————. "The Formfulness of Grief." *Interpretation* 31 (July 1977): 263–75.

————. *The Message of the Psalms: A Theological Commentary*. Minneapolis: Augsburg, 1984.

————. "Psalm 109: Three Times 'Steadfast Love.'" *Word and World* 5, no. 2 (1985): 144–54.

Bruhm, Steven. *Gothic Bodies: The Politics of Pain in Romantic Fiction*. Philadelphia: University of Pennsylvania Press, 1994.

Burke, Kenneth. *Permanence and Change: An Anatomy of Purpose*. 3d ed. Berkeley, Calif.: University of California Press, 1984.

Buss, Martin J. "Form Criticism." Pages 69–85 in *To Each Its Own Meaning*. Edited by Steven L. McKenzie and Stephen R. Haynes. Louisville, Ky.: Westminster John Knox, 1993.

————. "The Meaning of 'Cult' and the Interpretation of the Old Testament." *Journal of Bible and Religion* 32 (1964): 317–25.

Butler, Judith. *The Psychic Life of Power: Theories in Subjection*. Stanford, Calif.: Stanford University Press, 1997.

Campbell, J. K. *Honour, Family and Patronage: A Study of Institutions and Moral Values in a Greek Mountain Community*. Oxford: Clarendon, 1970.

Carr, David M. *Writing on the Tablet of the Heart: Origins of Scripture and Literature*. Oxford: Oxford University Press, 2005.

Carrithers, Michael, Steven Collins, and Steven Lukes. *The Category of the Person*. Cambridge: Cambridge University Press, 1985.

Cartledge, Tony W. "Conditional Vows in the Psalms of Lament: A New Approach to an Old Problem." Pages 77–94 in *The Listening Heart: Essays in Wisdom and the Psalms in Honor of Roland E. Murphy*. Edited by Kenneth G. Hoglund, Elizabeth F. Huwiler, Jonathan T. Glass, and Roger W. Lee. Journal for the Study of the Old Testament: Supplement Series 58. Sheffield: JSOT Press, 1987.

Cerulo, Karen A. *Deciphering Violence: The Cognitive Structure of Right and Wrong*. New York: Routledge, 1998.

Chance, John K. "The Anthropology of Honor and Shame: Culture, Values and Practice." *Semeia* 68 (1994): 139–51.

Clark, Gordon R. *The Word Hesed in the Hebrew Bible*. Journal for the Study of the Old Testament: Supplement Series 157. Sheffield: JSOT Press, 1993.

Clines, David J. A. "The Book of Psalms, Where Men are Men: On the Gender of Hebrew Piety." Paper presented at the annual meeting of the Society of Biblical Literature. Philadelphia, Pa., November 2005.

Coggins, Richard J. "The Old Testament and the Poor." *Expository Times* 99 (1987–88): 11–14.

Collins, John J. "The Zeal of Phinehas: The Bible and the Legitimation of Violence." *Journal of Biblical Literature* 122 (2003): 3–21.

Collins, Terence. "The Physiology of Tears in the Old Testament: Part I." *Catholic Biblical Quarterly* 33 (1971): 18–38.

———. "The Physiology of Tears in the Old Testament: Part II." *Catholic Biblical Quarterly* 33 (1971): 185–97.

Connell, R. W. *Gender and Power: Society, the Person, and Sexual Politics*. Stanford, Calif.: Stanford University Press, 1987.

Corrigan, Robert. Comedy, Meaning and Form. 2d ed. New York: Harper & Row, 1981.

Creager, Harold L. "Note on Psalm 109." *Journal of Near Eastern Studies* 6 (1947): 121–23.

Crenshaw, James. "Wisdom Psalms?" *Currents in Research: Biblical Studies* 8 (2000): 9–17.

Croft, Steven J. L. *The Identity of the Individual in the Psalms*. Journal for the Study of the Old Testament: Supplement Series 44. Sheffield: JSOT Press, 1987.

Csordas, Thomas, ed. *Embodiment and Experience: The Existential Ground of Culture and Self*. Cambridge: Cambridge University Press, 1994.

Dahood, Mitchell. *Psalms*. 3 vols. Anchor Bible 16–17A. Garden City, N.Y.: Doubleday, 1965–70.

Das, Veena, Arthur Kleinman, Mamphela Ramphele, and Pamela Reynolds, eds. *Violence and Subjectivity*. Berkeley, Calif,: University of California Press, 2000.

Daube, David. "The Culture of Deuteronomy." *Orita* 3 (1969): 27–52.

Davis, C. "Our Modern Identity: The Formation of the Self," *Modern Theology* 6 (1990): 159–71.

Davis, John. *People of the Mediterranean: An Essay in Comparative Social Anthropology*. London: Routledge & Kegan Paul, 1977.

Davison, Lisa W. "'My soul is like the weaned child that is with me': The Psalms and the Feminine Voice." *Horizons in Biblical Theology* 23, no. 2 (2001): 155–67.

Day, John. *Psalms*. Old Testament Guides. Sheffield: JSOT Press, 1993.

Delekat, Lienhard. *Asylie und Schutzorakel am Zionheiligtum: Eine Untersuchung zu den Privaten Feindpsalmen*. Leiden: Brill, 1967.

Dell, Katharine, J. "The Use of Animal Imagery in the Psalms and Wisdom Literature of Ancient Israel." *Scottish Journal of Theology* 53 (2000): 275–91.

DelVecchio Good, Mary-Jo, Paul E. Brodwin, Byron J. Good, Arthur Kleinman, eds. *Pain as Human Experience: An Anthropological Perspective*. Berkeley, Calif.: University of California Press, 1992.

Dhanaraj, Dharmakkan. *Theological Significance of the Motif of Enemies in Selected Psalms of Individual Lament*. Glückstadt: J. J. Augustin, 1992.

Dickson, C. R. "The Hebrew Terminology for the Poor in Psalm 82." *Hervormde teologiese studies* 51 (1995): 1029–45.

Di Vito, Robert A. "Old Testament Anthropology and the Construction of Personal Identity." *Catholic Biblical Quarterly* 61 (1999): 217–38.

Doi, Takeo. *Anatomy of Dependence*. Translated by John Bester. Tokyo: Kodansha International, 1973.

Downing, F. Gerald. "'Honor' Among Exegetes." *Catholic Biblical Quarterly* 61 (1999): 53–73.

Doyle, Brian. "Howling Like Dogs: Metaphorical Language in Psalm LIX." *Vetus Testamentum* 54 (2004): 61–82.

Duhm, Bernard. *Die Psalmen*. Tübingen: J.C.B. Mohr (Paul Siebeck), 1922.

Eaton, J. H. *Kingship and the Psalms*. London: S.C.M. Press, 1976.

Egmond, Florike, and Robert Zwijnenberg, eds. *Bodily Extremities: Preoccupations with the Human Body in Early Modern European Culture*. Burlington, Vt.: Ashgate, 2003.

Egwim, Stephen. "Determining the Place of vv. 6–19 in Ps. 109." *Ephemerides theologicae lovanienses* 80 (2004): 112–30.

Eisenstadt, S. N. "Ritualized Personal Relations, Blood Brotherhood, Best Friends, Compadres, Etc.: Some Comparative Hypotheses and Suggestions." *Man* 56 (July 1956): 90–95.

Eisenstadt. S. N. and René Lemarchand, eds. *Political Clientelism, Patronage and Development*. London: Sage, 1981.

Eisenstadt, S. N., and L. Roniger. *Patrons, Clients, and Friends: Interpersonal Relations and the Structure of Trust in Society*. Cambridge: Cambridge University Press, 1984.

———. "Patron–Client Relations as Model of Structuring Social Exchange." *Comparative Studies in Society and History* 22 (1980): 42–77.

Ellyson, Steve L., and John F. Dovidio, eds. *Power, Dominance, and Nonverbal Communication*. New York: Springer, 1985.

Emerton, J. A. "Looking on One's Enemies." *Vetus Testamentum* 51 (2001): 186–96.

Exum, Cheryl. *Fragmented Women: Feminist (Sub)Versions of Biblical Narratives*. Valley Forge, Pa.: Trinity, 1993.

———. *Tragedy and Biblical Narrative: Arrows of the Almighty*. Cambridge: Cambridge University Press, 1992.

Farmer, Kathleen. "Psalms." Pages 145–52 in *Women's Bible Commentary: Expanded Edition with Apocrypha*. Edited by Carol A. Newsom and Sharon H. Ringe. Louisville, Ky.: Westminster John Knox, 1998.

Featherstone, Mike, Mike Hepworth, and Bryan S. Turner, eds. *The Body: Social Process and Cultural Theory*. London: Sage, 1990.

Feher, Michel, Ramona Nadaff, and Nadia Tazi, eds. *Fragments for a History of the Human Body*. 3 vols. New York: Zone, 1989.

Felson, Richard B. "Mass Media Effects on Violent Behavior." *Annual Review of Sociology* 22 (1996): 103–28.

Fiebig-von Hase, Ragnhild, and Ursula Lehmkuhl, eds. *Enemy Images in American History*. Providence, R.I.: Berghahn, 1997.

Firth, D. G. "Context and Violence in Individual Prayers for Protection." *Skrif en Kerk* 18, no. 1 (1997): 86–96.

———. "Responses to Violence in Some Lament Psalms of the Individual." *Skrif en Kerk* 17, no. 2 (1996): 317–28.

Fisch, Harold. *Poetry With a Purpose*. Bloomington, Ind.: Indiana University Press, 1988.

Flint, Peter W., and Patrick D. Miller, eds. *The Book of Psalms: Composition and Reception*. Boston: Brill, 2005.

Fløoysvik, Ingvar. "When God Behaves Strangely: A Study in the Complaint Psalms." *Concordia Journal* 21 (1995): 298–304.

Forgacs, David. "Fascism, Violence, and Modernity." Pages 5–21 in Howlett and Mengham, eds., *The Violent Muse*.

Foss, Karen A., Sonja K. Foss, and Cindy L. Griffin. *Feminist Rhetorical Theories*. London: Sage, 1999.

Foucault, Michel. *Discipline and Punish: The Birth of the Prison*. Translated by Alan Sheridan. New York: Vintage, 1979.

Fowles, Jib. *Why Viewers Watch: A Reappraisal of Television's Effects*. Newbury Park, Calif.: Sage, 1992.

Fox, Nili S. "Clapping Hands as a Gesture of Anguish and Anger in Mesopotamia and in Israel." *Journal of Ancient Near Eastern Society* 23 (1996): 49–60.

Fretheim, Terence E. "God and Violence in the Old Testament." *Word and World* 24 (2004): 18–28.

Geertz, Clifford. "'From the Native's Point of View': On the Nature of Anthropological Understanding." Pages 221–37 in *Meaning in Anthropology*. Edited by K. H. Basso and H. A. Selby. Albuquerque: University of New Mexico Press, 1976.

———. *Local Knowledge*. New York: Basic, 1983.

Gellner, Ernest, and John Waterbury, eds. *Patrons and Clients in Mediterranean Societies.* London: Gerald Duckworth, 1977.

George, Mark K. "Body Works: Power, the Construction of Identity, and Gender in the Discourse on Kingship." Ph.D. diss., Princeton Theological Seminary, 1995.

Gerstenberger, Erhard S. *Psalms, Part I, With an Introduction to Cultic Poetry.* The Forms of the Old Testament Literature 14. Grand Rapids: Eerdmans, 1988.

———. *Psalms, Part 2, and Lamentations.* The Forms of the Old Testament Literature 15. Grand Rapids: Eerdmans, 2001.

———. "Theologies in the Book of Psalms." Pages 603–25 in Flint and Miller, eds., *The Book of Psalms.*

Gesenius, W., and E. Kautzch. *Gesenius' Hebrew Grammar.* Translated by A. E. Cowley. 2d. English ed. Oxford: Clarendon, 1910.

Gillingham, S. E. *The Poems and Psalms of the Hebrew Bible.* Oxford: Oxford University Press, 1994.

———. "The Poor in the Psalms." *Expository Times* 100 (1988): 15–19.

Gillmayr-Bucher, Susanne. "Body Images in the Psalms." *Journal for the Study of the Old Testament* 28 (2004): 310–26.

Gilmore, David. ed. *Honor and Shame and the Unity of the Mediterranean.* A Special Publication of the American Anthropological Association 22. Washington, D.C.: American Anthropological Association, 1987.

Glazov, Gregory Yuri. "The Significance of the 'Hand on the Mouth' Gesture in Job XL 4." *Vetus Testamentum* 52 (2002): 30–41.

Gluckman, Max. *Order and Rebellion in Tribal Africa: Collected Essays.* London: Routledge & Kegan Paul, 1963.

Glueck, Nelson. *Ḥesed in the Bible.* Translated by Alfred Gottschalk. Cincinnati, Ohio: The Hebrew Union College Press, 1967.

Good, Byron J. "A Body in Pain—The Making of a World of Chronic Pain." Pages 29–48 in DelVecchio Good et al., eds., *Pain as Human Experience.*

Gruber, M. I. *Aspects of Nonverbal Communication in the Ancient Near East.* Rome: Biblical Institute, 1980.

Guillaume, A. "A Note on Psalm CIX. 10." *Journal of Theological Studies* 14 (1964): 92–93.

Gunkel, Hermann. *Introduction to Psalms: The Genres of the Religious Lyric of Israel.* Completed by Joachim Begrich. Translated by James D. Nogalski. Macon, Ga.: Mercer University Press, 1998.

———. *The Psalms: A Form Critical Introduction.* Translated by T. M. Horner. Philadelphia: Fortress, 1967.

Gutiérrez, Gustavo. *We Drink From Our Own Wells.* Translated by Matthew J. O'Connell. Maryknoll, N.Y.: Orbis, 1984.

Halberstam, Judith. "Imagined Violence/Queer Violence: Representation, Rage, and Resistance." *Social Text* 37 (1993): 187–201.

Harrelson, Walter. "On God's Knowledge of the Self, Psalm 139." *Currents in Theology and Mission* 2 (1975): 261–65.

Hayes, John H. *Understanding the Psalms.* Valley Forge, Pa.: Judson, 1976.

Heller, T. C., M. Sosna, and D. E. Wellbery, eds. *Reconstructing Individualism: Autonomy, Individuality, and the Self in Western Thought.* Stanford, Calif.: Stanford University Press, 1986.

Henley, Nancy M., and Sean Harmon. "The Nonverbal Semantics of Power and Gender: A Perceptual Study." Pages 151–64 in Ellyson and Dovidio, eds., *Power, Dominance, and Nonverbal Communication.*

Herzfeld, Michael. "Honour and Shame: Problems in the Contemporary Analysis of Moral Systems." *Man* 15 (1980): 339–51.

Hobbs, T. R. "Reflections on Honor, Shame, and Covenant Relations." *Journal of Biblical Literature* 116 (1997): 501–3.

Hobbs, T. R., and P. K. Jackson. "The Enemy in the Psalms." *Biblical Theological Bulletin* 21 (1991): 22–29.

Hobilitzelle, W. "Differentiating and Measuring Shame and Guilt: The Relation Between Shame and Depression." Pages 207–36 in *The Role of Shame in Emotion Formation*. Edited by H. B. Lewis. Hillsdale, N.J.: Erlbaum, 1987.

Holland, Dorothy, and Andrew Kipnis. "Metaphors for Embarrassment and Stories of Exposure: The Not-So-Egocentric Self in American Culture." *Ethos* 22, no. 3 (1994): 316–42.

Holland, Dorothy, William Lachicotte, Jr., Debra Skinner, and Carole Cain. *Identity and Agency in Cultural Worlds*. Cambridge, Mass.: Harvard University Press, 1998.

Hoppe, Leslie J. *There Shall Be No Poor Among You: Poverty in the Bible*. Nashville, Ky.: Abingdon, 2004.

Howlett, Jana, and Rod Mengham, eds. *The Violent Muse: Violence and the Artistic Imagination in Europe, 1910–1939*. Manchester: Manchester University Press, 1994.

Huber, Lyn Bechtel. "The Biblical Experience of Shame/Shaming: The Social Experience of Shame/Shaming in Biblical Israel in Relation to its Use as Religious Metaphor." Ph.D. diss., Drew University, 1983.

Jacobsen, Thorkild. *The Treasures of Darkness, A History of Mesopotamian Religion*. New Haven: Yale University Press, 1976.

Jacobson, Rolf A. *"Many are Saying": The Function of Direct Discourse in the Hebrew Psalter*. Journal for the Study of the Old Testament: Supplement Series 397. London: T&T Clark, 2004.

Jacoby, Susan. *Wild Justice: The Evolution of Revenge*. New York: Harper & Row, 1983.

Janzen, Gerald J. "Another Look at Psalm XII 6." *Vetus Testamentum* 54 (2004): 157–64.

Jobling, David, Peggy L. Day, and Gerald T. Sheppard, eds. *The Bible and the Politics of Exegesis: Essays in Honor of Norman K. Gottwald on His Sixty-Fifth Birthday*. Cleveland, Ohio: Pilgrim, 1991.

Johnson, A. R. *Sacral Kingship in Ancient Israel*. Cardiff: University of Wales, 1967.

Johnson, Terry, and Christopher Dandeker. "Patronage: Relation and System." Pages 219–41 in Wallace-Hadrill, ed., *Patronage in Ancient Society*.

Jones, Serene. "'Soul Anatomy': Calvin's Commentary on the Psalms." Pages 265–84 in *Psalms in Community: Jewish and Christian Textual, Liturgical, and Artistic Traditions*. Edited by Harold W. Attridge and Margot E. Fassler. Atlanta: Society of Biblical Literature, 2003.

Kaltner, John. "Psalm 22:17b: Second Guessing 'the Old Guess.'" *Journal of Biblical Literature* 117 (1998): 503–6.

Keel, Othmar. *Feinde und Gottesleugner: Studien zum Image der Widersacher in den Individualpsalmen*. Stuttgart: Katholisches Bibelwerk, 1969.

———. *The Symbolism of the Biblical World: Ancient Near Eastern Iconography and the Book of Psalms*. Translated by Timothy L. Hallett. New York: Seabury, 1978.

Kerby, Anthony Paul. *Narrative and the Self*. Bloomington: Indiana University Press, 1991.

Keyishian, Harry. *The Shapes of Revenge: Victimization, Vengeance, and Vindictiveness in Shakespeare*. Atlantic Highlands, N.J.: Humanities, 1995.

Kim, Ee Kon. "'Outcry': Its Context in Biblical Theology." *Interpretation* 42 (July 1988): 229–39.

Kirkpatrick, A. F. *The Book of Psalms*. Cambridge: Cambridge University Press, 1901.

Kirouac, G., and U. Hess. "Group Membership and Decoding Nonverbal Behavior." Pages 182–210 in *The Social Context of Nonverbal Behavior*. Edited by Pierre Philippot, Robert S. Feldman, and Erik J. Coats. Cambridge: Cambridge University Press, 1999.

Kleinman, Arthur. *The Illness Narratives: Suffering, Healing, and the Human Condition*. New York: Basic, 1988.

———. *Social Origins of Distress and Disease: Depression, Neurasthenia, and Pain in Modern China*. New Haven: Yale University Press, 1986.

———. "The Violences of Everyday Life: The Multiple Forms and Dynamics of Social Violence." Pages 226–241 in Das et al., eds., *Violence and Subjectivity*.

Klingbeil, Martin. *Yahweh Fighting from Heaven: God as Warrior and as God of Heaven in the Hebrew Psalter and Ancient Near Eastern Iconography*. Fribourg, Switzerland: University Press; Göttingen: Vandenhoeck & Ruprecht, 1999.

Klopfenstein, Martin A. *Scham und Schande nach dem Alten Testament*. Abhandlungen zur Theologie des Alten und Neuen Testamentes 62. Zurich: Theologischer Verlag, 1972.

Koester, Helmut. *Introduction to the New Testament: History, Culture, and Religion of the Hellenistic Age*. 2 vols. 2d ed. New York: de Gruyter, 1995.

Korte, Barbara. *Body Language in Literature*. Toronto: University of Toronto Press, 1993.

Kraus, Hans-Joachim. *Die Königsherrschaft Gottes im Alten Testament* (Tübingen: J. C. B. Mohr, 1951).

———*Psalms 1–59: A Commentary*. Translated by Hilton C. Oswald. Minneapolis: Augsburg, 1988.

———. *Psalms 60–150: A Commentary*. Translated by Hilton C. Oswald. Minneapolis: Augsburg, 1989.

———. *Theology of the Psalms*. Translated by Keith Crim. Minneapolis: Augsburg, 1979.

Kruger, Paul A. "Nonverbal Communication and Symbolic Gestures in the Psalms." *Bible Translator* 45 (April 1994): 213–22.

Kselman, John S. "'Why Have You Abandoned Me?' A Rhetorical Study of Psalm 22." Pages 172–98 in *Art and Meaning: Rhetoric in Biblical Literature*. Edited by David J. A. Clines, David M. Gunn, and Alan J. Hauser. Journal for the Study of the Old Testament: Supplement Series 19. Sheffield: JSOT Press, 1982.

Kugel, James L. "Topics in the History of the Spirituality of the Psalms." Pages 113–44 in *Jewish Spirituality From the Bible Through the Middle Ages*. Edited by Arthur Green. New York: Crossroad, 1987.

Kwakkel, Gert. *"According to My Righteousness": Upright Behavior as Grounds for Deliverance in Psalms 7, 17, 18, 26, and 44*. Oudtestamentische Studiën 46. Leiden: Brill, 2002.

Laniak, Timothy S. *Shame and Honor in the Book of Esther*. Atlanta: Scholars Press, 1998.

Lapsley, Jacqueline E. *Can These Bones Live? The Problem of the Moral Self in the Book of Ezekiel*. Berlin: de Gruyter, 2000.

Layton, Scott C. "'Head on Lap' in Sumero-Akkadian Literature." *Journal of Ancient Near Eastern Society* 15 (1983): 59–62.

Lee, Sung-Hun. "Lament and the Joy of Salvation." Pages 224–47 in Flint and Miller, eds., *The Book of Psalms*.

Lemche, Niels Peter. "From Patronage Society to Patronage Society." Pages 106–20 in *The Origins of the Ancient Israelite States*. Edited by Volkmar Fritz and Philip R. Davies. Journal for the Study of the Old Testament: Supplement Series 228. Sheffield: Sheffield Academic Press, 1996.

———. "Kings and Clients: On Loyalty Between the Ruler and the Ruled in Ancient 'Israel.'" *Semeia* 66 (1994): 119–32.

Lepore, Jill. *The Name of War: King Philip's War and the Origins of American Identity*. New York: Knopf, 1998.

Levine, Herbert J. "An Audience with the King: The Perspective of Dialogue." Pages 79–129 in *Sing Unto God a New Song: A Contemporary Reading of the Psalms*. Bloomington: Indiana University Press, 1995.

————. "The Dialogic Discourse of Psalms." Pages 145–61 in *Hermeneutics, the Bible, and Literary Criticism.* Edited by Ann Loades and Michael McLain. New York: Saint Martin's, 1992.

Lewis, I. M. *Social Anthropology in Perspective: The Relevance of Social Anthropology.* New York: Penguin, 1976.

Lewis, Michael. *Shame: The Exposed Self.* New York: The Free Press, 1992.

Lindström, Fredrik. *Suffering and Sin: Interpretations of Illness in the Individual Complaint Psalms.* Stockholm: Almqvist & Wiksell, 1994.

Linville, James R. "Psalm 22:17B: A New Guess." *Journal of Biblical Literature* 124 (2005): 733–44.

Liverani, Mario. "Political Lexicon and Political Ideologies in the Amarna Letters." *Berytus* 31 (1983): 41–56.

————. *Prestige and Interest, International Relations in the Near East ca. 1600–1100 B.C.* Padova: Sargon, 1990.

Long, Gary. Review of Gordon R. Clark, *The Word Hesed in the Hebrew Bible. Journal of Near Eastern Studies* 58 (1999): 67–69.

Lynd, Helen Merrell. *On Shame and the Search for Identity.* New York: Harcourt Brace, 1958.

Malina, Bruce J. *The New Testament World: Insights from Cultural Anthropology.* Atlanta: John Knox, 1981.

Malina, Bruce J., and Jerome H. Neyrey, "Honor and Shame in Luke–Acts: Pivotal Values of the Mediterranean World." Pages 25–65 in Neyrey, ed., *The Social World of Luke–Acts.*

Mandolfo, Carleen. *God in the Dock: Dialogic Tension in the Psalms.* Journal for the Study of the Old Testament: Supplement Series 357. Sheffield: Sheffield Academic Press, 2002.

Marshall, Cynthia. *The Shattering of the Self: Violence, Subjectivity, and Early Modern Texts.* Baltimore: The Johns Hopkins University Press, 2002.

Mays, James L. "The Place of the Torah-Psalms in the Psalter." *Journal of Biblical Literature* 106 (1987): 3–12.

————. "The Question of Context in Psalm Interpretation." Pages 14–20 in *The Shape and Shaping of the Psalter.* Edited by J. Clinton McCann. Journal for the Study of the Old Testament: Supplement Series 159. Sheffield: Sheffield Academic Press, 1993.

McAlpine, Thomas H. *Sleep, Divine and Human, in the Old Testament.* Journal for the Study of the Old Testament: Supplement Series 38. Sheffield: JSOT Press, 1987.

McCann, J. Clinton. "The Psalms as Instruction." *Interpretation* 46 (1992): 117–28.

————, ed. *The Shape and Shaping of the Psalter.* Journal for the Study of the Old Testament: Supplement Series 159. Sheffield: Sheffield Academic Press, 1993.

Menn, Esther M. "No Ordinary Lament: Relecture and the Identity of the Distressed in Psalm 22." *Harvard Theological Review* 93 (2000): 301–341.

Meskell, Lynn. "The Irresistible Body and the Seduction of Archaeology." Pages 139–161 in *Changing Bodies, Changing Meanings: Studies on the Human Body in Antiquity.* Edited by Dominic Montserrat. London: Routledge, 1998.

Miller, Patrick D. "The Hermeneutics of Imprecation." Pages 153–63 in *Theology in the Service of the Church: Essays in Honor of Thomas W. Gillespie.* Edited by Wallace M. Alston, Jr. Grand Rapids: Eerdmans, 2000.

————. "Prayer as Persuasion: The Rhetoric and Intention of Prayer." *Word and World* 13 (Fall 1993): 356–62.

————. *They Cried to the Lord: The Form and Theology of Biblical Prayer.* Minneapolis: Fortress, 1994.

————. "Things Too Wonderful: Prayers Women Prayed." Pages 233–43 in *They Cried to the Lord.*

————. "Trouble and Woe: Interpreting the Biblical Laments." *Interpretation* 37 (1983): 32–45.

————. "*Yāpiaḥ* in Psalm XII 6." *Vetus Testamentum* 29 (1979): 495–501.

Morris, David B. *The Culture of Pain*. Berkeley, Calif.: University of California Press, 1991.
———. "The Languages of Pain." Pages 89–99 in *Exploring the Concept of the Mind*. Edited by Richard M. Caplan. Iowa City: University of Iowa Press, 1986.
Morrison, A. P. "The Eye Turned Inward: Shame and the Self." Pages 271–91 in *The Many Faces of Shame*. Edited by D. L. Nathanson. New York: Guilford, 1986.
Morson, Gary Saul, and Caryl Emerson. *Mikhail Bakhtin: Creation of a Prosaics*. Stanford, Calif.: Stanford University Press, 1990.
Mowinckel, Sigmund. *Offersang og Sangoffer*. Oslo: Aschehoug, 1951.
———. *The Psalms in Israel's Worship*. Translated by D. R. Ap-Thomas. 2 vols. Grand Rapids: Eerdmans; Dearborn: Dove, 2004.
———. *Psalmstudien*. 6 vols. Kristiania: Jacob Dybwad, 1921–24.
Moxnes, Halvor. "Patron–Client Relations and the New Community in Luke–Acts." Pages 241–68 in Neyrey, ed., *The Social World of Luke–Acts*.
Mueller, Janel M. "Pain, Persecution, and the Construction of Selfhood in Foxe's *Acts and Monuments*." Pages 161–87 in *Religion and Culture in Renaissance England*. Edited by Claire McEachern and Debora Shuger. Cambridge: Cambridge University Press, 1997.
Nasuti, Harry Peter. *Defining the Sacred Songs: Genre, Tradition and the Post-Critical Interpretation of the Psalms*. Journal for the Study of the Old Testament: Supplement Series 218. Sheffield: Sheffield Academic Press, 1999.
Nessan, Craig L. "Sex, Aggression, and Pain: Sociobiological Implications for Theological Anthropology." *Zygon* 33 (1998): 443–54.
Newsom, Carol A. "Apocalyptic Subjects: Social Construction of the Self in the Qumran Hodayot." *Journal for the Study of the Pseudepigrapha* 12 (2001): 3–35.
———. "The Moral Sense of Nature: Ethics in the Light of God's Speech to Job." *The Princeton Seminary Bulletin* 15 (1994): 9–27.
———. "Woman and the Discourse of Patriarchal Wisdom: A Study of Proverbs 1–9." Pages 142–60 in *Gender and Difference in Ancient Israel*. Edited by Peggy L. Day. Minneapolis: Fortress, 1989.
Neyrey, J. H., ed. *The Social World of Luke–Acts: Models for Interpretation*. Peabody, Mass.: Hendrickson, 1991.
Nowell, Irene. "Psalm 88: A Lesson in Lament." Pages 105–18 in *Imagery and Imagination in Biblical Literature: Essays in Honor of Aloysius Fitzgerald, F.S.C.* Edited by Lawrence Boadt and Mark S. Smith. Washington, D.C.: The Catholic Biblical Association of America, 2001.
Odell, Margaret S. "An Exploratory Study of Shame and Dependence in the Bible and Selected Near Eastern Parallels." Pages 217–33 in *The Biblical Canon in Comparative Perspective*. Edited by K. L. Younger, Jr., William W. Hallo, and Bernard F. Batto. Ancient Near Eastern Texts and Studies 11. New York: Edwin Mellen, 1991.
———. "The Inversion of Shame and Forgiveness in Ezekiel 16:59–63." *Journal for the Study of the Old Testament* 56 (1992): 101–12.
O'Donovan-Anderson, Michael, ed. *The Incorporated Self: Interdisciplinary Perspectives on Embodiment*. New York: Rowman & Littlefield, 1996.
Olyan, Saul. "Honor, Shame, and Covenant Relations in Ancient Israel and its Environment." *Journal of Biblical Literature* 115 (1996): 201–18.
Parsons, Ian Ross McKenzie. "Evil Speaking in the Psalms of Lament." Ph.D. diss., Drew University, 1969.
Peels, H. G. L. *The Vengeance of God; The Meaning of the Root NQM and the Function of NQM-Texts in the Context of Divine Revelation in the Old Testament*. Leiden: Brill, 1995.
Peristiany, J. G. *Honor and Shame: The Values of Mediterranean Society*. London: Weidenfeld and Nicholson, 1965.
Peristiany, J. G., and J. Pitt-Rivers. *Honor and Grace in Anthropology*. Cambridge: Cambridge University Press, 1992.

Pincikowski, Scott. *Bodies of Pain: Suffering in the Works of Hartmann von Aue.* New York: Routledge, 2002.

Pitt-Rivers, Julian. "The Anthropology of Honour." Pages 1–17 in *The Fate of Shechem, or The Politics of Sex: Essays in the Anthropology of the Mediterranean.* Cambridge: Cambridge University Press, 1977.

————. "Honour and Social Status." Pages 21–78 in Peristiany, ed., *Honour and Shame.*

Pleins, J. David. "Poor, Poverty." Pages 402–12 in vol. 5 of *The Anchor Bible Dictionary.* Edited by David Noel Freedman. 6 vols. New York: Doubleday, 1992.

————. *The Social Visions of the Hebrew Bible: A Theological Introduction.* Louisville, Ky.: Westminster John Knox, 2001.

Porter, Roy. "History of the Body." Pages 206–32 in *New Perspectives on Historical Writing.* Edited by Peter Burke. University Park, Pa.: The Pennsylvania State University Press, 1992.

Potter, W. James. *The 11 Myths of Media Violence.* Thousand Oaks, Calif.: Sage, 2003.

————. *On Media Violence.* Thousand Oaks, Calif.: Sage, 1999.

Pressler, Carolyn. "Certainty, Ambiguity, and Trust: Knowledge of God in Psalm 139." Pages 91–99 in *A God So Near: Essays in Old Testament Theology in Honor of Patrick D. Miller.* Edited by Brent A. Strawn and Nancy R. Bowen. Winona Lake, Ind.: Eisenbrauns, 2003.

Prudovsky, Gad. "Can We Ascribe to Past Thinkers Concepts They Had No Linguistic Means to Express?" *History and Theory* 36 (1997): 15–31.

Rey, Roselyne. *The History of Pain.* Cambridge, Mass.: Harvard University Press, 1995.

Rieber, Robert W., ed. *The Psychology of War and Peace: The Image of the Enemy.* New York: Plenum, 1991.

Riede, Peter. *Im Netz des Jägers: Studien zur Feindmetaphorik der Individualpsalmen.* Wissenschaftliche Monographien zum Alten and Neuen Testament 85. Neukirchen–Vluyn: Neukirchener, 2000.

Rigby, Cynthia L. "Someone to Blame, Someone to Trust: Divine Power and the Self-Recovery of the Oppressed." Pages 79–102 in *Power, Powerlessness, and the Divine: New Inquiries in Bible and Theology.* Edited by Cynthia L. Rigby. Atlanta: Scholars Press, 1997.

Roberts, J. J. M. "A New Root for an Old Crux, Ps. XXII 17c." *Vetus Testamentum* 23 (1973): 247–52.

Rogerson, J. W. "The Enemy in the Old Testament." Pages 284–93 in *Understanding Poets and Prophets.* Edited by A. Graeme Auld. Sheffield: JSOT Press, 1993.

Roniger, Luis. *Hierarchy and Trust in Mexico and Brazil.* New York: Praeger, 1990.

Roniger, Luis, and Ayşe Güneş-Ayata, eds. *Democracy, Clientelism, and Civil Society.* London: Lynne Rienner, 1994.

Rosenbaum, Stanley. "The Concept 'Antagonist' in Hebrew Psalmography: A Semantic Field Study." Ph.D. diss., Brandeis University, 1974.

Routledge, Robin. "Ḥesed as Obligation: A Re-Examination." *Tyndale Bulletin* 46 (1995): 179–196.

Sabourin, L. *The Psalms: Their Origin and Meaning.* New York: Alba, 1974.

Sakenfeld, Katharine Doob. *Faithfulness in Action; Loyalty in Biblical Perspective.* Philadelphia: Fortress, 1985.

————. *The Meaning of Ḥesed in the Hebrew Bible: A New Inquiry.* Harvard Semitic Monographs 17. Missoula, Mont.: Scholars Press, 1978.

Saller, Richard P. *Personal Patronage Under the Early Empire.* Cambridge: Cambridge University Press, 1982.

Sawyer, John F. A. *Semantics in Biblical Research: New Methods of Defining Hebrew Words for Salvation.* London: S.C.M. Press, 1972.

Scarry, Elaine. *The Body in Pain: The Making and Unmaking of the World.* New York: Oxford University Press, 1985.

Schaefer, Konrad. *Psalms*. Collegeville: Liturgical, 2001.

Schmidt, Hans. *Das Gebet der Angeklagten im Alten Testament*. Giessen: Töpelmann, 1928.

———. *Die Psalmen*. Tübingen: J. C. B. Mohr (Paul Siebeck), 1934.

Scott, James. "Patronage and Exploitation." Pages 21–39 in Gellner and Waterbury, eds., *Patrons and Clients in Mediterranean Societies*.

Seybold, Klaus. *Introducing the Psalms*. Translated by R. Graeme Dunphy. Edinburgh: T. & T. Clark, 1990.

Shanin, T., ed. *Peasants and Peasant Societies*. New York: Penguin, 1971.

Shepherd, John. "The Place of the Imprecatory Psalms in the Canon of Scripture." *Churchman* 111 (1997): 27–47.

Sheppard, Gerald T. "'Enemies' and the Politics of Prayer in the Book of Psalms." Pages 61–82 in Jobling, Day, and Sheppard, eds., *The Bible and the Politics of Exegesis*.

———. "Theology and the Book of Psalms." *Interpretation* 46 (Apr. 1992): 143–55.

Shilling, Chris. *The Body and Social Theory*. London: Sage, 1993.

Siker, Jeffrey S. "Uses of the Bible in the Theology of Gustavo Gutiérrez: Liberating Scriptures of the Poor." *Biblical Interpretation* 4 (1996): 40–71.

Silva, David A. de. "Exchanging Favor for Wrath: Apostasy in Hebrew and Patron-Client Relationships." *Journal of Biblical Literature* 115 (1996): 91–116.

———. *Honor, Patronage, Kinship and Purity: Unlocking New Testament Culture*. Downers Grove, Ill.: InterVarsity, 2000.

Simkins, Ronald A. "Patronage and the Political Economy of Monarchic Israel." *Semeia* 87 (1999): 123–44.

———. "'Return to Yahweh': Honor and Shame in Joel." *Semeia* 68 (1994): 41–54.

Simon, Uriel. *Four Approaches to the Book of Psalms: From Saadiah Gaon to Abraham Ibn Ezra*. Translated by Lenn J. Schramm. Albany: State University of New York Press, 1991.

Singer, Peter. "Unspeakable Acts": Review of Elaine Scarry, *The Body in Pain: The Making and Unmaking of the World*, and Edward Peters, *Torture. New York Review of Books* 33, no. 3, February 27, 1986.

Smend, Rudolf. "Uber das Ich der Psalmen." *Zeitschrift für die altestamentliche Wissenschaft* 8 (1888): 49–147.

Sondergard, Sidney L. *Sharpening Her Pen: Strategies of Rhetorical Violence by Early Modern English Writers*. London: Associated University Presses, 2002.

Stansell, Gary. "Honor and Shame in the David Narratives." *Semeia* 68 (1994): 55–79.

Staubli, Thomas, and Silvia Schroer. *Body Symbolism in the Bible*. Collegeville: Liturgical, 2001.

Stiebert, Johanna. *The Construction of Shame in the Hebrew Bible: The Prophetic Contribution*. Journal for the Study of the Old Testament: Supplement Series 346. London: Sheffield Academic Press, 2002.

Stone, Ken. *Sex, Honor, and Power in the Deuteronomistic History*. Journal for the Study of the Old Testament: Supplement Series 234. Sheffield: Sheffield Academic Press, 1996.

Strawn, Brent A. "Psalm 22:17b: More Guessing." *Journal of Biblical Literature* 119 (Fall 2000): 439–51.

———. *What is Stronger than a Lion?: Leonine Image and Metaphor in the Hebrew Bible and the Ancient Near East*. Fribourg: Academic Press; Göttingen: Vandenhoeck & Ruprecht, 2005.

Swenson, Kristin M. *Living Through Pain: Psalms and the Search for Wholeness*. Waco, Tex.: Baylor University Press, 2005.

———. "Psalm 22:17: Circling Around the Problem Again." *Journal of Biblical Literature* 123 (2004): 637–48.

Synnott, Anthony. *The Body Social: Symbolism, Self and Society*. London: Routledge, 1993.

Tangney, June Price, and Ronda L. Dearing. *Shame and Guilt*. New York: Guilford, 2002.

Tanner, Laura E. *Intimate Violence: Reading Rape and Torture in Twentieth-Century Fiction*. Bloomington: Indian University Press, 1994.

Taylor, Charles. *Sources of the Self: The Making of the Modern Identity*. Cambridge, Mass.: Harvard University Press, 1989.

Thomas, D. Winton. "Psalm XXXV. 15f." *Journal of Theological Studies* 12 (1961): 50–51.

Tournay, R. "Note sur le Psaume 22:17." *Vetus Testamentum* 23 (1973): 111–12.

Tucker, Dennis. "Democratization and the Language of the Poor in Psalms 2–89." *Horizons in Biblical Theology* 25 (2003): 161–78.

———. "Is Shame a Matter of Patronage in the Communal Laments?" Paper presented at the annual meeting of the Society of Biblical Literature. Atlanta, November, 2003.

Turner, Bryan. *The Body and Society*. New York: Basil Blackwell, 1984.

Vall, Gregory. "Psalm 22:17b: 'The Old Guess.'" *Journal of Biblical Literature* 116 (1997): 45–56.

Wallace-Hadrill, Andrew, ed. *Patronage in Ancient Society*. London: Routledge, 1989.

Weingrod, Alex. "Patronage and Power." Pages 41–51 in Gellner and Waterbury, eds., *Patrons and Clients in Mediterranean Societies*.

Weintraub, K. J. *The Value of the Individual: Self and Circumstance in Autobiography*. Chicago: University of Chicago Press, 1978.

Weiser, A. *The Psalms: A Commentary*. London: Westminster, 1962.

Westermann, Claus. *The Praise of God in the Psalms*. Translated by Keith R. Crim. Richmond, Va.: John Knox, 1965.

Wette, W. M. L. de. *Kommentar über die Psalmen*. Heidelberg: Mohr & Zimmer, 1811.

White, James Boyd. *When Words Lose Their Meaning: Constitutions and Reconstitutions of Language, Character, and Community*. Chicago: University of Chicago Press, 1984.

Wiig, Arne. *Promise, Protection, and Prosperity: Aspects of the 'Shield' as a Religious Relational Metaphor in an Ancient Near Eastern Perspective, An Iconographical and Textual Analysis*. Translated by Jennifer Evans. Lund: Novapress, 1999.

Wikan, Unni. "Shame and Honour: A Contestable Pair." *Man* 19, no. 4 (1984): 635–52.

Williams, James G. *The Bible, Violence, and the Sacred: Liberation from the Myth of Sanctified Violence*. New York: Harper Collins, 1991.

Williams, Simon J., and Gillian Bendelow, eds. *The Lived Body: Sociological Themes, Embodied Issues*. London: Routledge, 1998.

Wiltshire, John. *Jane Austen and the Body: The Picture of Health*. Cambridge: Cambridge University Press, 1992.

Wolf, Eric R. "Kinship, Friendship, and Patron-Client Relations in Complex Societies." Pages 1–22 in *The Social Anthropology of Complex Societies*. Edited by M. Banton. London: Tavistock, 1966.

Wolff, Hans Walter. *Anthropology of the Old Testament*. Philadelphia: Fortress, 1974.

Wright, David P. "The Gesture of Hand Placement in the Hebrew Bible and in Hittite Literature." *Journal of the American Oriental Society* 106 (1986): 433–46.

———. "Ritual Analogy in Psalm 109." *Journal of Biblical Literature* 113 (1994): 385–404.

Zenger, Erich. *A God of Vengeance? Understanding the Psalms of Divine Wrath*. Louisville, Ky.: Westminster John Knox, 1996.

INDEX OF REFERENCES

INDEX OF AUTHORS